ADVANCES IN CLINICAL BEHAVIOR THERAPY

Other books from Banff International Conferences on Behavior Modification available from Brunner/Mazel

Behavior Modification and Families (Banff VI)
Behavior Modification Approaches to Parenting (Banff VI)
The Behavioral Management of Anxiety, Depression and Pain (Banff VII)
Behavioral Self-management: Strategies, Techniques and Outcome (Banff VIII)
Behavioral Systems for the Developmentally Disabled: I. School and Family Environments (Banff IX)
Behavioral Systems for the Developmentally Disabled: II. Institutional, Clinic and Community Environments (Banff IX)
Behavioral Medicine: Changing Health Lifestyles (Banff X)
Violent Behavior: Social Learning Approaches to Prediction, Management and Treatment (Banff XI)
Adherence, Compliance and Generalization in Behavioral Medicine (Banff XII)

ADVANCES IN CLINICAL BEHAVIOR THERAPY

Edited by

Kenneth D. Craig
and
Robert J. McMahon

Department of Psychology,
University of British Columbia
Vancouver, B.C.

BRUNNER/MAZEL, *Publishers* • New York

Library of Congress Cataloging in Publication Data
Main entry under title:

Advances in clinical behavior therapy, ed. by Kenneth D. Craig.

Based on papers presented at the 14th Banff International Conference on Behavior
Modification, held in spring 1982 in Banff, Can.
Includes bibliographies and index.
1. Behavior therapy—Congresses. I. Craig, Kenneth D., 1937-   . II. McMahon, Robert
J. (Robert Joseph), 1953-   . III. Banff International Conference on Behavior Modifi-
cation (14th : 1982 : Banff, Alta.)
[DNLM: 1. Behavior therapy—Congresses. W3 BA203 14th 1982 / WM 425 B215 1982a]
RC489.B4A34   1983   616.89′142   83-10161
ISBN 0-87630-338-6

Copyright © 1983 by Brunner/Mazel, Inc.

Published by
BRUNNER/MAZEL, INC.
19 Union Square
New York, New York 10003

MANUFACTURED IN THE UNITED STATES OF AMERICA

Preface

This is one in a continuing series of publications sponsored by the Banff International Conferences on Behavior Science. The conferences have been held each spring since 1969 in Banff, Alberta, Canada. They serve the purpose of bringing together outstanding behavioral scientists and professionals in a forum where they can present and discuss data related to emergent issues and topics in the field of behavior modification. Thus, the International Conferences, as a continuing event, have served as an expressive "early indicator" of the developing nature and composition of behavioristic science and scientific application.

Distance, schedules, and restricted audience preclude wide attendance at the conferences. Consequently, the publications have equal status with the conferences proper. They are not, however, simply publications of the papers presented at the conference. Major presenters at the Banff Conferences are required to specifically write a chapter for the forthcoming book, separate from their informal presentation and discussion at the conference itself.

The original conference had as its theme "Ideal Mental Health Services." The policy consciously adopted at that conference, and followed ever since, was to identify for each year's theme those behavioral researchers who could best identify the state of the art. In 1969, the conference faculty were Nathan Azrin, Ogden Lindsley, Gerald Patterson, Todd Risley, and Richard Stuart! The conference topics for the first five years were as follows:

1969: I. IDEAL MENTAL HEALTH SERVICES
1970: II. SERVICES AND PROGRAMS FOR EXCEPTIONAL CHILDREN AND YOUTH
1971: III. IMPLEMENTING BEHAVIORAL PROGRAMS FOR SCHOOLS AND CLINICS
1972: IV. BEHAVIOR CHANGE: METHODOLOGY, CONCEPTS, AND PRACTICE
1973: V. EVALUATION OF BEHAVIORAL PROGRAMS IN COMMUNITY, RESIDENTIAL AND SCHOOL SETTINGS

Beginning in 1974, the Banff Conference books have been published by Brunner/Mazel, and the interested reader may obtain copies of these earlier publications from the publisher. The conference topics were:

1974: VI. BEHAVIOR MODIFICATION AND FAMILIES and BEHAVIOR MODIFICATION AP-
      PROACHES TO PARENTING
1975: VII. THE BEHAVIORAL MANAGEMENT OF ANXIETY, DEPRESSION AND PAIN
1976: VIII. BEHAVIORAL SELF-MANAGEMENT: STRATEGIES, TECHNIQUES AND OUTCOMES
1977: IX. BEHAVIORAL SYSTEMS FOR THE DEVELOPMENTALLY DISABLED:
      I. SCHOOL AND FAMILY ENVIRONMENTS
      II. INSTITUTIONAL, CLINIC, AND COMMUNITY ENVIRONMENTS
1978: X. BEHAVIORAL MEDICINE: CHANGING HEALTH LIFESTYLES
1979: XI. VIOLENT BEHAVIOR: SOCIAL LEARNING APPROACHES TO PREDICTION, MANAGE-
      MENT AND TREATMENT
1980: XII. ADHERENCE, COMPLIANCE, AND GENERALIZATION IN BEHAVIORAL MEDICINE

The Banff Conferences have been more than places at which theories and research data are presented and discussed. The magnificence of the Banff natural environment and recreation opportunities, as well as the pleasurable ambience and resources of The Banff Centre where the conference is held, contribute enormously to the vigor and stimulation of the conference. It has encouraged substantial program development and evaluation and helped to bring together policymakers, program administrators, researchers and clinicians in an effort to stimulate the adoption in practical settings of many of the programs that have been discussed during the conference proceedings.

Over the past 13 years, the conference has yielded many papers that described innovative service delivery and research in the fields of behavioral dysfunction and health psychology. Because clinical behavior therapy has become firmly established, but continues to rapidly evolve, Banff XIV was chosen as the occasion to provide major summative and prospective statements. Invitations to prepare papers describing critical developments and their research basis were extended to a group of clinicians who had distinguished themselves through innovative practice, research, and professional contributions. This volume presents the product of the conference.

Many people have contributed notably to the success of these conferences. Those who have attended the conferences and participated so vigorously in the presentations and discussions, both formally and informally, contribute enormously to its success. Other members of the conference Planning Committee who contributed substantial help and guidance to Banff XIV were Dr. Ray deV. Peters and Dr. L. A. Hamerlynck.

Editing of this volume was supported in part by a grant from the Social Sciences and Humanities Research Council of Canada.

K. D. C.
R. J. M.

Vancouver, B.C.
December, 1982

Contents

Contributors

JAMES F. ALEXANDER
University of Utah

LAURENCE H. BAKER
*University of Connecticut
Health Center*

DAVID H. BARLOW
*State Univerity of New York at
Albany*

COLE BARTON
University of Utah

NED L. COONEY
*University of Connecticut
Health Center*

JULIET DARKE
Queen's University

CHRISTOPHER M. EARLS
Queen's University

DAVID W. FOY
*Brentwood V.A. Medical Center
U.C.L.A. Medical School*

ARTHUR E. HOLDEN
*State University of New York at
Albany*

NEIL S. JACOBSON
University of Washington

CYNTHIA G. LAST
*State University of New York at
Albany*

ROBERT P. LIBERMAN
*Brentwood V.A. Medical Center
U.C.L.A. Medical School*

MICHAEL J. MAHONEY
Pennsylvania State University

WILLIAM L. MARSHALL
Queen's University

C. HAYDEE MAS
University of Utah

GERALD T. O'BRIEN
*State University of New York at
Albany*

CLARE PHILIPS
Institute of Psychiatry
London, England
    and
Shaughnessy Hospital
Vancouver, British Columbia

OVIDE F. POMERLEAU
University of Connecticut
School of Medicine

STANLEY J. RACHMAN
Institute of Psychiatry
London, England
    and
University of British Columbia

TED L. ROSENTHAL
University of Tennessee
College of Medicine

RENATE H. ROSENTHAL
University of Tennessee
College of Medicine

ZINDEL SEGAL
Queen's University

LINDA C. SOBELL
Addiction Research Foundation
University of Toronto

MARK B. SOBELL
Addiction Research Foundation
University of Toronto

HOLLY WALDRON
University of Utah

CHARLES J. WALLACE
Brentwood V.A. Medical Center
U.C.L.A. Medical School

Introduction

Developments within the field of clinical behavior therapy over the past several decades represent remarkable achievements. Prior to the 1960s, behavioral practitioners were not unknown (Kazdin, 1978), but they were uncommon and would be reasonably characterized as pioneers of the field (Kanfer & Phillips, 1970; Ullman & Krasner, 1965). Their vision grasped the attention of practitioners and students dissatisfied with both the level of effectiveness of existing treatment strategies and the theoretical foundations of psychotherapy as it was then practiced. Those who were steeped in the knowledge-base and methodologies of the behavioral sciences observed and acted upon the opportunity to examine and evaluate innovative treatment strategies. At that time, the behavioral intervention strategies as we know them today were but a promise. The successes have been substantial (Rachman & Wilson, 1980) and have led to major reorganizations of the attitudes and practices of health practitioners over the past two decades. Behavioral intervention strategies have become assimilated into the intervention strategies used by most practitioners. However, smug satisfaction and self-congratulations would be inappropriate. Major problems exist. Within the field, there is substantial diversity of opinion concerning the nature of many disorders and how they should be best dealt with. The social and personal needs that provoked the development of behavior therapy have barely been touched. The papers in this volume document deficiencies in the field and the efforts of notable scientists and clinicians to resolve them.

This brief introduction to the volume provides the reader with an overview of its contents and an outline of the principles that governed the selection of the chapters. The intent was to present current work of investigators who could provide knowledgeable, well-considered accounts of new developments with considerable real-life relevance, rather than to provide dry and technical descriptions of techniques presented elsewhere in retrospective textbooks.

Stress is a ubiquitous explanatory construct in accounts of the behavior disorders, but too often it is ill-defined, poorly measured, and refractive to efforts at change. Rosenthal and Rosenthal have integrated current concepts and empirical findings and describe the therapeutic strategy and clinical procedures that have emerged. The integration of social learning theory and biobehavioral constructs is of particular interest. Clinicians concerned with many behavior disorders are obliged to undertake a similar exercise and may find comparisons of their strategies with the programmatic approach of these active and experienced clinicians of value.

Mahoney provides a lucid critical analysis of current behavioral and cognitive formulations of behavior therapy, drawing upon such far-ranging fields as philosophy, theoretical physics, economics, and cognitive psychology. It becomes apparent that underlying theoretical concepts have not kept pace with the development of therapeutic strategies. Indeed, many theoretical concepts implicit in the work of behavior therapists appear to reflect positions that have been rejected as outmoded by experimental psychologists and other behavioral scientists. One suspects that many successes have been the fortuitous result of the insistence upon empirical analyses, thereby staying close to the natural order. Mahoney observes that careful attention to newly emerging concepts in experimental psychology and a greater interface with philosophy would prove a more satisfactory explanatory basis for existing techniques and contribute to the development of a more satisfactory system for helping people.

The inadequacies of therapeutic formulations limited to accounts of client characteristics and clinical techniques are underscored by Alexander, Barton, Waldron, and Mas. The field has developed through careful attention to specific techniques and their evaluation. This perhaps is illustrated in the training of behavior therapists by the priorities attached to technical proficiency. Less attention has been devoted to the subtleties of therapist characteristics, interpersonal process, and the familial and sociocultural contexts in which the clinician's agency and client's problems are embedded. These represent rich fields deserving of the attention of behavioral scientists and clinicians committed to the improvement and development of therapeutic strategies. The chapter by Alexander and his colleagues systematically describes the current status of systems approaches to behavioral management, along with the conceptual model that has governed their development in family therapy.

Detailed exposition of the elements of this heuristic model in the context of marriage and families and over the course of treatment highlights their important work.

Few recent developments in behavior therapy have grasped the attention of clinicians as has behavioral marital therapy. This field has grown enormously as a result of empirical analyses of the inadequacies of traditional behavioral concepts in a family systems context, along with the development of new strategies. Jacobson and his colleagues reflect this tradition of hard-nosed analysis and creative advances. Jacobson's conference presentation evoked a reaction of "right on." The reader may find of special interest the discussions of the decline of contingency contracting, efforts to incorporate cognitive intervention procedures into behavior therapy, and the analyses of therapist behaviors critical in producing positive outcomes.

The next two chapters describe at least partially successful attacks on perhaps the most intransigent anxiety-mediated disorders.

Barlow, O'Brien, Last, and Holden demonstrate the merit of adapting broader systems perspectives of therapy and examining the interaction of family patterns and behavior problems. Agoraphobia was long construed as a disorder without a satisfactory treatment. In recent years, *in vivo* exposure therapies have proven to be the treatment of choice, but they have not proven universally effective, nor have treatment effects demonstrated wholly satisfactory maintenance and generalization. Barlow and his colleagues provide an appraisal of exposure therapies and describe the merits of the couples treatment approach which takes into account the broad social context in which treatment is provided.

Rachman's attack on obsessive-compulsive disorders draws inspiration from sensitive observations as a behavior therapist and research analyses of the impact of a variety of therapeutic strategies on these disorders. The paper illustrates the power of programmatic, step-wise empirical analyses in the development of therapeutic strategies. Several forms of compulsive behavior have yielded to the innovative intervention strategies described; moreover, the characteristics of those disorders requiring different approaches are now better understood. The reader will discover detailed descriptions of the most effective strategies available for treating obsessive and compulsive disorders, as well as sobering accounts of unsatisfactory results with some disorders.

The capacity of the behavior therapies to respond to societal needs and demands for better programs for the assessment and treatment of sexual aggressors has been well-documented by Marshall, Earls, Segal, and Darke. Traditional approaches of physical restraint and custodial care have proven ineffective and people have remained vulnerable to sexual assault because of difficulties in predicting and controlling the risk. Unpredictably dangerous people are too often unrecognized or released to the streets from the prison system. In the best tradition of the researcher/clinician, these authors provide a comprehensive survey of work in the area and describe the development of treatment programs superior to many that continue to be used. The treatment model described here encompasses the full range of affective (e.g., eroticism, anxiety, and anger), cognitive (e.g., fantasies and social perception), and behavioral (e.g., sexual and social skills) processes.

Alcoholism and the addictive disorders represent an area desperately needing new assessment and treatment techniques. The economic and psychological costs of these disorders are staggering. Sobell and Sobell meticulously examine prevalent traditional concepts and paradigms from the behavioral perspective and find them wanting in contrast to promising alternatives. Traditional paradigms and beliefs frequently remain refractive to efforts at change, and the field of alcoholism is no exception. This paper systematically outlines and details the grounds for current controversies. The behavioral formulation has opened the door to new methods of investigation, alternative sources of data, and new treatment approaches, such as those focusing on the problem drinker, controlled drinking, skills training, and relapse prevention.

Maintenance of alcoholism treatment effects has become the focus of particularly interesting and important behavioral theories of relapse (Marlatt, 1982). Cooney, Baker and Pomerleau review basic research on stimulus control, and the outcome of cue exposure strategies to prevent the recurrent relapses that so strongly characterize the behavior of alcoholics and those suffering other substance use disorders. Details of current assessment and intervention techniques have been provided.

Earlier volumes in the Banff International Conference series, *Behavioral Medicine: Changing Health Lifestyles* (Davidson & Davidson, 1980) and *Adherence, Compliance and Generalization in Behavioral Medicine* (Stuart, 1982), highlight applications of behavioral principles to the problems of physical health and illness. No survey of clinical behavior therapy could omit consideration of problems in health psychology. It is appropriate that Philip's paper should address the formidable challenges of pain, since it precipitates most visits to health professionals, and headache, in particular, since it is one of the most prevalent forms of chronic pain. Through empirical analyses of treatment research, Philips concludes that existing theoretical formulations of tension headache and biofeedback treatment are inadequate, leading to the development of a broader model incorporating dimensions of behavioral models of pain that have led to substantial improvements in pain management in the past decade.

At the forefront of contributions of behavior therapy to the treatment of chronic mental patients has been the work of Foy, Wallace, and Liberman. Their paper describes in detail the considerations that led to their current social skills training program. Social skills have been recognized as the elements of effective social adaptations, but the field has been beset by the complexity of the skills and the patience that is required to teach them. The authors have developed and provide their overarching conceptual system and a systematic instructional program that has been adopted by other agencies and institutions. The authors make it clear that within the short time span of 10 years social skills training for chronic mental patients has progressed from training a few topographic or content responses in a few problem situations to comprehensive social and independent living skills training in many broad functional areas.

A careful reading of these chapters leaves one with the impression that clinical behavior therapy has come a long way since it began to acquire general acceptance in the 1960s, but a great deal more needs to be done. Practitioners have become far less preoccupied with the specifics of technique and have come to incorporate in their models of behavior change systems concepts that include the social contexts of clients' lives, clinicians' practices, and interpersonal relationships. Behavior therapists who had been sensitive to these processes and were obliged to turn to alternative therapeutic paradigms can now find them incorporated within the behavioral framework. Also, they can now find the basic canons of behavioral measurement and evaluation applied to these broader concepts. In this manner, clinical behavior therapy will continue to grow.

Kenneth D. Craig

REFERENCES

DAVIDSON, P. O., & DAVIDSON, S. M. (Eds.). *Behavioral medicine: Changing health lifestyles.* New York: Brunner/Mazel, 1980.

KANFER, F. H., & PHILLIPS, J. S. *Learning foundations of behavior therapy.* New York: Wiley, 1970.

KAZDIN, A. E. *History of behavior modification: Experimental foundations of contemporary research.* Baltimore: University Park Press, 1978.

MARLATT, G. A. Relapse prevention: A self-control program for the treatment of addictive behaviors. In R. B. Stuart (Ed.), *Adherence, compliance, and generalization in behavioral medicine.* New York: Brunner/Mazel, 1982.

RACHMAN, S. J. and WILSON, G. T. *The effects of psychological therapy.* Oxford: Pergamon, 1980.

STUART, R. B. (Ed.). *Adherence, compliance and generalization in behavioral medicine.* New York: Brunner/Mazel, 1982.

ULLMAN, L. P., & KRASNER, L. *Case studies in behavior modification.* New York: Holt, Rinehart and Winston, 1965.

ADVANCES IN CLINICAL BEHAVIOR THERAPY

1
Stress: Causes, Measurement, and Management

TED L. ROSENTHAL and
RENATE H. ROSENTHAL

In this chapter, we mainly want to proceed as working clinicians. Rather than attempting to review an extensive literature on stress, dating from before Selye and burgeoning since, we will provide some general references that cover the ground very well. An excellent chapter by Novaco (1979) surveys the history of the subject and formulates the issues in ways that have influenced our thinking, as has a discussion of the related topic of pain regulation (Turk & Genest, 1979).

Our colleague, Dr. Hagop Akiskal, has taught us his conception of affective disorder as a "final common pathway" which expresses the *conjoint* effects of genetic, phenomenological, neurochemical, and life event variables. In vulnerable persons, for example, a full-blown depression may emerge under conditions that most peers can take in stride. Reciprocally, there may be some conspiracies of circumstance—such as

This chapter is dedicated to John W. Thibaut, Ph.D., mentor, friend, homme leger. The Tennessee Department of Mental Health and Mental Retardation, J. Brown, M.D., Commissioner, and the Memphis Mental Health Institute, R.D. Fink, M.D., Superintendent, are gratefully acknowledged for funding to the first author that partly supported completion of this chapter.

chronic, debilitating illness—that provoke affective hazard for all but the hardiest souls. In either case, it is probably a mistake to conceive the problem in univariate terms and seek its single cause. Most often, a complex tissue of *biobehavioral* factors kindles affective disturbance, with covariants exacerbating or mitigating each other. Stressful life experiences can be potent sparks for persons predisposed by fragile adjustment to life or affective temperaments or both (Akiskal, 1979; Depue, 1979). For instance, in some chronic depressions, malaise that seems the result of jaded attitudes and pessimistic philosophical convictions responds to medication that conceivably alters brain chemistry; other forms of chronic dysphoria resist antidepressant drugs but seem the continuing legacy of such developmental stressors as unstable adjustment at home and stormy parental modeling during the patient's formative years (Akiskal, Rosenthal, Haykal, Lemmi, Rosenthal, & Scott-Strauss, 1980; Rosenthal, Akiskal, Scott-Strauss, Rosenthal, & David, 1981). Yet either variant of affective vulnerability can be inflamed by loss or crisis in such important spheres as marital, career, or parenting roles.

There is some evidence to suggest that the network of psychophysiological intercausation is more intricate but better unified than was held by formerly accepted views. Since the data are still emerging, only an illustrative sample is given. It appears that the immune and endocrine systems influence one another through a bidirectional linkage (Besedovsky & Sorkin, 1977). Interrupting the usual sympathetic nervous innervation can inhibit protective immune response. Also, neuroendocrine changes serve to regulate or modulate immunoregulation to a degree not previously supposed (Besedovsky, Del Rey, Sorkin, Da Prada, & Keller, 1979). In turn, various medical therapies—lithium, tricyclic antidepressants, *and* electroconvulsive therapy—that have treated affective disorders successfully can each alter the permeability of the blood-brain barrier, which appears to be regulated by central adrenergic (sympathetic) signals (Preskorn, Irwin, Simpson, Friesen, Rinne, & Jerkovich, 1981). It has long been held that stress, by depleting or shifting the neuroamine balance, may trigger depression (e.g., Anisman & Zacharko, 1982). There are also new data suggesting that subjective self-perceptions and experiences can stimulate sympathetic activity to alter the release of catecholamines (Bandura, Reese, & Adams, 1982). Whatever may be the ultimate conceptualization when all the data are in, it appears that reciprocal, network-like, biobehavioral influences maintain—across the cellular, neurophysiological, and experiential levels of organization in human systems—a striking degree of two-way communication.

Reciprocity in causation among environmental situations, overt behavior, and the person's stored experiences, values, decision-making standards, and interpretations is also a hallmark of social learning theory (Bandura, 1977a, 1982; Rosenthal & Bandura, 1978). By pointing out that bodily acts—such as neurotransmitter production—are part of what the behaving organism does, and that bodily cues—such as emotional arousal, perhaps an adrenergic response to perceived stress—offer compelling information about one's high or low state of well-being, one can see there is an affinity between interactive, biobehavioral thought and the perspective of social learning theory, which informs much of the discussion to follow. If we henceforth emphasize the cognitive-phenomenological aspects of a complex equation, this vantage is taken for convenience. For any personally important mental events, we assume biological concomitants are reciprocally interwoven.

Moreover, in the present state of emergent knowledge, identifying some variable as a "cause" versus an "effect" versus a "concomitant ripple" can present formidable *chicken or egg?* quandaries. Such decisions can be taxing enough for normative, group phenomena, but become more opaque when the goal is to parse the threads of causation stirring the individual patient. For instance, chronic insomniacs attribute their wakeful preoccupations to both somatic and cognitive cues, but more often to the latter (Lichstein & Rosenthal, 1980). Given new data that weather changes which shift the incidence of small positive ions in the air can increase irritability and alter mood for ion-sensitive persons (Charry & Hawkinshire, 1981), and that the intensity of photic stimuli—such as created by amount of daylight changing with the seasons—can also affect mood (Wehr, Wirz-Justice, Goodwin, Duncan, & Gillin, 1979; see also Goodwin & Wehr, 1982), one can see that a division between cognitive and somatic intrusions on sleep may be too crude a distinction. Untangling the causal skeins which, collectively, combine to incite adjustment strains will be no mean feat for the future. It seems most realistic just to reiterate that stressors will likely involve conjoint, *biobehavioral* impact on the person. (For an overview of research on the physiological consequences of stress—as mediated via pituitary secretion after emotional activation of the adrenal cortex—see Riley, 1981.)

Conceptualizing Subjective Stress

Beauty lies in the eye of the beholder. So does a great deal of stress. What one person construes as pressure-laden or noxious, another may calmly take in stride or enjoy. In part, this will depend on the person's *standards* for making judgments and decisions. These, in turn, will reflect the impact of others' precedents on one's own social learning history. Craig's (1978) work on pain illustrates how the same external stimuli can create more distress when social models first exemplify intolerance to pain, and less distress when people first observe stoic fortitude exemplified. Not just experimenter-defined operations—such as the physical parameters of faradic shock or the time a hand is immersed in ice water—but also subjective weighings and definitions determine the aversiveness of painful experiences. For example, many chronic pain patients react to increased discomfort after physical therapy with great alarm and emotionality if they infer that the pain cues indicate further deterioration. The same cues will be well tolerated if interpreted as a temporary, self-limiting "flare-up" due to increased physical activity.

Most important human events span multiple facets. Since the person's own expectations, priorities, and interpretations often count just as heavily, or more heavily, as the "objective" external stimuli, it is probably a mistake to seek to define psychological stress only by reference to explicit stimulus features. A good example of this pitfall concerns the perception of danger during the Blitz of England in the Second World War. The people who lived where bombs fell in greatest numbers and most often, such as London, were not the populations that developed the strongest fears. Instead, the people in outlying areas who were never or rarely bombed were the most worried. They could not predict if and when their turn might come, and this uncertainty seemed to keep the remote danger preying on their minds (Rachman, 1978). True, there may be some circumstances—such as the loss of a person dearly loved—that will count as heavy blows for most humans, but even this illustration does not assure maximal stress for the bereaved. For instance, if the loved one has been enduring prolonged pain or other great adversity, as from a fatal illness, the sufferer's death may come as a comparative relief to close kith and kin.

For such reasons, we have clinical reservations about defining stress in terms of purely overt circumstance and our reservations extend to applying any life event metrics that seek to quantify the stress level of objective events when treating individual patients. The mean impact of defined events may have normative value in weighting a stressor for populations and still not fit well with an individual's subjective perception of the event(s). There have been recent attempts to quantify the *subjective* impact of life events (see Depue, 1979), which may be more clinically viable as a strategy.

Nor in our experience are all very stressful events negative in valence.

They may also be positive but overly arousing. For example, a patient during many years had been highly involved in coaching a competitive sport within the community. The "diversion" brought many kinds of satisfaction. Yet before, during, and after meets the patient was tense as a drum, worked up into an excited pitch of subjectively much-valued arousal. Added to considerable job pressures, which were inescapable since most were inherent in the patient's work situation, this frenzied leisure-time activity was, in overall context, medically hazardous to the patient's health. It was no simple feat, over time, to persuade the person that the psychophysiological costs much outweighed the indisputable gratifications. Yet, when the patient finally passed the coach's mantle to another—and after a period of mourning this retirement and learning to replace it with calmer diversions—there was a visible drop in complaints of feeling chronically weary and overburdened during the coaching season.

Obviously, what one can enjoy and take in stride will in large part depend on the rest of one's life: What else is one doing? What toll is it taking? In short, the view of stress that we espouse and try to teach patients, from the time of their referral, involves the additive, cumulative balance of their lives: What is the total pattern of how one spends time and pursues recurrent involvements? How does one perceive and react to the sum of one's activity pattern or lifestyle? This is explicitly a complex, multivariate framework. It would be fair to acknowledge that our conception of stress is constructivistic and reflects the assumptions of social learning theory regarding how people build up and maintain their personal realities (Bandura, 1977a, 1982; Rosenthal, 1982, 1983; Rosenthal & Bandura, 1978).

A Metastrategy to Reduce Stress

Stemming from the reasoning sketched above, we have no automatic menu of interventions. Treatment procedures (discussed in more detail later) will depend on the person's needs and options, which are carefully assessed, and also—inevitably—on the clinician assigned to the case. However, an array of target changes can be provisionally assembled, and methods selected or devised as needed, to follow a simple, governing principle: Any combination of discrete elements that can be changed for the better improves the total sum.

It will often happen that people can do rather little directly to eliminate or reduce their one or two main hassles. In an otherwise good job, a grouchy supervisor may be a cross that must be borne, especially during the current hard economic times. There are many other burdens that people feel can only be altered by cutting off their nose to spite their face: A rigid and stubborn but otherwise cherished spouse may resist all efforts at joint negotiation and compromise in certain spheres. A job may demand enduring long hours, making tough decisions promptly from limited information, and assuming other heavy responsibilities; yet in pay, chances for advancement, and career satisfaction the job may still offer more than any other feasible position. Some social and community leadership roles may drain an already-busy person's time and resilience, yet remain duties that could only be surrendered at the risk of alienating significant peers, such as customers or colleagues who exert control over the patient's fate. The foregoing are realistic cases in point.

In contrast, the person potentially may be able to shift the balance by improving the manner of handling a number of more minor burdens which, if collectively eased, can make a real difference. Phrased differently, the most *pressing* stressors are sometimes the least amenable to change, while other contributing factors may be readily altered. To communicate this idea vividly, among our copyrighted guidance materials is a diagram showing many different pipes—labeled marital conflicts, financial troubles, tight deadlines, etc.—each pouring fluid at varying rates onto an overloaded, racing turbine. The points being made are 1) that a combination of changes is usually desirable and possible, but 2) that reducing several smaller stress conduits can have substantial benefit for a system whose major strains may not be easily altered.

Some concrete examples are called for. We maintain a file of reasonably priced local restaurants that serve tasty food, and we keep track of which have take-out services and which stay open late and when most others are closed, e.g., Mondays. Such information enables working couples on tight budgets to stop for supper on the way home from work or to phone in advance and have their meal ready to pick up, as a way to lighten the burdens of kitchen chores. We have taught more affluent patients ways to reduce conflicts between wanting to maintain lofty standards when entertaining guests and the excessive drain on a busy professional that can be created by epicurean aspirations. One option is for the host(ess) to prepare one or two courses of high quality, but to obtain the remaining dishes from a caterer or restaurant.

Here is another homely instance from clinical practice. Memphis sits on a very—almost painfully—flat flood plain. The Mississippi river aside, it is hard to deny the scenic limitations of our geology. This has led to a local stereotype that diversity in the settings for such outdoor recreation as hiking cannot be achieved without traveling for the better part of a day, e.g., to the Smoky or Ozark mountains. For someone who needs to learn to get away, to take breaks, and to move the sedentary body, it becomes easy to invoke the monotonous terrain as an excuse for inaction and procrastination, since rarely is there time to visit the mountains. Fortunately, less than one hour's drive west, a narrow ridge juts up and runs some 200 miles. It contains high, rolling land for walking (amidst farms and fruit orchards) and offers marked contrast in topography and vegetation. Since most Memphis residents somehow remain unaware of this nearby ridge, we can open a new vista for people who truly believe the only uplands lie hundreds of miles distant.

Likewise, we stay informed about tourist sites near Memphis, keep handy at the office maps of adjacent regions that can be explored in a weekend, and ride herd on the many pleasant—but poorly publicized—audience events that just play for a few nights, or occur regularly but only once per week, or require advance preparation and reservations to assure access to a limited number of seats.

In a much larger, more crowded metropolis, the specific tactics would differ but the principles at issue would stay much the same. Perhaps one analogy might be inertia justified by the formidable traffic strains that must be overcome in order to get out of town for a change of scene. The legitimate exodus worries might be forestalled by urging the wary patient to try departing when traffic is light, e.g., before dawn, and delaying breakfast until in the hinterlands, etc. In such ways, therapists can help to enrich an environment by modeling solutions not often spontaneously discerned by overtaxed, stress-prone people. Playing "travel agent" or entertainment consultant may seem an unorthodox activity for a therapist. However, we consider such counseling an integral part of stress management. As the discussion proceeds, other concrete examples of ways to surmount resistance, negativism, or apathy will be provided for their heuristic value.

THE UNIVERSITY OF TENNESSEE PSYCHIATRY PROGRAM

Part of what clinical scientists emphasize and neglect will depend on the population they seek to serve and on the program goals of their agency. To understand the frame of reference in which we operate and the boundary conditions demarking our activities, a sketch is needed of the Stress Management Program at the University of Tennessee College of Medicine, Department of Psychiatry. The program is new, having "formally" begun in 1981. Unlike programs at other settings, our priorities are, first, to generate fee-producing services to our clientele; next, to make these services the basis for educating psychiatry residents, psychology interns, and medical students; and eventually, to conduct and support systematic research. We still are very much in the first phase, seeking to build a referral base for patients able to afford private fees or covered by insurance for our services. Getting started has not been an easy task for three reasons: Above all, we came into being during a sustained economic recession which has curtailed "elective" treatment throughout the College of Medicine facilities and the local community. Second, there is the need to steer around historical "town-gown" jealousies between the University and private practitioners, while at the same time attempting to develop referral sources from private practice physicians who, by tradition, refer patients mainly to colleagues also in private practice; this requires us to tread lightly in various spheres. Finally, the cultural values of the Memphis/Mid-South region breed suspicion or disinclination toward psychiatry and psychotherapy of all forms. We have tried to diminish such sociocultural reluctance by emphasizing 1) that we hope to serve people who, essentially, are psychiatrically normal—not "mental patients"—but are showing physical or experiential signs of stress; 2) that we mainly use rather brief, practical techniques; and 3) that many of our goals—such as promoting constructive lifestyle changes—strive to prevent physical illness and to enrich life, not merely to remove glaring or dramatic symptoms.

We thus aim just at the private sector and at a spectrum of persons for whom stress effects may be either the primary problem or an added risk in the face of serious or life-threatening illness. The cases we have seen to date have ranged from self-referred executives to heart patients referred by their cardiologist after bypass surgery because their pattern of life was further worsening their already slim chances of functional recovery. Despite the practical obstacles earlier noted, we have achieved some growth, but a good deal more slowly than we would have wished. For this reason, it is not yet possible to present meaningful outcome data. Nonetheless, there has been enough clinical material to allow us to sharpen our intervention tactics, to check and refine some of our assessment devices, and—tentatively and loosely—to test out our theoretical conceptualizations; so far we are encouraged to find that they bear up well. Hence, we work hard to teach our patients our conception of the issues, and have devised and copyrighted a schematic to aid us by interrelating what we deem the key factors. There is evidence that supplying an organized framework to explain the principles and reasons which underlie and steer therapy can improve treatment outcomes (e.g., Davis, Rosenthal, & Kelley, 1981).

Moreover, when patients find that seemingly discrete symptoms and pressures—which they have noticed and worried about—can be integrated into a coherent picture, the burdens of mystery and uncertainty (themselves stressful) diminish, and optimism and cooperation rise. Strange as it may sound, patients are often genuinely surprised and relieved to learn, for instance, that excessive ruminations accompanied by muscle tension and hyperventilation can indeed account for the *physical* sensations which spur worry, fear, and distress in already overburdened individuals. Since many of the changes we seek to promote are cognitively simple, but demand making efforts to dispel the inertia of long-ingrained habits, patients' confidence in us, and especially in their own perceived self-efficacy about undertaking change, becomes a critical factor in treatment. For these reasons, we feel that giving a coherent explanation of cause and remediation is essential, at least for our well-educated and intellectually curious modal patient (Rosenthal, in press). A summary view of our conceptual premises is now needed.

THE TERRAIN OF VICIOUS STRESS CYCLES

Since the functional stressors include the person's perception that some event(s) are threatening or overtaxing *and* his reactions to that perception, it is natural for the person to attempt actively to grapple with the problems—insults, dangers, losses, etc.—as perceived. However, cognitive preoccupation invites emotionality, worry, negative anticipation, and much self-referent rumination, which itself can become a prime maintaining mechanism of subjective misery (Bandura, 1982; Rosenthal & Bandura, 1978). If hypervigilance to stressful content continues long enough, an exacerbation cycle is initiated in which four interrelated but separable elements can be distinguished.

Physiological Cues

The person interprets circumstance as dire or threatening and the body reacts accordingly with sympathetic innervation. Heart rate may speed up and the person notices that. The familiar manifestations of anxiety—including muscle tension, tightness or "butterflies" in the stomach, sweaty palms, dizziness, etc.—may occur, and the person notices them. The arousal so manifested will often interfere with sleep functions. Insomnia and shallow sleep are frequent complaints and can spawn cumulative fatigue. The person notices these, too, and usually worries about them as well. The sensations of noxious emotional arousal (and their physiological coeffects earlier surveyed) are not only intrinsically unpleasant, but the typical effects or covariates themselves become legitimate further sources of concern. The manifestations of prolonged hypervigilance both validate that the person is in a crisis *and* intensify the perceived gravity of the stress-related cues being scrutinized.

Attention

   In this way, attention comes to focus on emotionality, worry, physical illness, and the perceived stressors which, collectively, dominate cognition. The person may rehearse provocations—such as strains or unfairness at work—and thus multiply them manyfold in subjective duration compared to their duration in real time. The person may elaborate failure-laden scenarios in which anticipated threats and the person's own inability to master them loom as dominant themes; objective difficulties nearly always become exaggerated. Virtually always, the burdened person cannot leave job troubles at the office or marital conflicts at home. Selective attention to arousal content can further raise emotional arousal. Yet, despite various efforts, the person is not able to divert attention away from the selected, stressful content without resort to alcohol or other drugs. Often, the person's efforts and exhortations from family and friends to "get it off your mind" are ill advised. There may be conflictful internal dialogues ongoing, with the person trying to "fight" the attentional malfocus and, by so doing, keeping the adversary, stressful content salient.

   The scientific literature on the role of attention in maintaining distress and means to counteract such mental sets is reviewed in detail elsewhere (Rosenthal, 1980). The clinical reality is that most patients we see present such complaints in varying forms but do not know how to alleviate them and often adopt strategies that are counterproductive. For example, a patient who was preoccupied with cardiac symptoms took to feeling her pulse for reassurance each time she noted her heart "pound," "jump," or "skip a beat."

Thought and Memory

   Perceiving stressful cues and preoccupation with them can have a number of harmful effects that continue or worsen such cycles. First, there are data to show that memory has state-dependent features. For instance, positive mood facilitates retrieval of positive memories from storage and negative states facilitate negative memories (see Rosenthal, 1980, 1983). This systematic bias toward recalling unpleasant content combines with the self-referent fixation on "worry and danger thoughts." In effect, the sampling balance of cognition is shifted toward a dominance of negative information being processed and attended to, whether the specifics are dysphoric, fearful, threatening, hopeless, or angry in quality—or some combination thereof. This pattern of negative ideation—accompanied by emotional arousal, sleep disturbance, etc.—is fatiguing, and as it continues the person can become very weary. Many patients with no real history of alcohol abuse report that, if they fall into the kind of exacerbation cycle being depicted, they will turn to alcohol (or other chemicals) as a way to self-medicate in order to sleep. Further, preoccupation with negative phenomenology competes with the opportunity *and* the willingness to actively seek out constructive diversions.

Recreation

If one perceives oneself in crisis, or "under the gun," or enduring "intolerable" provocations, it is not surprising if the pursuit of "good clean fun" loses perceived value. One tells oneself one cannot afford the time, one doesn't have the energy, or that there is nothing one would enjoy. As a result, one abdicates leisure interests that might, if continued, distract attention away from the negative content (see Rosenthal, 1980), create a "breathing spell," and perhaps even introduce some positive reactions that could somewhat shift the negative experiential balance. Despite the mystique of our allegedly affluent and leisure-oriented society, the legacy of the Puritan Ethic endures for stress-prone people. Rarely do we treat a person who maintains a good balance of regular physical exercise, active social involvements, and valued, hobby-like, *noncompetitive* diversions. Our patients in large part have never cultivated such buffer activites earnestly or, if they have, these "frivolous" distractions are the first activities dropped when the going gets tough for the person. It is *not* that most patients lack recreational interests; they often report many interests which they rarely enact because they haven't the time or are too tired at the end of a day, etc.

In other words, as potential buffers to compete with stressful cues, recreational activities are very much underused by our stressed population *and* various cognitive rationales (no time; too tired) support their belief that such diversions are expendable. We often see situations where both husband and wife remain bogged down in their respective stresses and burdens. One spouse may be unwilling to consider alternative modes of action, citing the long litany of duties which must be fulfilled. The other may be ready to contemplate increasing recreation but, in the face of the other's intransigence, feel too guilty to initiate enjoyable pastimes while the mate persists in toiling. For such cases, conjoint sessions are in order.

In overview, then, we see people who are characterized by 1) high states of arousal and its physical effects, perhaps most notably poor sleep and repetitive monitoring of physical stress symptoms; 2) attentional and 3) ideational fixation on the mental representations of the perceived stressors *and* their own elaborations in terms of anticipated bad consequences, doubts of personal adequacy to alter the situation, etc.; and 4) a tendency to allow a stressful focus to drive out such constructive—and potentially stress-reducing—activities as physical exercise, social recreation, and low-key hobbies and diversions. These conclusions stem from a variety of data, including what we have learned during therapy efforts. However, we are pleased that much of the picture now emerges, at least in main outlines, rather quickly from our initial assessment procedures.

MEASURING STRESS AND ITS PHENOMENOLOGY

An advantage of our setting in a medical school is that we are able to work closely with physicians in various specialties. A psychiatrist, Dr. Neil Edwards, is an active member of our stress program staff. As a result, we ordinarily can have access to various physiological measures, such as blood pressure, or, when indicated, can obtain the results of sophisticated laboratory tests. As a matter of policy, we try to obtain referrals from physicians and, when a patient is self-referred, urge that a full physical workup be obtained. This sort of close, interdisciplinary collaboration does more than foster good professional relationships. More than once, such somatic complaints as tachycardia and hyperventilation have turned out to be partly created by adrenergic overactivity. When placed on beta-blocking medication, a chunk of the patient's distress promptly abated.

Even assuming that physical contributions have been assessed and treated by medical colleagues, it can be a mistake to attribute detached objectivity to all physical measures. One suspects it might be difficult for subjective state to have much *immediate* impact on physiological assays of endocrine or neurochemical levels. However, there are a number of common measures—e.g., heart rate and galvanic skin response—that are used in research because they do promptly reflect emotionality. By the same token, blood pressure readings would appear quite open to the influence of subjective experience. One would not expect the same levels from someone who dwells on highly stressful versus tranquil covert events while the pressures are being measured. In the long run, it may be that general medicine can benefit, and diagnostic accuracy improve, if some apt measures of covert subjective state were to become part of routine physical exams. At any rate, and concordant with our multivariate perspective, it seems best to treat physiological data as one important source of assessment information, but not to assign automatically a privileged status to laboratory indices. The day when "the" prime measures of stress have been validated and consensually accepted lies far in the future.

Appraisal at the University of Tennessee

In addition to the lab data available, and to extensive interviews tuned to the individual circumstances, we routinely obtain three inventory measures from each patient. The first is the Eysenck Personality Questionnaire (Eysenck & Eysenck, 1975), which will be familiar to many readers. We use this for several reasons, which include its brevity (less than 100 true-false items), its relevance to personality theory (since it reduces to three, conceptually-validated, orthogonal factorial dimensions), and its promise as a convenient device for eventual comparative research. Both other self-report instruments seek to depict personalized (rather than nomothetic) reality; both have been developed and copyrighted in conjunction with our U.T. Program.

The BAROMAS stress scales were developed jointly with Professor Albert Bandura and are extensions of his theorizing and research on *self-efficacy,* which is a person's judgment or prediction about being able to execute some defined act with greater or less confidence (see Bandura, 1977b, 1978, 1982). Among the component BAROMAS scales, the following are representative: Tolerance of Telephone Urgency requires the person to rate own ability and confidence about performing each item of a task hierarchy that starts with putting an "urgent" telephone call on hold and concludes with deferring the "urgent" call until the next week. Reducing Time Pressures begins with asking if the person can comfortably goof off for five minutes, and the hierarchy mounts by a series of time intervals up to comfortably goofing off all day. Physical Exercise starts with doing some chosen sport 30 minutes each week, and its steps ascend to doing some sport(s) for an hour on most days and several evenings of the week. Unwinding asks if, at the end of a long, hard, tension-arousing day, but *without* the use of drugs or alcohol, the person can unwind self 5%, 10%, etc. in steps until 100%. Priorities is a measure of preoccupation and ability to maintain elective attention focus. It begins by asking if the person can divide the many tasks needing completion into high versus low priority groups. The item hierarchy then proceeds to assess if the person can give *full attention* to the first task chosen (for 15, then 45, then 90 minutes) *without* worrying about the other tasks not yet begun. This format continues across finishing the first, starting and finishing a second, and then a last task. The penultimate item is as follows: "Can you congratulate (praise) yourself for finishing the things you HAVE done WITHOUT thinking of the things you still have not done?" On all such items, the person must judge if the act can be managed and, if so, what is the confidence in doing the step as described.

Across the domains sampled, we feel these self-efficacy scales give a very useful map or picture of the patient's phenomenology regarding representative events that may—but need not—be perceived and reacted to with subjective manifestations of stress. For example, a patient who was at life-threatening cardiovascular risk reported (on a scale of 0 to 100) confidence levels of 40 in perceived self-efficacy for putting an "urgent" phone call on hold for half an hour, for comfortably goofing off for 15 minutes, and for doing an hour's physical exercise four days per week. Confidence levels of 30 were given for being able to unwind self 60% after a hard day, for picking a final task for the workday and starting it without worry about those not done, and for working on that last task for 45 minutes, giving it full attention, without worrying about the others.

To illustrate individual differences, let us compare the foregoing ratings with those of a same-sexed peer seen, in part, for stress resulting from the effects of spouse's illness. This person's confidence was 100 about delaying an urgent call for half an hour and comfortably goofing off for 15 minutes; it dropped to only 30 if goofing-off were to last one hour. This second patient felt there was zero chance of doing an hour's physical exercise four days per week, unwinding self 60% without alcohol or drugs after a long, hard day, and likewise no chance of picking a last task, or giving it full attention for 45 minutes, without worrying about the other tasks not completed.

Our second copyrighted device is the Leisure Interests Checklist (LIC) which consists of 135 categorical activity items, such as #11. "Making jams, jellies, preserves, pickles, etc." and #109. "Sewing, knitting, crocheting, needlepoint, etc." For each item, the person must rate own degree of interest on a four-point scale from Very Much to Not at All. The activities range from #100. "P.T.A., Scouting, or other work with children" and #98. "Attending Church or Bible Study" to #38. "Looking at sex books, films, or magazines" and #4. "Betting and gambling," with the items deployed in a purely randomized order. As with the BARO-MAS, we do not as yet have criterion validity data, but the LIC (Form B) appears to be quite content valid. Its last page has space for the respondent to supply up to eight interests not in the checklist. We have given it to participants at several group workshops. Only rarely have any interests been added, and then the added option itself perhaps contained diagnostic clues. For instance, one addition read "watching the snow and the rain fall." The final section of the LIC asks the respondent to pick his or her "5 favorite (strongest or least disliked) interests" and then to estimate how many hours are currently spent pursuing each interest in a typical week.

As we use it, the LIC serves a number of functions. It gives a duration estimate of how much recreational time the patient is now spending. This also becomes a pre- to posttreatment measure of duration changes. It allows us to identify which kinds of diversions (if more are needed) the patient is most likely to implement or least likely to detest. It has mnemonic value in reminding people about former pastimes they have let slide and potential pastimes they have thought might be enjoyable but have never gotten around to trying. Finally, we have used it with spouses—who each complete it independently—as a means of locating joint diversions that are mutually agreeable or at least tolerable. We have been surprised that couples will often acknowledge and complain of boredom and claim they have no or few common recreational interests, but they will never have made serious efforts to explore common ground. When we match their individual checklists with them, we have found that unsuspected mutual options may in fact exist. In this manner, assessment can be closely tied to facets of treatment. Similarly, the BAR-OMAS responses help point up concrete spheres of self-modulation in which the person is having difficulty and needs intervention efforts.

DEVISING TREATMENT

Before discussing the more visible stress-reduction techniques that can be combined for the individual patient, it is germane to illustrate a class of problems which can be termed *logjams.* Just as a horseshoe nail may cost the rider and hence the battle, sometimes an impasse in achieving constructive changes may derive from obstacles not often delineated in most texts on conducting treatment. In order to detect and resolve such logjams, the clinician will need a vivid and accurate mapping of the context and patterning of the patient's everyday life.

At times, interview procedures will utterly fail to disclose the actual milieu realities. A vivid example of this concerns a distressed family (treated some years ago) whose fragmented interaction pattern seemed to persist "mysteriously" despite a number of office visits to rectify it. Only after a series of observations in the home did it emerge that each of the several children had a television set in his or her own room, as did the parents. Another color set placed in the living room had become a de facto battle zone. Much of the family members' "free" time was spent either in isolation, glued to their private sets, or in arguing about choice of programs for the color set in their common space. Only after the therapist discovered that seven TVs exerted centrifugal impact on joint interaction and imposed strict limits on the amount of television-viewing subsequently allowed was progress possible.

Here are some further clinical examples. Sometimes a patient's inertia toward making an admittedly needed change can be overcome if the desired new conduct is embedded in undertakings perceived as necessary for the welfare of loved ones. A patient who resists all our efforts to promote commencing some regular physical exercise may find the time and make the effort if, instead of an individual project, exercise is recast as a family endeavor. For instance, the patient may participate more willingly in parent-child biking or swimming to assist the youngsters' physical well-being and socially relevant recreation skills.

Parenting concerns, reciprocally, can underlie some blatantly self-damaging behavior. One cardiovascular patient, with serious risk of mortality after open-heart surgery, resisted making many needed changes, including reducing massive daily consumption of alcohol. It eventually emerged that the patient and an adult child, living in the home, were locked in continual combat over the offspring's escapades, which included drug abuse, promiscuity, and deception. It further emerged that the miscreant met full DSM-III criteria for Antisocial Personality. Only after showing the patient and later the spouse the DSM-III description of the syndrome, along with its poor prognosis, and discussing those implications with them in detail, was it possible to help the patient abandon hope of "straightening out" the erring offspring, whose adventures typically led the patient to sedate himself with whiskey. A plan was jointly developed to induce the miscreant to move to another city, a plan which the spouse (who was able to view the situation with greater detachment), rather than the patient, was to execute. Once these changes were accomplished, hitherto "impossible" alterations in lifestyle were achieved by the patient rather rapidly.

Incipient divorce will often elicit vengeful provocations between estranged spouses. In one case, a patient whose career entailed sudden duty phone calls, which the person was to answer promptly, was besieged by the angry ex-spouse. Despite the advice of legal counsel, the ex-spouse would telephone at odd hours, disturb the patient's sleep, and lure the patient into acrimonious debates. Not only was the patient exhausted, but the ex-spouse's intrusions kept issues (such as the welfare of the children), which were already negative preoccupations for the patient, as a focus of attention. We solved this problem by advising the patient to install a telephone recording device. Not only did this allow screening wanted phone calls needing rapid response from the ex-spouse's belligerent assaults, but the legal ramifications of having statements recorded acted to curb the ex-spouse's intrusions.

A final example concerns how material possessions can tyrannize their owners by encroaching on personal space. For some time, the couple in question despaired of implementing our strong suggestion that more personal diversion for the wife was needed as a counterweight to her domestic responsibilities. The couple was doing well financially and interpersonally, yet somehow hobby projects at home could not be accomplished. Over time, and with considerable embarrassment, they confessed that there was no space in their large home to execute the jointly preferred diversion because it required space and every nook and cranny in each room was crammed with a horde of objects. Many of these had economic value but were rarely used. After the couple was eventually persuaded to identify the surplus items and to dispose of them via a garage sale, it became possible for the hobby to proceed. Despite some initial reluctance toward the sale, both spouses expressed relief once it was accomplished. In addition, burdens of dusting, cleaning, and otherwise maintaining the rarely used objects were reduced after their sale, hence reducing the wife's domestic chores, which had been oppressing her.

STRESS-REDUCTION MEDLEYS

We suspect that our approach to treating stress may be more comprehensive than some other perspectives, but we have no brand-new stress-reduction techniques to offer. This is partly because a visible kinship exists among most "cognitive-behavioral" interventions (Rosenthal, 1982, 1983). For instance, there appear to be two key types of overlap across a host of relaxation techniques. A list of them might include 1) Jacobsen's progressive muscle relaxation, 2) his newer *self-operations* approach, (Jacobsen, 1938, 1970), 3) symbolic relaxation via positive imagery, 4) yoga, 5) transcendental and other meditation techniques, 6) certain forms of martial arts "mental discipline" procedures, 7) autogenic training, and related methods. First, all appear to introduce a state of relative calmness, whose depth will depend on such factors as the patient's skill in applying the method and diligence in practicing it regularly. Second, all have the capacity to divert the patient's attention *away from* stressful content, and distraction has been shown to have arousal-reducing properties (Rosenthal, 1980). By the same token, regular vigorous but noncompetitive physical exercise has similar effects—often more strongly—if it becomes woven into a person's lifestyle. On the assumption that "half a loaf is better than none," we try to assess what works best for the person *and* what is best enjoyed or least resisted, and then emphasize those options. For instance, some persons do not generate vivid covert images; for them, muscle relaxation or meditation seem better bets. Some persons may loathe jogging or biking but accept swimming or dance as viable, etc.

Likewise, assertiveness training by various means, Novaco's (1979) anger management extension of the method, cognitive restructuring—especially to reduce unrealistic self-standards and perfectionistic expectations—and a substantial amount of persuasive social influence (Rosenthal, 1980, in press) may all be used and combined as indicated. We often supply conjoint marital counseling and sometimes provide guidance to our patient about ways to better handle a spouse or a child. As earlier mentioned regarding the psychopathic offspring, we may urge or advise major milieu changes. Other examples have included helping a couple confront very intrusive grandparents by giving them the choice of negotiating explicit limits on impinging on the younger generation's privacy or instead having the couple accept a job in another state, i.e., depriving their elders of the opportunity for frequent contacts. Often we engage in task analyses to help the person simplify and lighten burdens at work or at home. Such efforts usually involve seeking to change patients' cognitive standards for self-regulation (Bandura, 1977a; Rosenthal & Bandura, 1978) in terms of how many, and how rapidly, duties can realistically be undertaken. For this purpose, we have evolved the mnemonic slogan "slower not lower standards" and invoke it and its governing principles repeatedly until the message begins to sponsor at least provisional changes, which, in turn, can give the patient evidence that wiser self-pacing can reduce perceived stress. A corollary entails helping people to delimit their own versus others' responsibilities more wisely, rather than assuming an unfair share of burdens. For instance, an estranged spouse facing divorce may need aid to redefine as the other's responsibility explanations to children or kin, as well as efforts to maintain peace during the interim before the divorce is final, rather than uncritically accepting a disproportionate share of divorce-related strains.

In most cases, various points arise at which interventions must be improvised to deal with concrete particularities. There is no manual to guide such instances, which span a motley host of specifics. These have included a "crash course" in systematic desensitization—largely self-administered after the principles have been learned—for a patient living out of town who faced an important career-related speaking engagement with anticipatory worry. We continually apply exemplary symbolic modeling, and sometimes participant modeling, to ease the transition to newer styles of conduct. We help patients develop stepwise task hierarchies and schedules for diverse activities, and assist in devising strategies and plans to facilitate change.

A simple example involves a patient with a physical ailment for which medication for symptomatic relief had been prescribed to be taken "as needed," but the patient grew concerned about becoming dependent on the medicine. We agreed on this decision rule: Wait 15 minutes and reassure yourself as best you can that the discomfort does not signal a major flare-up. If the symptom worsens, take the medicine; if the symptom mainly abates, do not take the medicine; if the symptom remains ambiguous, wait another 15 minutes and apply the same rule.

A much more complicated example of planning involves helping lonely patients to find suitable dating partners and to make new friends. In such cases, we try to analyze with the patient where congenial partners have higher-than-random likelihood of congregating. Depending on the person's values and tastes, this may render church, sports, civic, nature (e.g. Sierra Club, Audubon Society), philanthropic, crafts, performing arts, or educational settings more promising and salient. Of course, no guarantee exists that, for instance, becoming involved with a little theater group will assure access to suitable heterosocial partners. Back-up alternatives and an iterative process of "if at first you don't succeed, try, try again" are usually necessary.

Finally, we sometimes find ourselves engaging in what amount to philosophical discussions with patients. The topics may involve what kinds of sexual activities are "legitimate" or how soon after meeting is any erotic intimacy "seemly." (Where strong religious convictions are at issue, we may get the patient's clergyman or one of the same denomination to consult on doctrinal aspects.) Or, the issue may be what is "fair" to another person, such as an estranged spouse. In this sphere of value judgments, we are most like conventional psychotherapists, seeking to aid patients in exploring the issues fully and reaching their own best decisions without abridging their value options because of our own personal biases. Decisions about abortion, getting married or divorced, career plans or changes, and choice of schools for children would fall into this category, except where matter of fact or consensus enter, e.g., obtaining informed data about the academic quality and atmosphere of one school versus another. In sum, 1) we tune interventions to the individual and 2) help patients to change or improve the collective impact of myriad—presently or potentially—stressful aspects of their lives. We doubt that an approach much more narrow in scope will prove clinically viable.

An Epistemological Mini-epilogue

We are sometimes asked by colleagues and students if our foregoing clinical perspective is a shift toward "eclecticism" or an abandonment of "behaviorism." From our standpoint, the answer is "No" for a number of reasons. First, utilization of a technique does not mean acceptance of its parent viewpoint. If, for instance, perhaps from lack of a more cogent alternative, one may utter an "um-hmm" to a patient, this does *not* indicate acceptance of such Rogerian premises as belief in a positive, unidirectional tendency toward personal "growth." There is no doubt that we routinely use interventions that, loosely, can be accurately labeled "cognitive-behavioral," *but*—as a conceptual scheme—social learning theory is amply distinct from many, perhaps most, of the conceptual frameworks which share those same methods (Rosenthal, 1982). Second, social learning theory is not a static or "complete" system, but continues to evolve and expand (Bandura, 1982; Rosenthal, 1983). A good illustration would be the biobehavioral developments that opened this chapter: They are congenial enough to social learning views that the promise of eventual dalliance and ultimate cohabitation should not be dismissed prematurely. Third, social learning theory cannot "abandon" Behaviorism since it is not, and has not been, a Behaviorism—as that term is presently used most widely. In the technical sense, social learning theory is a *constructivistic* position (Bandura, 1977a, 1982; Rosenthal, 1982, 1983; Rosenthal & Bandura, 1978; Zimmerman, 1980), and further, in current taxonomies of theory, probably qualifies as a contextualistic position as well (Zimmerman, 1983).

However, the issue of "behaviorism" or not is more complex. In current parlance, "behavioral" has become a term with so broad a spread of meaning that further specificity is necessary. Social learning theory, emphatically, is not and has never been a Behaviorism of the sort exemplified by operant "theory." One could, indeed, argue (as others have) that operant research may have spurred exciting discoveries, but as *theory* the position is not much more than deft embroidery upon Thorndike's *law of effect*. Likewise, one may accept empirical principles—such as the Yerkes-Dodson law—that have become identified with neoHullian thought, and yet not adopt the larger, "conditioning," frame of reference exemplified by such scholars as Hans Eysenck. Historically, there have been "behaviorisms" with which social learning theory has closer affinity. The best example, antedating both Hull's and Skinner's systems, is Tolman's. Tolman as a thinker and a writer—who dedicated his major book on the topic of learning to the white laboratory rat—showed by that jest a very different *stylistic* approach to science than is found in current operant technology. Yet Tolman explicitly labeled his views as a "behaviorism." In brief, Tolman conceived complex mediating acts to intervene between overt stimuli and responses. He even credited the lowly rat with some measure of the capacity to form expectancies and engage in decision-making. Further, Tolman and Kurt Lewin did, eventually, mutually agree that they were saying much the same (and quite cognitive) things. From that tradition sprang much of the germinal work in experimental social psychology. For example, Thibaut and Kelley's (1959) research and theorizing on an "exchange" approach to social interaction are fruits of the Tolman-Lewin position, as is Thibaut's research on the development of social norms (e.g., Thibaut, Friedland, & Walker, 1974). Unlike its main contemporaries, social learning theory has been strongly influenced by ideas and data drawn from experimental social psychology which, in large part, was first actively sparked by Lewin, his students, and theirs.

Moreover, psychologists are too often ahistorical in their purview and transmit inadvertent stereotypes about their intellectual forebears. Thorndike is usually credited with parenting the experimental psychology of learning. Yet close reading of his work in the original or in *detailed* secondary sources (especially the several editions of Hilgard's *Theories of Learning*, which we draw upon below), discloses greater flexibility than might be supposed. For instance, Thorndike suggested a number of supplementary "laws" of learning. Those included: 1) multiple response, by which learners make *active* efforts to solve problems by trying one solution after another until some strategy works; 2) responding by analogy to new situations with conduct that brought satisfaction in similar past situations; 3) selective response, by which people can *discern* the key features of a new problem or challenge and then react accordingly; and 4) attitude or mental set, in which cultural and temperamental factors help determine action and also *contrast* principles (Rosenthal, 1980) which help fix the value of an achievement, hence akin to Lewin's *level of aspiration*. Thus, some stereotypes notwithstanding, Thorndike himself (especially when seeking to provide practical advice for applied education) was less of a "behaviorist" than is often assumed. The strands in Thorndike just noted, were—in some sense—transmitted to or rediscovered by both Tolman and Lewin, and subsequent developments from similar reasoning are often woven throughout current social learning theory (Bandura, 1977a; Rosenthal, 1983; Rosenthal & Bandura, 1978). In conclusion, then, the "behavioral" credentials of social learning theory—and applications drawn therefrom—will depend on which "behavioral" lineage(s) the reader chooses to emphasize.

REFERENCES

AKISKAL, H.S. (Ed.). Affective disorders: Special clinical forms. *Psychiatric Clinics of North America*, 1979, *2*, whole No. 3, pp. 417-629.

AKISKAL, H.S., ROSENTHAL, T.L., HAYKAL, R.F., LEMMI, H., ROSENTHAL, R.H., & SCOTT-STRAUSS, A. Characterological depressions: Clinical features of "dysthymic" versus "character-spectrum" subtypes. *Archives of General Psychiatry*, 1980, *37*, 777-783.

ANISMAN, H., & ZACHARKO, R.M. Depression: The predisposing influence of stress. *The Behavioral and Brain Sciences*, 1982, *5*, 89-137.

BANDURA, A. *Social learning theory.* Englewood Cliffs, N.J.: Prentice-Hall, 1977(a).

BANDURA, A. Self-efficacy: Toward a unifying theory of behavioral change. *Psychological Review*, 1977(b), *84*, 191-215.

BANDURA, A. Reflections on self-efficacy. *Advances in Behaviour Research and Therapy*, 1978, *1*, 237-269.

BANDURA, A. Self-efficacy mechanisms in human agency. *American Psychologist*, 1982, *37*, 122-147.

BANDURA, A., REESE, L. & ADAMS, N.E., Microanalysis of action and fear arousal as a function of differential levels of perceived self-efficacy. *Journal of Personality and Social Psychology*, 1983, *43*, 5-21.

BESEDOVSKY, H.O., DEL REY, A., SORKIN, E., DA PRADA, M., & KELLER, H.H. Immunoregulation mediated by the sympathetic nervous system. *Cellular Immunology*, 1979, *48*, 346-355.

BESEDOVSKY, H.O., & SORKIN, E. Network of immune-endocrine interactions. *Clinical and Experimental Immunology*, 1977, *27*, 1-12.

CHARRY, J.M., & HAWKINSHIRE, F.B.W. Effects of atmospheric electricity on some substrates of disordered social behavior. *Journal of Personality and Social Psychology*, 1981, *41*, 185-197.

CRAIG, K.D. Social modeling influences on pain. In R.A. Sternbach (Ed.), *The Psychology of Pain*. New York: Raven Press, 1978.

DAVIS, A.F., ROSENTHAL, T.L., & KELLEY, J.E. Actual fear cues, prompt therapy, and rationale enhance participant modeling with adolescents. *Behavior Therapy*, 1981, *12*, 536-542.

DEPUE, R.A. (Ed.). *The psychobiology of the depressive disorders: Implications for the effects of stress.* New York: Academic Press, 1979.

EYSENCK, H.J., & EYSENCK, S.B. *Manual: Eysenck Personality Questionnaire.* San Diego, CA: Educational and Industrial Testing Service, 1975.

GOODWIN, F.K., & WEHR, T.A. (Eds.). *Circadian rhythms in psychiatry.* Pacific Grove, CA: Boxwood Press, 1982.

JACOBSEN, E. *Progressive relaxation.* Chicago: University of Chicago Press, 1938.

JACOBSEN, E. *Modern treatment of tense patients.* Springfield, IL: Charles C. Thomas, 1970.

LICHSTEIN, K.L., & ROSENTHAL, T.L. Insomniacs' perceptions of cognitive versus somatic determinants of sleep disturbance. *Journal of Abnormal Psychology*, 1980, *89*, 105-107.

NOVACO, R.W. The cognitive regulation of anger and stress. In P.C. Kendall & S.D. Hollon (Ed.), *Cognitive-behavioral interventions: Theory, research, and procedures.* New York: Academic Press, 1979. Pp. 241-286.

PRESKORN, S.H., IRWIN, G.H., SIMPSON, S., FRIESEN, D., RINNE, J., & JERKOVICH, G. Medical therapies for mood disorders alter the blood-brain barrier. *Science*, 1981, *213*, 469-471.

RACHMAN, S.J. *Fear and Courage.* San Francisco: Freeman, 1978.

RILEY, V. Psychoneuroendocrine influences on immunocompetence and neoplasia. *Science*, 1981, *212*, 1100-1109.

ROSENTHAL, T.L. Social cueing processes. In M. Hersen, R.M. Eisler, & P.M. Miller (Eds.), *Progress in Behavior Modification*, Vol. 10 New York: Academic Press, 1980. Pp. 111-146.

ROSENTHAL, T.L. Social learning theory. In G.T. Wilson & C.M. Franks (Eds.), *Contemporary behavior therapy: Conceptual and empirical foundations.* New York: Guilford Press, 1982, pp. 339-363.

ROSENTHAL, T.L. Cognitive social learning theory. In N.S. Endler & J. McVicker Hunt (Eds.), *Personality and the behavior disorders*, revised ed. New York: John Wiley, 1983.

ROSENTHAL, T.L. Some organizing hints for communicating applied information. In B.J. Gholson & T.L. Rosenthal (Eds.), *Applications of cognitive-developmental theory.* New York: Academic Press, in press.

ROSENTHAL, T.L., AKISKAL, H.S., SCOTT-STRAUSS, A., ROSENTHAL, R.H., & DAVID, M. Familial and developmental factors in characterological depressions. *Journal of Affective Disorders*, 1981, *3*, 183-192.

ROSENTHAL, T.L., & BANDURA, A. Psychological modeling: Theory and practice. In S.L. Garfield & A.E. Bergin (Eds.), *Handbook of psychotherapy and behavior change* (2nd ed.). New York: John Wiley, 1978. Pp. 621-658.

THIBAUT, J.W., FRIEDLAND, N., & WALKER, L. Compliance with rules: Some social determinants. *Journal of Personality and Social Psychology*, 1974, *30*, 792-801.

THIBAUT, J.W., & KELLEY, H.H. *The social psychology of groups.* New York: Wiley, 1959.

TURK, D.C., & GENEST, M. Regulation of pain: The application of cognitive and behavioral techniques for prevention and remediation. In P.C. Kendall & S.D. Hollon (Eds.), *Cognitive-behavioral interventions: Theory, research, and procedures.* New York: Academic Press, 1979. Pp. 287-318.

WEHR, T.A., WIRZ-JUSTICE, A., GOODWIN, F.K., DUNCAN, W., & GILLIN, J.C. Phase advance of the circadian sleep-wake cycle as an antidepressant. *Science*, 1979, *206*, 710-713.

ZIMMERMAN, B.J. Social Learning Theory and cognitive constructivism. In I.E. Siegel, R.M. Golinkoff, & D. Brodzinsky (Eds.), *Piagetian theory and research: New directions and applications*. Hillsdale, N.J.: L. Erlbaum, 1980.

ZIMMERMAN, B.J. Social Learning Theory: A contextualist account. In C.J. Brainerd (Ed.), *Recent advances in cognitive-developmental theory*. New York: Springer, 1983.

2
Cognition, Consciousness, and Processes of Personal Change

MICHAEL J. MAHONEY

Historians of psychology will probably look back upon the decade of the 1960s as having ushered in the first widespread application of scientific methodologies and experimentally derived strategies for the modification of human behavior. Behavior therapy clearly moved from a young and pioneering endeavor to one of the fastest growing and most energetic developments of twentieth century psychology (Kazdin, 1978). As pioneering behavior therapists moved from the laboratory to clinical and field settings, they were faced with a range of challenges that were to have an indelible impact on the directions of their thinking, research, and services. Indeed, one could argue that the impressive conceptual and technical evolution that has characterized behavior therapy in the last three decades offers one of the clearest examples of what theoreticians in the physical, biological, and related sciences have termed spontaneous self-organization (or, more technically, "autopoiesis" (cf. Jantsch, 1980; Prigogine, 1980; Zeleny, 1980). The behaviorist's response to the numerous challenges, ambiguities, and impinging forces of applied service have, of course, ranged widely. My intent here is not to attempt a delineation of the historical and developmental processes involved; rather, I will briefly review where behavioral researchers appeared to have begun their pioneering efforts and how these efforts have been shaped by subsequent events and enigmas.

The rate of change within behavior therapy in the past few decades has been almost phenomenal. There are probably a number of different viable historiographic analyses of these changes and the themes they represent. Allow me to take a moment here to share some of my own personal impressions on the developmental sequences that seem to have characterized this field. To begin with, one cannot look back upon the behavior therapy of the 1960s without being impressed by its relatively undifferentiated endorsement of the law of effect, the veridicality of conditioning, and the undisputed power of logical empiricism as an adequate metatheory of scientific knowledge. Desensitization was the favored topic of experimental research and the most frequent technique employed in outpatient clinical intervention. The hottest theoretical controversy had to do with some of the continuing debates around two-factor learning theory, the role of verbal behavior and awareness in change, and the critical parameters of counterconditioning. Needless to say, we have come a long way since then. Although several of these issues remain controversial, the majority have had to make room for more pressing and contemporary challenges to behavioral theory and practice.

One of the earliest and most dramatic shifts in both theory and practice had to do with the area of self-control. Aside from the important work that had been gestating in the laboratories of people like Albert Bandura and Frederick Kanfer, the only attempts to address self-regulatory processes had been sparse and, for the most part, conceptual rather than experimental (cf. Ferster, Nurnberger, & Levitt, 1962; Goldiamond, 1965; Skinner, 1953). Richard Stuart's (1967) data-based report of a behavioral strategy for treating problems in weight control remains one of the classic pioneering efforts in this area. Nevertheless, when Cautela (1969) rendered the first review of behavioral self-control, there was not a sizeable empirical literature upon which to draw. The situation had not changed much when I offered my own review of the area in 1972 (Mahoney, 1972).

It is worth noting that the appearance of self-control as an area of interest also marked the first real attempts to incorporate private events into theory and techniques in behavior therapy. Lloyd Homme's (1965) provocative little paper on "coverants, the operants of the mind" represented one of the first daring steps in that direction. At about the same time, Joseph Cautela (1966, 1967) introduced the technique of "covert sensitization," the first of a subsequent family of covert conditioning techniques. These developments were not initially presented as criticisms of the conventional views regarding conditioning, human learning, and clinical practice. On the contrary, they were offered as logical and empirically testable derivations from the writings of such people as Skinner, Guthrie, and Pavlov. The private events discussed by these early "covert conditioners" were explicitly defined as miniature stimuli and responses.

When Bandura published his classic volume on the *Principles of Behavior Modification* in 1969, the field was ripe for a comprehensive theoretical integration. Besides offering such an integration, Bandura presented a strong argument, both theoretically and empirically, for the critical role of central (as opposed to peripheral) processes in human learning. While it was soon recognized as one of the most important volumes of the decade, Bandura's book was met with mixed reactions both within and outside behavioral quarters. Its controversial status was illustrated by the fact that the book was actually banned on some campuses where its unorthodox contentions were considered threatening. It was already becoming clear to behavior therapists that much of the ideological unity that they had experienced in the late '50s and early '60s was soon becoming an historical remembrance. The field was unquestionably enmeshed in conceptual differentiation processes.

In the decade of the '70s, the themes of self-control and cognitive processes became even more central in the maturation of behavior therapy. Publications in the area of self-regulation began to appear with increasing frequency in the first half of that decade, and they have since become one of the main themes in contemporary behavioral research. When the book *Cognition and Behavior Modification* (Mahoney, 1974) appeared in 1974 it was still difficult to publish a cognitive or mediational treatise in the behavioral journals. It was not long, however, before those journals and the behavioral conferences were expanding to accommodate the growing interest in this area. By the time behavior therapy entered the decade of the 1980s, cognition and self-regulation had become major areas of contribution and continuing development. The writings of such people as Aaron Beck (1970, 1976), Albert Ellis (1962), and Donald Meichenbaum (1977) had begun to have a significant impact on the direction and nature of these developments. This movement of behavior therapy in the direction of self-control and cognitive processes could itself consume a volume of reflections and evaluative commentary. There were certainly more things going on in behavior therapy than these two trends, and some of their personal and paradigmatic consequences may someday merit historical analysis.

The decade of the '80s will surely present historians of behavior modification with ample material for contemplation and interpretation. Besides significant developments in behavioral medicine, community applications, behavioral assessment, and professional training issues, the field is marked by more heterogeneity and differentiation than at any previous point in its development. There is talk of technical eclecticism, rapprochement with psychoanalysis, collaboration with nonbehavioral therapies, and a substantially heightened awareness of some of the ethical and sociocultural dimensions which any applied science must eventually confront. There have already been a number of commentaries, both critical and favorable, regarding specific themes and controversial issues in the immediate and distant future of behavior therapy. Judging from the vicissitudes of the last two decades, any predictions about the future of this energetic discipline must be offered with a generous dose of tentativeness and an open acknowledgment of uncertainty.

Let me therefore shift my focus away from this brief commentary on the recent development of behavior modification and move toward the basic points that I would like to share in this paper. While I cannot predict where behavior therapy may be going in the 1980s, I would like to think that I have a somewhat clearer idea about the current directions of my own thinking and research. Since I have belabored some of these themes elsewhere (Mahoney, 1982, in press), I will confine my remarks here to a brief overview of two broad navigational themes: 1) recent developments in cognitive psychology, and 2) disequilibrium and emotive processes in personal change. Following my overview of these themes, I will conclude with a brief comment on unifying themes amidst our developmental diversity. Without further preview, then, let me broach the first theme.

RECENT DEVELOPMENTS IN COGNITIVE PSYCHOLOGY

It is interesting, and somewhat ironic that, while most areas in psychology have been becoming more cognitive during the last two decades, cognitive psychology has itself been experiencing a theoretical revolution. What has been particularly interesting to me has been the extent to which modern cognitive psychology has moved in the direction of emphasizing active behavioral processes. Indeed, the major paradigm clash between what I would call "old" and "new" cognitive psychology has been termed by specialists in that area as a controversy between "sensory" and "motor" models of cognition (Weimer, 1977). Without belaboring some of the subtleties and technical points in this competition, let me suggest that the major features which differentiate these two approaches might be enumerated along three dimensions:

1) the relative activity of the central nervous system, particularly as such activity is expressed in the construction rather than passive registration of experience;
2) the adequacy of associationism as a dominant metatheory of ordering processes in the nervous system;
3) the critical significance of a hierarchical approach to consciousness and brain functions.

Some of these themes become a bit technical in their finer points, and I shall not presume to render them in detail here. What I will offer, instead, is a brief exposition on each of these three points. For a more complete and comprehensive discussion, I recommend the original sources.

CNS Activity in the Construction of Experience

The first and perhaps most fundamental dimension of controversy has to do with the role of the nervous system as an active participant in its own experience. Sensory theories of cognition, which are characterized by information-processing and cybernetic models, presume that the human nervous system is a relatively passive recorder of events and relationships. I say "relatively" because many of the sensory theories argue that the brain is a very active recorder (Anderson, 1980; Haugeland, 1981; Neisser, 1976). In other words, they suggest that the nervous system is very active in its relatively passive task of mapping the world. As Weimer (1977) has aptly noted, these sensory theories tend to study cognition and define its processes from "the outside inward" and in a manner that is reminiscent of the doctrine of naive realism. Reality is assumed to really be "out there" rather than "in here."

Sensory approaches to cognition, which have been dominant for several decades in cognitive psychology, presume that the stimulus is a specifiable entity independent of the nervous system. Thus, most of the analyses that are endorsed by such a perspective attempt to trace a stimulus input through iconic storage, a buffer system, short-term memory, encoding processes, and, in some cases, retention in long-term memory. Cybernetic feedback loops are invoked as a means of explaining the organism's regulation and direction of purposive activity. This is the basic prototype of information-processing that was the focus of my theoretical analysis in *Cognition and Behavior Modification* (Mahoney, 1974). At that time, it was not clear to me (or to most cognitive psychologists) that there might be a more viable alternative to sensory theories of human cognitive processes. The move to central processes in the nervous system was a quantum leap in and of itself. It soon became obvious to increasing numbers of the cognitivists that the cybernetic portrayals of information flow did not address such core issues as the construction of meaning, novelty, motivation, and choice. A more adequate alternative was needed.

The emergence of such an alternative may be a topic that will intrigue historians for some time to come. It turns out that—as in many other instances of scientific "discovery" (Mahoney, 1976)—the seeds of an alternate view of cognition not only were present during the monarchy of sensory theories, but had actually been elucidated in the early writings of such people as Wilhelm Wundt (Blumenthal, in press). Indeed, the growing popularity of "action theory" in Europe at this point in time is partly a reflection of the belated appreciation of some of the work of Wundt and early workers at the Wurzberg School (cf. Hacker, Volpert, & von Cranach, in press). The contemporary rendition of this approach in cognitive psychology has been termed "motor theory" and is ironically "behavioral."

Although there are some important issues of controversy within and among motor theorists, this approach is best represented in the writngs of Bransford (1979), Hayek (1952, 1978), and Weimer (1977, 1982). In essence, motor theories of cognition stress the fact that the human nervous system actively participates in creating the stimulation to which it is responsive.

> What the motor metatheory asserts is that there is no sharp separation between sensory and motor components of the nervous system which can be made on functional grounds and that the mental or cognitive realm is intrinsically motoric, like all the nervous system. The mind is intrinsically a motor system, and the sensory order by which we are acquainted with external objects as well as ourselves . . . is a product of what are, correctly interpreted, constructive motor skills (Weimer, 1977, p. 272).

The clearest example of this active and constructive participation might be what are called "feedforward mechanisms" which are invoked as a supplement to (and not a replacement of) the feedback processes that figure so prominently in sensory theories. Feedforward mechanisms, whose operation has been corroborated in both cognitive and psychobiological research, effectively "prepare" the organism for certain categories of experience. They are preperceptual and predominantly tacit. By the time a human infant is seven months of age, for example, he or she is capable of abstract concepts which involve invariant features (Cohen, 1979). After being shown a series of pictures of different birds, infants will show habituation to the category and fail to exhibit an orienting response. When a stimulus from outside the category of birds is presented to them, however, they will immediately exhibit focal attentive behavior. Although the invariant features of the category may be unspecifiable, it is clear that even the nascent brain is developing perceptual and conceptual expectations regarding experience. It is when those expectations are phenomenologically violated that the organism has an opportunity for learning. According to motor theories, reality is neither and both "out there" and "in here"—it is, in a theoretical as well as a practical sense, the ongoing dynamic *relationship* between these boundaries.

The practical and clinical significance of feedforward mechanisms and some of the other concepts in motor theories of cognition are probably well beyond our current appreciation. It is not too large a leap, however, from the basic operation of these mechanisms to such phenomena as self-fulfilling prophecies (Jones, 1977), confirmatory bias (Mahoney, 1974, 1976), and expectancy or placebo processes (Shapiro & Morris, 1978). It is tempting and, I believe, warranted to draw parallels between these processes and the painful tenacity of many "neurotic" and otherwise limiting patterns in human behavior. The anxious individual tends to prepare for danger, the depressive often prepares for helplessness, and the violent or hostile person seems to prepare for some form of violation. Since I have spelled out some of my speculations about the far-reaching implications of feedforward mechanisms and motor theories of cognition elsewhere (Mahoney, in press), I shall allow the preceding comments to suffice for the moment and move on to the second point of contention between sensory and motor theories.

The Inadequacies of Associationism

Although the doctrine of associationism has a long and relatively venerable history, its limited usefulness and heuristic inadequacies have become increasingly apparent in the last few decades. In their lengthy discussion of the relationship between brain functions and human experience, for example, philosopher Karl Popper and psychobiologist John Eccles concur on the theoretical and empirical bankruptcy of associationism (Popper & Eccles, 1977). Indeed, as Popper makes clear in his comments on the topic, contemporary psychology may well be suffering unnecessary limitations in its stubborn preoccupation with molecular associationism and billiard-ball determinism: "[Associationism], I suggest, is the most terribly misleading doctrine which has emerged from Cartesian dualism. . ." (p. 194).

The formal (theoretical) limitations of associationism were elucidated by Bever, Fodor, and Garrett (1968) in a brief but incisive analysis of "the terminal metapostulate" of associationism. I don't think it would be misrepresentative of their argument to translate it into the simple assertion that associationism can never hope to offer an adequate theoretical vantage point because—by its own explicit rule—it cannot transcend the linear sequence of particulars. In other words, associationism is an inherently two-dimensional doctrine of orderly relationships. Its popularity among behavioral and neobehavioral thinkers has probably derived in part from its intrinsic two-dimensionality, which complements attempts to remain at a single level of analysis and to avoid mediational (three-dimensional) propositions (Mahoney, 1974; Skinner, 1950, 1959).

The problems of associationism could consume a volume in and of themselves. They range from the esoterics of explanatory power (which is absent in associationism and other purely descriptive doctrines) to the embarrassments of empirical disconfirmation. For the present point, all that need be emphasized is that the "new look" in cognitive psychology recognizes the limitations of a metatheory that cannot accommodate the complex hierarchical nature of human behavior. Associationism is by its own criteria two-dimensional. It can only deal with dimensions of before and after or left and right in one's mathematical analyses; because it can only be two-dimensional it is inherently limited to a weakly predictive and superficially descriptive level of analysis. It cannot offer an adequate account. It cannot move to the abstract, since all statements about variables within the system have to be kept at the same level of analysis. Skinner (1950) chose to endorse associationism because he did not want to leave the level of analysis of input and output. If you stay at that level of analysis, you are staying at a descriptive two-dimensional level.

Another problem with associationism is that it encourages something that I will call the "tyranny of technique." This refers to our continuing homage to the power of technique despite its relatively poor showing in the parceling of outcome variance. The percentage of variance attributed to various techniques is hotly debated, and the problems of drawing valid inferences from the extant clinical research are all too clear (cf. Kazdin, 1980, 1982; Kazdin & Wilson, 1978). On the whole, however, the attribution of therapeutic power to techniques per se would seem to be a risky undertaking:

> It appears that . . . personal factors are crucial ingredients even in the more technical therapies. . . . This is not to say that techniques are irrelevant but that their power for change pales when compared with that of personal influence. . . . We believe the hypothesis is supportable that the largest proportion of variation in therapy outcome is accounted for by preexisting client factors, such as motivation for change and the like. Therapist personal factors account for the second largest proportion of change, with technique variables coming in a distant third (Bergin & Lambert, 1978, p. 181).

This same conclusion was reiterated by Jerome Frank (1982) in his recent observation that "more of the determinants of therapeutic success lie in the personal qualities of and the interaction between patient and therapist than in the particular therapeutic method used" (p. 15). When one looks at our journals, however, one finds that most of the research is focused on technique variables. It is time, I believe, to reappraise our conception of technique and to distinguish persuasive messengers and their basic message (Frank, 1982; Mahoney, 1981; Strupp, 1982). One can use a lot of different messengers to get a point across in a therapeutic situation.

Bringing all of this back to the problems of associationism, it is interesting to note how we in the social sciences have tried to align ourselves with and to imitate the physical sciences. Much of this flattering imitation has involved a mechanistic billiard ball approach—the kind that highlights vector analyses and simple techniques of influence. Unfortunately, our imitation of the physical sciences—which is ill-advised given the greater levels of complexity in our subject matter (Hayek, 1967, 1978; Weimer, Note 1)—is likewise embarrassingly outdated. Billiard ball determinism went out in 1927 with the Copenhagen Interpretation of quantum mechanics. The physicists gave it up, but psychology still hopes to discover the mechanics of particulate influence. This is illustrated by our continuing preoccupation with particulars versus systems and with content over process. We seem to be much more preoccupied with content than we are with the processes involved in the generation and specification of that content.

The point I am trying to make here is that sensory theories are basically deterministic and associationistic while motor theories are basically determinate and hierarchical. In deterministic analyses one is generally presuming a billiard ball model of a system, whether that system be the universe or an atom. The basic mechanism of influence in such a system is the simple summation of linear forces of different magnitudes and directions. In determinate order the contention is that there are certain constraining rules which place limits on the range of events that can come out of a particular interaction, but the specific outcome cannot be accurately predetermined. One can estimate probabilities of events and classes of events, but a complete and adequate prediction of particulars will always remain beyond the practical and conceptual capacities of any theory of complex phenomena. This means, of course, that our quest for simple laws of human behavior—and for pure techniques of influence—is inherently misguided. As Hayek (1967) has noted:

> the search for the discovery of laws is not an appropriate hallmark of scientific procedure but merely a characteristic of the theories of simple phenomena . . . in the field of complex phenomena the term "law" as well as the concepts of cause and effect are not applicable without such modification as to deprive them of their ordinary meaning. . . . And the prejudice that in order to be scientific one must produce laws may yet prove to be one of the most harmful of methodological conceptions (p. 42).

The most viable alternative to laws of particulate prediction are abstract rules of constraint which specify broad classes of interactive influence. The heuristic implications of a shift away from naive determinism and associationism are, in my opinion, among the more optimistic developments in recent scientific history (cf. Weimer, Note 1).

Hierarchy Theory

The third major distinction between sensory and motor theories of cognition is the relative importance they assign to a hierarchical approach to complex phenomena. The sensory theories are associationistic and therefore cannot use a hierarchical approach. They stay at a two-dimensional level of analysis, which is potentially descriptive but inherently non-explanatory. Motor theories, on the other hand, subscribe to something that I would call "hierarchical structuralism," which is basically the contention that the ordering processes within the central nervous system are themselves ordered. Another way of saying this is that they are functionally stratified. One of the most cogent and comprehensible arguments for this is a book called *The Sensory Order* by Friedrich Hayek (1952), a Nobel laureate in economics. I will be surprised if future historians do not view that book as one of the major theoretical works in twentieth century psychology. While it is still relatively unknown except in progressive quarters of cognitive psychology, Hayek's analyses of the central nervous system are some of the most revolutionary and heuristic treatments yet offered. Likewise, his major contentions are consistent with much of what has come about in psychobiology and experimental cognitive psychology in the three decades since their publication (cf. Eccles, 1971; Pribram, 1971; Popper & Eccles, 1977; Shaw & Bransford, 1977; Weimer & Palermo, 1974, 1982).

One of the most sweeping and incisive arguments that Hayek offers has to do with "the primacy of the abstract." It has direct bearing on our foregoing discussion of the analysis of particulars.

> The contention which I want to expound and defend here is that . . . all the conscious experience that we regard as relatively concrete and primary, in particular all sensations, perceptions and images, are the product of a super-imposition of many classifications of the events perceived. . . . What I contend, in short, is that the mind must be capable of performing abstract operations in order to be able to perceive particulars and that this capacity appears long before we can speak of a conscious awareness of particulars. . . . When we want to explain what makes us tick, we must start with the abstract relations governing the order which, as a whole, gives particulars their distinct place (Hayek, 1978, pp. 36-37).

The basic contention here is that the human brain is essentially an organ of classification and order and that the processes involved in these functions are inherently abstract and therefore tacit. From this perspective, all experience is an active construction of the nervous system and all particulars of content are a reflection of the abstract rules (tacit processes) which are a prerequisite to them.

Any discussion of tacit processes leads, of course, into the highly charged realm of "the unconscious." There is often a reflexive reaction

to this term in behavioral quarters. Unconscious processes conjure up
Sigmund Freud, mentalistic speculation, and unscientific sophistry. I
have elaborated elsewhere on my own initial reactions and resistance to
the accreditation of unconscious processes and to some of the excess
meaning we seem to attach to such accreditation (Mahoney, 1980, 1982).
In brief, there is nothing inherently unscientific about such processes
and there is no rational imperative that we equate them with Freud's
conjectures. Despite my belated appreciation for his clinical genius and
theoretical innovations, I continue to reject—among other things—the
Freudian reification of the unconscious. The contrast between Freud's
view of tacit processes and the perspective taken by motor theorists is
illustrated by yet another gem from Hayek:

> It is generally taken for granted that in some sense conscious ex-
> perience constitutes the "highest" level in the hierarchy of mental
> events, and that what is not conscious has remained "sub-conscious"
> because it is not yet risen to that level. . . . If my conception is
> correct . . . [we are not aware of much that happens in our mind]
> not because it proceeds at too low a level but because it proceeds
> at too high a level. It would seem more appropriate to call such
> processes not "sub-conscious" but "super-conscious" because they
> govern the conscious processes without appearing in them (1978,
> p. 45).

The potential relevance of unconscious processes for our understanding
of human change will probably remain controversial for a long time. It
will take time and reflection to get past some of the associations, if you
will pardon the pun, that have been built up around anything associated
with Freud. The need to reappraise our notions in this area is, however,
quite apparent. Besides the compelling theoretical arguments of such
writers as Hayek (1952, 1967, 1978), Polanyi (1966), and Weimer (1977,
Note 1), there is a growing body of clinical and experimental evidence
emphasizing the importance of tacit processes in human experience (e.g.,
Bowlby, 1979; Guidano & Liotti, 1982; Nisbett & Wilson, 1977; Shaw
& Bransford, 1977; Shevrin & Dickman, 1980).

By way of wrapping up this discourse on recent developments in
cognitive psychology, let me offer the following review and commentary.
Sensory theories of cognition are basically passive, associative, deterministic, and preoccupied with concrete particulars. The newer motor
theories of cognition are active, hierarchical, subscribe to determinate
order rather than naive determinism, and emphasize the abstract proc-

esses that generate concrete particulars. A legitimate question is whether this shift within cognitive psychology is a progressive one. That is, do the motor theories serve us better than their sensory predecessors in our attempts to understand human behavior and its change? That, of course, is the debate. I won't presume to decide it for you. My own opinion on it should be pretty obvious, in that I am excited about the expanded capacities of the newer cognitive approaches. Possible clinical implications of the motor perspective are worth briefly noting.

One of the most salient here is the idea that we are active participants in our own experience—far more active than we had previously assumed. This contention suggests that the person acts as a co-creator in problem formation and resolution as well as in general well-being. As Cris Williamson says in a song about process, "we are the changer and the changed." The motor approach is congruent with—but moves well beyond—behavioral participation and reciprocal determinism because it analyzes moment-to-moment experience as a dynamic exchange. The feedforward and feedback processes blend together so that the separation between input and output becomes anything but obvious. The motor theories also fit well with our clinical impressions about clients being extensively involved in the creation and maintenance of life stresses. This point is reminiscent of Walt Kelly's famous line that "we have met the enemy and they are us." With motor theories, however, the enemy is also the ally. That is, much of the power for change is within the individual, not the technique. This has clear implications for our notions of personal responsibility and our approach to personal counseling.

A second clinical implication is that the motor theories invite us to move beyond the problem level of analysis. In my current clinical work, I view a personal problem as a felt discrepancy between the way things are and the way one would like them to be. That is the problem level and it is the focus of most contemporary Western approaches to therapy. Pattern level is reflected by an orderly repetition of the problem or problems. Process level has to do with the functional significance and personal meaning of the problems and patterns. Moving from problem to pattern to process invites a progressive and facilitating shift in our approach to counseling. As I have suggested elsewhere (Mahoney, 1982), significant personal change seems to inherently involve changes in personal meaning. Regardless of theory or technique, all forms of therapy strive to produce changes in meaning. It may be the meaning of a stimulus, the meaning of a performance, the meaning of a relationship, and so on, but it is clear that the client seeks and the therapist offers a shift in meaning. At pattern and process levels of analysis, it is much easier to recognize and work with shifts in personal meaning. This does not, in my opinion, deny the significance of problems or "symptoms" in therapy, but it suggests that our attention and professional energies might be more effectively focused on the ordering processes which generate and/or maintain problematic patterns.

DISEQUILIBRIUM AND EMOTIVE PROCESSES

The concepts of balance and equilibrium are pervasive in our theories and treatment. We assume, rightfully so, that the brain is wired with negative feedback logic. This is most apparent in the lower and midbrain structures where homeostatic mechanisms are operative any time a critical variable assumes a value that is outside our latitude of acceptance. The system then kicks in like a thermostat and regulates for balancing. At the cortical level the negative feedback logic takes the form of discrepancy. The only way one can challenge a feedforward mechanism is to produce a discrepancy, to produce something that wasn't expected; it is my hunch that a lot of what we are doing in therapy is just that. We are often producing incongruities which the individual must work to assimilate into his/her old belief system, or he/she must accommodate the discrepancy by changing that system.

It is interesting to note how order and balance converge in our theories. We talk about behavioral disorder, emotional imbalance, and psychological dysfunction. We also frequently invoke opponent processes to describe or explain the dynamics of order and balance. The history of Western and Eastern thinking reflects a high frequency—across disciplines and across ideologies—of hypothesized opponent processes. Lao-Tze introduced this notion in Eastern writing with his elaboration of the doctrine of *Tao* and the complementary principles of *yin* and *yang* (Tomlin, 1963). The same concept of "the attunement of opposite tensions" appeared at about the same time in Western philosophy (ca. 500 B.C.) in the writings of Heraclitus. The appeal of this idea of competing forces is quite apparent in such diverse areas as the dialectics of Hegel, Piaget's notions of assimilation and accommodaton, Mowrer's two-factor learning theory, and Solomon's opponent process theory of motivation. At the sociology of science level, Thomas Kuhn (1977) has called it "the essential tension"—an apt term for our pursuit of theoretical models that emanate from a metatheory of conflict or complementarity. The "sodium pump" is but one illustration of our resort to hypothetical opponent processes to explain an observed violation of the principle of entropy.

The strands of thought that are being here woven into a primitive tapestry are as follows:

1) Our nervous systems are dependent on contrast for all levels of their functioning—from the simplest act of perception to the most complex act of conceptualizing.
2) The current cognitive and psychobiological literatures are beginning to favor dynamic over static models of CNS ordering processes—e.g., metaphors of interference waves and holistic representation are gaining popularity over the linear flow diagrams and storage metaphors of the cyberneticians.
3) The metaphor of dynamic opponent processes may be a heuristic one for our understanding of such phenomena as psychological "disorder," "emotional imbalance," and certain patterns of cyclicity in human development.

I don't claim to have reached any confident conclusions about opponent processes, other than that they are the undeniable substrate of most, if not all, human experience. David Hume once noted that ignorance and surprise are incompatible, since surprise entails an expectancy based on presumed knowledge. Surprise is a phenomelogical registration of discrepancy, and discrepancy appears to be an essential feature of learning.

At the gross anatomical level, it is easy to find complementary opponent processes in system regulation—e.g., the phenomenon of reciprocal innervation of agonistic and antagonistic muscle groups or the contrasting functions of ascending and descending reticular bundles. And if we leap to the clinical level it is not difficult to identify opponent process assumptions. A more pertinent theme here, however, is that of disequilibrium and our tacit models of balance. Our implicit function as therapists is that of protecting and/or restoring balance. The majority of our clients present with the complaint of disequilibrium, usually experienced and expressed emotionally, and our goal has understandably been to help them restore equilibrium and reduce suffering. How do we do that? Our strategy depends, of course, on our notions about "emotional processing" (Rachman, 1980). The three most basic approaches are probably insight, discharge, and control. In all insight-based strategies of intervention, the basic assumption is that reason is more powerful than emotion—that disequilibrium can be analyzed, understood, and cognitively reordered. The strategy of emphasizing emotional discharge is probably best represented by people like Arthur Janov (1970), Harvey Jackins (1965), and Stanley Keleman (1979). The basic idea here is to discharge the excess of negative affect. The third approach to disequilibrium is the strategy of control, which involves manipulating the controlling parameters of the feelings. Behavior therapy has been a prototypic representative of the controlling strategy.

In actuality, of course, all of our extant theories include combinations of the above three strategies. For the most part, however, they continue to share the illusion that these three spheres of experience—thoughts, feelings, and actions—can be meaningfully isolated. I would not be surprised if future historians were to chuckle at our preoccupation with this relatively parochial segregation of cognition, affect, and behavior. There were people—they might write—who thought you focused on changing behavior and could assume that the affect and cognition would follow; they were called behavior therapists. And then there were the cognitive therapists who said that changing cognitions was the efficient route since cognition is the substrate of all behavior and affect. The affective or provocative therapists said that changes in feelings would alter cognitive and behavioral processes. But, as we already appreciate, the nervous system is simply not divided that way, functionally or structurally. It is time that we stop feeding the less heuristic debates and invest our inquisitive energy in the more holistic models of experience.

My major concern around the issue of disequilibrium and emotive processes is that we may be misdirecting our commendable humanitarian intentions to help an individual in suffering. The danger is that we may be tacitly endorsing our clients' prejudices against anxiety, depression, and anger—the three most salient forms of "negative affect." Our culture has not been egalitarian in its prescriptions and proscriptions regarding these presumably darker dimensions of human feeling processes. Besides being associated with self-limiting, self-destructive, and violent patterns of action, the dysphoric emotions are usually unpleasant or intensely painful. It is therefore not surprising that we struggle to avoid or escape their experience and that much of contemporary therapy is aimed at the control, discharge, and rationalistic realignment of negative feelings. My concern here is that our understanding of human affect is still very primitive and preliminary. We have some intriguing theories and valuable research directions (e.g., Lewis & Rosenblum, 1978; Plutchik & Kellerman, 1980; Zajonc, 1980), but we are still relatively ignorant of the complex patterns and relationships that characterize emotional phenomena. Thus, we don't really know whether our therapeutic attempts are as clearly "in the client's best interest" as we would like. By attempting to artificially "equilibrate" a client we may be unknowingly exacerbating an emotional episode or, more seriously, interfering with a poorly understood natural expression of emotional processing.

This class of phenomenon could be illustrated on a number of clinical dimensions. The client who seeks therapy in order to develop better control of his or her negative affect is a case in point. To the extent that the quest for control has become part of the problem pattern, this client may be vulnerable to potentially self-defeating solutions. If he or she works with a therapist who shares a "controlling" philosophy of life, their collaboration may evolve along the lines of developing progressively greater control over feelings. I have worked with a number of clients who fit this description, and their struggles are often painful and enduring. Their limited ability to control their unpleasant feelings often becomes a secondary source of frustration and stress. They are frightened of their own emotional processes and frustrated with their inability to perfectly regulate them. In my work with them, such themes as control, limits, and "dangerous" feelings often move to the foreground.

The point of all of this is that our tacit notions about emotional processes exert a pervasive influence on how we approach and conduct therapy. There are now ample signs that emotional disequilibrium may serve a vital role in energizing and directing personal development (Frank, 1982; Mahoney, 1980, 1982). There are also recent developments—ranging from "pendulum theory" in linguistic development (Nelson & Nelson, 1978) to "order through fluctuation" in chemistry and physics (Prigogine, 1980)—that suggest the need for a more dynamic conception of balance and the role of disorder in systems development. Prigogine's work on negentropic self-ordering processes in open systems has already spawned some exciting ideas about reappraising our traditional strategies of intervention and artificial equilibration (cf. Jantsch, 1980; Zeleny, 1980).

Whatever else they may be, emotional processes serve a critical role in personal knowing. The limbic and pre-limbic structures of the human brain seem to be powerful participants in learning processes. Our experience of "desynchrony"—the imperfect covariation between cortical and subcortical phenomena—is a frequent and sometimes frustrating reminder of the fact that we are comprised of partially independent subsystems. The harmony of head and heart remains an elusive ideal, and it has become increasingly clear that changes in cognition, behavior, and affect may proceed with generous gaps in timing, intensity, and integration. My main point in this section has been to suggest that we reappraise some of our basic ideas about the nature and regulation of emotional processes and the painful disequilibrium that is so often associated with significant personal change. We will, I believe, be more helpful to our clients as we develop a deeper appreciation of those processes and their functions in adjustment and well-being.

CONCLUDING REMARKS

I have talked about recent developments in cognitive psychology and, more briefly, about the role of emotive processes and disequilibrium in personal change. These are two of the more fascinating themes in our current attempts to understand and facilitate individual development. They interconnect, I believe, with such significant issues as resistance to change, the role of attention, and the limiting parameters of effort as a monolithic strategy for coping (Mahoney, 1982, in press). The ultimate yield of these research themes remains, of course, a future historical issue. Rather than further belabor their promise, I would like to close with a comment on these "changing times."

Whether we choose to call it revolution or evolution, it seems increasingly clear that behavior therapy is in the process of changing. The growing popularity of cognitive approaches is only one expression of that change. It is also important to note that the broader field of psychotherapy is showing signs of dramatic development (Garfield & Kurtz, 1976; Harvey & Parks, 1982). These are, indeed, exciting times. My closing comment has to do with the importance of our appreciating the values and intentions that underlie our rapidly changing expressions of professional service. Amid the rallying cries of this and that competing paradigm, it is all too easy to lose touch with the enduring pulse of progress. Let us therefore move forward—perhaps to different drummers—with an acknowledgment of the unity of our intent, if not always our models and methods. Beneath the diversity of theory and technique there remains a strong and unifying commitment to helping people in their personal development. It is in this sense that I believe our technical differences are much less important than our humanitarian similarities. A deep appreciation of shared intentions may help to facilitate our professional participation in the dialectics of the next decade. If history is any indication, we will probably change in unanticipated ways. Change—as we know all too well—is seldom simple, easy, or painless, but it is an inherent aspect of all growth, individual and theoretical. And it is often in the process of change that we develop a deeper appreciation of that which is most enduring.

REFERENCE NOTE

1. WEIMER, W.B. *Rationalist constructivism, scientism, and the study of man and society*. Manuscript in preparation.

REFERENCES

ANDERSON, J.R. *Cognitive psychology and its implications*. San Francisco: W.H. Freeman, 1980.

BANDURA, A. *Principles of behavior modification*. New York: Holt, Rinehart & Winston, 1969.

BECK, A.T. Cognitive therapy: Nature and relation to behavior therapy. *Behavior Therapy*, 1970, *1*, 184-200.

BECK, A.T. *Cognitive therapy and the emotional disorders*. New York: International Universities Press, 1976.

BERGIN, A.E., & LAMBERT, M.J. The evaluation of therapeutic outcomes. In S.L. Garfield & A.E. Bergin (Eds.), *Handbook of psychotherapy and behavior change*. 2nd ed. New York: Wiley, 1978. Pp. 139-189.

BEVER, T.G., FODOR, J.A., & GARRETT, M. A formal limit of associationism. In T.R. Dixon and D.L. Horton (Eds.), *Verbal behavior and general behavior theory*. Englewood Cliffs, NJ: Prentice-Hall, 1968.

BLUMENTHAL, A.L. Wilhelm Wundt: Psychology as the propadeutic science. In C. Buxton (ed.), *Points of view of the history of modern psychology*. New York: Academic Press, in press.

BOWLBY, J. Knowing what you are not supposed to know and feeling what you are not supposed to feel. *Canadian Journal of Psychiatry*, 1979, *24*, 403-408.

BRANSFORD, J.D. *Human cognition: Learning, understanding, and remembering*. Belmont, CA: Wadsworth, 1979.

CAUTELA, J.R. Treatment of compulsive behavior by covert sensitization. *Psychological Record*, 1966, *16*, 33-41.

CAUTELA, J.R. Covert sensitization. *Psychological Reports*, 1967, *20*, 459-468.

CAUTELA, J.R. Behavior therapy and self-control: Techniques and implications. In C.M. Franks (Ed.), *Behavior therapy: Appraisal and status*. New York: McGraw-Hill, 1969. Pp. 323-340.

COHEN, L.B. Our developing knowledge of infant perception and cognition. *American Psychologist*, 1979, *34*, 894-899.

ECCLES, J.C. *The understanding of the brain*. Englewood Cliffs, NJ: Prentice-Hall, 1971.

ELLIS, A. *Reason and emotion in psychotherapy*. New York: Stuart, 1962.

FERSTER, C.B., NURNBERGER, J.I., & LEVITT, E.B. The control of eating. *Journal of Mathetics*, 1962, *1*, 87-100.

FRANK, J.D. Therapuetic components shared by all psychotherapies. In J.H. Harvey & M.M. Parks (Eds.), *Psychotherapy research and behavior change*. Washington, DC: American Psychological Association, 1982.

GARFIELD, S.L., & KURTZ, R. Clinical psychologists in the 1970's. *American Psychologist*, 1976, *31*, 1-9.

GOLDIAMOND, I. Self-control procedures in personal behavior problems. *Psychological Reports*, 1965, *17*, 851-868.

GUIDANO, V.V., & LIOTTI, G. *Cognitive processes and emotional disorders: A structural approach to psychotherapy*. New York: Guilford, 1982.

HACKER, W., VOLPERT, W., & VON CRANACH, M. (Eds.), *Cognitive and motivational aspects of action*. Amsterdam: North Holland Publishing Co., in press.

HARVEY, J.H., & PARKS, M.M. (Eds.), *Psychotherapy research and behavior change*. Washington, DC: American Psychological Association, 1982.

HAUGELAND, J. (Ed.), *Mind design: Philosophy, psychology, artificial intelligence.* Montgomery, VT: Bradford Books, 1981.

HAYEK, F.A. *The sensory order.* Chicago: University of Chicago Press, 1952.

HAYEK, F.A. *Studies in philosophy, politics, and economics.* Chicago: University of Chicago Press, 1967.

HAYEK, F.A. *New studies in philosophy, politics, economics, and the history of ideas.* Chicago: University of Chicago Press, 1978.

HOMME, L.E. Perspectives in psychology: XXIV. Control of coverants, the operants of the mind. *Psychological Record,* 1965, *15,* 501-511.

JACKINS, H. *The human side of human beings: The theory of re-evaluation counseling.* Seattle: Rational Island Publishers, 1965.

JANOV, A. *The primal scream: Primal therapy, the cure for neurosis.* New York: Putnam, 1970.

JANTSCH, E. *The self-organizing universe: Scientific and human implications of the emerging paradigm of evolution.* New York: Pergamon, 1980.

JONES, R.A. *Self-fulfilling prophecies: Social, psychological, and physiological effects of expectancies.* Hillsdale, NJ: Lawrence Erlbaum Associates, 1977.

KAZDIN, A.E. *History of behavior modification.* Baltimore: University Park Press, 1978.

KAZDIN, A.E. *Research design in clinical psychology.* New York: Harper & Row, 1980.

KAZDIN, A.E. Methodology of psychotherapy outcome research: Recent developments and remaining limitations. In J.H. Harvey & M.M. Parks (Eds.), *Psychotherapy research and behavior change.* Washington, DC: American Psychological Association, 1982.

KAZDIN, A.E., & WILSON, G.T. *Evaluation of behavior therapy: Issues, evidence, and research strategies.* Cambridge, MA: Ballinger, 1978.

KELEMAN, S. *Somatic reality.* Berkeley: Center Press, 1979.

KUHN, T.S. *The essential tension: Selected studies in scientific tradition and change.* Chicago: University of Chicago Press, 1977.

LEWIS, M., & ROSENBLUM, L.A. (Eds.), *The development of affect.* New York: Plenum, 1978.

MAHONEY, M.J. Research issues in self-management. *Behavior Therapy,* 1972, *3,* 45-63.

MAHONEY, M.J. *Cognition and behavior modification.* Cambridge, MA: Ballinger, 1974.

MAHONEY, M.J. *Scientist as subject: The psychological imperative.* Cambridge, MA: Ballinger, 1976.

MAHONEY, M.J. Psychotherapy and the structure of personal revolutions. In M.J. Mahoney (Ed.), *Psychotherapy process: Current issues and future directions.* New York: Plenum, 1980. Pp. 157-180.

MAHONEY, M.J. Clinical psychology and scientific inquiry. *International Journal of Psychology,* 1981.

MAHONEY, M.J. Psychotherapy and human change processes. In J.H. Harvey & M.M. Parks (Eds.), *Psychotherapy research and behavior change.* Washington, DC: American Psychological Association, 1982.

MAHONEY, M.J. *Personal change processes: Notes on the facilitation of human development.* New York: Basic Books, in press.

MEICHENBAUM, D. *Cognitive behavior modification.* New York: Plenum, 1977.

NEISSER, U. *Cognition and reality: Principles and implications of cognitive psychology.* San Francisco: W.H. Freeman, 1976.

NELSON, K.E., & NELSON, K. Cognitive pendulums and their linguistic realization. In K.E. Nelson (Ed.), *Children's language.* Vol. 1. New York: Gardner Press, 1978. Pp. 223-285.

NISBETT, R.E., & WILSON, T.D. Telling more than we can know: Verbal reports on mental processes. *Psychological Review,* 1977, *84,* 231-259.

PLUTCHIK, R., & KELLERMAN, H. *Emotion: Theory, research, and experience.* Vol. 1. New York: Academic Press, 1980.

POLANYI, M. *The tacit dimension.* New York: Doubleday, 1966.

POPPER, K.R., & ECCLES, J.C. *The self and its brain: An argument for interactionism.* New York: Springer, 1977.

PRIBRAM, K.H. *Languages of the brain.* Englewood Cliffs, NJ: Prentice-Hall, 1971.

PRIGOGINE, I. *From being to becoming: Time and complexity in the physical sciences.* San Francisco: W.H. Freeman, 1980.

RACHMAN, S. Emotional processing. *Behaviour Research and Therapy,* 1980, *18,* 51-60.

SHAPIRO, A.K., & MORRIS, L.A. Placebo effects in medical and psychological therapies. In S.L. Garfield & A.E. Bergin (Eds.), *Handbook of psychotherapy and behavior change.* 2nd ed. New York: Wiley, 1978. Pp. 369-410.

SHAW, R., & BRANSFORD, J. (Eds.), *Perceiving, acting, and knowing: Toward an ecological psychology.* Hillsdale, NJ: Lawrence Erlbaum, 1977.

SHEVRIN, H., & DICKMAN, S. The psychological unconscious: A necessary assumption for all psychological theory? *American Psychologist,* 1980, *35,* 421-434.

SKINNER, B.F. Are theories of learning necessary? *Psychological Review,* 1950, *57,* 193-216.

SKINNER, B.F. *Science and human behavior.* New York: Macmillan, 1953.

SKINNER, B.F. Freedom and the control of men. In B.F. Skinner, *Cumulative Record.* New York: Appleton-Century-Crofts, 1959. Pp. 3-18. Originally published in *The American Scholar,* 1955-56.

STRUPP, H.H. The outcome problem in psychotherapy: Contemporary perspectives. In J.H. Harvey & M.M. Park (Eds.), *Psychotherapy research and behavior change.* Washington, DC: American Psychological Association, 1982.

STUART, R.B. Behavioral control of overeating. *Behaviour Research and Therapy,* 1967, *5,* 357-365.

TOMLIN, E.W.F. *The oriental philosophers: An introduction.* New York: Harper & Row, 1963.

WEIMER, W.B. A conceptual framework for cognitive psychology: Motor theories of the mind. In R. Shaw & J. Bransford (Eds.), *Perceiving, acting, and knowing.* Hillsdale, NJ: Lawrence Erlbaum Associates, 1977. Pp. 267-311.

WEIMER, W.B. Hayek's approach to the problems of complex phenomena: An introduction to the theoretical psychology of *The Sensory Order.* In W.B. Weimer & D.S. Palermo (eds.), *Cognition and the symbolic processes.* Vol. 2. Hillsdale, NJ: Lawrence Erlbaum Associates, 1982. Pp. 241-285.

WEIMER, W.B., & PALERMO, D.S. (Eds.), *Cognition and the symbolic processes.* Vol. 1, Hillsdale, NJ: Lawrence Erlbaum Associates, 1974.

WEIMER, W.B., & PALERMO, D.S. (Eds.), *Cognition and the symbolic processes.* Vol. 2, Hillsdale, NJ: Lawrence Erlbaum Associates, 1982.

ZAJONC, R.B. Feeling and thinking: Preferences need no inferences. *American Psychologist,* 1980, *35,* 151-175.

ZELENY, M. (Ed.), *Autopoiesis, dissipative structures, and spontaneous social orders.* Washington, DC: American Association for the Advancement of Science, 1980.

3
Beyond the Technology
of Family Therapy:
The Anatomy of Intervention Model

JAMES F. ALEXANDER, COLE BARTON,
HOLLY WALDRON, and C. HAYDEE MAS

BEHAVIOR CHANGE TECHNOLOGY AND THE CHANGE AGENT

The nine-year-old daughter of one of the authors didn't particularly like participating in the first two weeks of the Junior Development Tennis Program. This father was a bit disappointed in her attitude, since he knew how hard the three instructors had worked to develop the program and because he enjoys tennis a great deal. He had, nevertheless, resigned himself to his daughter's lack of enthusiasm and the assumption she would not like to play tennis; then, after the third session, she came home quite excited. Surprised, he asked her what she was excited about; she responded, "I played a lot better today . . . it was a lot of fun." He asked her what the group had done differently that week, but her answer was, "We did the same drills as the other times." So he asked her why she had played better, and she answered, "Lori was our teacher today." Naturally he then asked how Lori made such a difference. His daughter clarified the entire situation by explaining, "She's pretty!"

We imagine it might have been disconcerting for the instructors to hear that comment. Teaching tennis has become a major industry, requiring the development of a sophisticated technology for providing information, for analyzing both the technical and psychological aspects of the game, for modeling appropriate stroke production, and for providing corrective feedback to students or helping them learn how to provide feedback to themselves. In addition to this technology, teaching programs include various types of apparatus, such as ball machines, teaching lanes, videotape systems, and a variety of visual aids to be used on the tennis court. In this case, the father was aware of how carefully the instructors had planned the teaching sessions so that the instructors were comparable to each other and how carefully they had developed the programmed skill-building exercises. Yet, despite all this technology, the daughter had attributed her increased enthusiasm and higher level of performance to a dimension that the tennis instructors had not identified as relevant—Lori's looks. Since the father had considered withdrawing his daughter from the program, Lori's qualities had more than a simple additive impact on the effectiveness of the program. Instead, they may have created a *necessary condition* for his daughter's participation.

It is our contention that therapists in the behavior change process may play a similar role. While the analogy between tennis and marriage/family therapy can be taken only so far, some interesting similarities do exist. Some participants are "self-referred" and are enthusiastic about change. Others, like the daughter, have been referred by someone else and are not particularly enthusiastic about (and may even be resistant to) the change process. And like tennis, family intervention is a complex understanding which involves a number of conceptual models and technologies. These models and technologies are only as salient, attractive, and effective as the service delivery system (therapists, teachers, and the like) allows them to be. Thus, while the behavioral family intervention literature has focused almost exclusively on the technology of change, for many family members a number of additional variables, particularly therapist qualities, may be operating to determine how effective the technologies will be. Such nontechnical variables represent the major focus of this paper.

To create an oversimplified and extreme example, consider the case where the therapist says, "I'd like you to fill out this form about what you two did together during the past 24 hours and indicate how you felt about each of the activities." Husband then responds, "Hey, I'm too damn busy and tired to think about every little thing that has gone on.

Besides, if she'd just stop being such a bitch we wouldn't have to be so picky about each and every little thing." Now consider the following potential responses by the therapist:

- "Hey, turkey, we're not gonna get anywhere with your attitude!"
- "Gee, we can't even know what to change if we don't know what actually happens."
- "Sounds like you're so upset that it doesn't feel like doing anything is worth it."
- "Well, Sharon, will you fill out yours?"

Any therapist would recognize that these different statements will elicit many different immediate responses from the couple. Beyond these immediate reactions, these different therapist statements will also create or enhance a number of attributional and motivational reactions in both members of the couple—reactions whose effects may extend far beyond the immediate interchange and thereby facilitate or inhibit the effects of subsequent interventions.

To continue the vignette, if the therapist could immediately contact a supervisor for advice about what to do next, we doubt that most supervisors would be so strictly "goal oriented" as to say, "Just get the data!" Instead, most supervisors would give advice (or model responses, or ask questions, or whatever) about how to deal with this husband's angry refusal and blaming. Supervision is based on a blend of the supervisor's clinical model, experience, and what is unfortunately often called "intuition." Yet, while the supervisor's advice can be critical to successful accomplishment of the assessment phase, this content is rarely described, dimensionalized, or researched in the literature. Instead, the entire process is often summarized in such phrases as "The instrument was administered to the couple, and their responses were used to develop. . . ."

To the extent that the theorists and researchers adopt this ostrich approach, many important clinical phenomena will continue to be seen as involving "soft clinical skills," "intuition," "experience," or similar magical qualities that operate according to principles other than the scientific ones that are supposed to underlie our models, techniques, and even our profession! This is unnecessary, inconsistent, and deleterious to the field. Instead, we must treat these phenomena in the same way we treat other phenomena: acknowledge, conceptualize, describe, dimensionalize, manipulate, evaluate, and predict them (not necessarily in that order).

It appears that some of the individually oriented psychotherapy models assume that therapist qualities alone can account for most of the outcome variance in the change process (Pope, 1977). While most major reviewers of individual psychotherapy process and outcome studies do not necessarily share this extreme view, these reviewers nevertheless consistenly emphasize the importance of therapist characteristics (Berzins, 1977; Frank, 1979; Parloff, Waskow, & Wolfe, 1978; Strupp, 1978; Strupp, Hadley, & Gomes-Schwartz, 1977).

In a similar vein, an increasing number of reviewers and theorists in the behavioral and systems literature have argued that technology alone is not sufficient to produce change effectively. Over a decade ago, Wilson, Hannon and Evans (1968) attempted to illustrate how critical interpersonal variables were being underplayed by behavior therapists. More recently, Wilson and Evans (1977) have reviewed the therapist-client relationship in behavior therapy and again called for an increased focus on nontechnical therapist activities. Jacobson and Margolin (1979, p. 51) assert that *"the most desirable goal of an initial interview is not to gather assessment information but rather to set the stage for therapeutic change,"* and they suggest the use of therapist relationship skills to accomplish this. Wolpe (1958) stated that behavior therapists do acknowledge the value of some aspects of the therapist-patient relationship. He suggests that communicating unconditional acceptance and the feeling that the therapist is on the patient's side are particularly beneficial.

Additional representative quotes further reflect the attention to therapist behaviors and relationship issues in the behavioral and systems literature.

> . . . the quality of the helper-client relationship can serve as a powerful positive influence upon communication, openness, persuasibility and, ultimately, positive change in the client (Kanfer & Goldstein, 1980, pp. 19-20).

> . . . behavior therapists, while increasingly recognizing the importance of the therapeutic relationship, regard it primarily as a vehicle for effecting behavioral or cognitive change. . . . (Strupp, 1978, p. 6).

> . . . relationship skills . . . made the most significant contribution to outcome variance [and] Relationship skills also differentiate good from poor outcome therapists (Alexander, Barton, Schiavo, & Parsons, 1976, p. 672.).

Several explanations have been offered about how therapist relationship skills can be beneficial in the context of behavior therapy. Shoben (1949) sees the client-therapist relationship as a platform or source for modeling and reinforcing new behavior and Watchtel (1977) sees it as enabling the client to participate in the therapeutic process. Gelder, Marks, and Wolff (1967) see the client-therapist relationship as a means of engaging the cooperation of the client. Goldstein, Heller, and Sechrest (1966) describe the relationship as a means of heightening the therapist's ability to influence the patient towards therapeutic ends. Truax and Carkhuff (1967) suggest that therapists who are high in relationship skills are more effective in psychotherapy because they themselves are more potent positive reinforcers. In addition, when therapists exhibit relationship skills, they presumably elicit reciprocal affect in the patient; for example, therapist warmth elicits patient warmth (Strupp & Bergin, 1969). Reciprocated positive affect serves to increase the level of the patient's positive self-reinforcement, to decrease anxiety, and to increase the level of positive affect communicated to others. This in turn increases the positive affect and positive reinforcement received from others.

Yes, But . . .

To the extent that the reviewers and theorists listed above have identified important issues, one would expect the behavioral research and treatment literature to contain a significant number of descriptive and evaluative articles on therapists' behaviors (for example, in the tradition of Truax and Carkhuff's [1967] work with client-centered therapy). Jacobsen and Margolin (1979), in fact, reject as untrue the stereotype that behaviorists, compared to other orientations, are more concerned with technology than with relationship building. In light of this stance and the assertions made above, a review of five major behaviorally oriented journals provides interesting and humbling data. Every article published in the journals *Behavior Therapy, Journal of Applied Behavior Analysis, Behavior Modification, Behavior Research and Therapy,* and *American Journal of Family Therapy* was reviewed for the years 1980 and 1981. Articles were categorized according to the following dimensions based on a title and abstract reading: therapy or behavior change article, nontherapy or behavior change article, and therapy or behavior change article dealing with therapist characteristics. Table 1 summarizes the findings.

Taken together, the articles described above and in Table 1 present inconsistencies between some theorists' suggestions and published research. While many major review articles and books note the importance

TABLE 1

Summary of Primary Content in Five Major Behaviorally Oriented Journals

Name of Journal	Type and number of articles			
	Therapy or behavior change	Non therapy or behavior change	Therapist Characteristics	Total Number
Amer. J. of Family Therapy	20	20	1	40
Behavior Modification	30	28	0	58
Behaviour Research and Therapy	71	52	0	123
Behavior Therapy	84	45	0	129
J. of Applied Behavior Analysis	60	39	0	99
TOTAL	265	184	1	449

of nontechnical therapist behaviors, specific clinical and research articles reflect a startling paucity of prescriptive guidelines or descriptive and evaluative data regarding this aspect of service delivery. To the extent that we as behaviorists believe that how people behave accurately reflects their motivations, belief systems, or environmental influences, it is clear that we either don't want to or are unable to study the therapist delivery system.

We doubt that most behaviorists believe the therapist delivery system or its study is unimportant. We know that different therapists can experience markedly different outcomes when using the very same intervention model with the same amount of training and with homogeneous clients. Certainly most (if not all) behavioral clinicians are aware of the impact of a variety of nontechnical therapist characteristics, be they attractiveness, gender, value systems, self-confidence, ability to be persuasive, ability to engender trust, and the like.

Behavioral clinicians also know that their impact can differ dramatically when they are elated versus depressed, when they are working in a supportive environment versus a hostile environment, and when they really like their clients versus dislike them. As trainers we also know that our trainees spend considerable time asking questions about and struggling with "how to" issues that go far beyond the mechanics of applying a certain technique. Preventing or dealing with resistance, dropouts, and clients' failure to maintain change seems often to require the type of therapist skills that Reid, Patterson, and Lorber (1980) have called "soft clinical skills."

A number of factors have impeded the study of these nontechnical aspects of the change process. These factors include the time and cost involved, the transactional nature of family therapy (Garfield, 1978), which requires conceptual and statistical/analytical models of multivariate and bidirectional causality (Alexander & Barton, 1980), and the tendency for the early behavior change theorists and researchers to eschew a focus on "traditional" change factors such as "empathy."

Although these factors have impeded research, contemporary developments facilitate the study of therapists' characteristics and the service delivery system. For example, statistical tools such as contingency analysis (Castellan, 1979), lag analysis (Sackett, 1977), and time-series analysis (McCleary & Hay, 1980) allow researchers to examine interdependent and reciprocally causative processes in more descriptive and at the same time more statistically correct ways. Behavioral and family systems intervention models have expanded their explanatory power by incorporating variables such as cognition as a causal mechanism or independent variable in their models (Alexander & Parsons, 1982).

Further, rather than relying solely on incomplete or inadequate adaptions of traditional univariate Fisherian statistics, some behavioral and family systems researchers are adopting interactive and multivariate analytic techniques. These techniques better fit the characteristics of interpersonal data, while at the same time increasing descriptive power (Alexander & Barton, 1980). As a result, the study of therapists' characteristics is both more timely and possible than previously was the case.

To avoid rushing into this area of study in an unsystematic way, behavioral and family systems models must articulate a conceptual framework for how therapists' characteristics interact with intervention models and the clients being seen. To that end, the rest of this paper will articulate a global model of clinical intervention with families. Using the research and theoretical literature (when possible) and intuition and clinical experience (when necessary), we will propose a number of therapists' skills and characteristics which are necessary to attain the goals and perform the tasks that are required in each phase of the clinical intervention model.

THE ANATOMY OF INTERVENTION MODEL

The heuristic model developed below is designed to describe the major phases of clinical intervention. While *all* forms of clinical intervention may involve similar phases and activities, the scope of the Anatomy of Intervention (AIM) approach will be restricted to marriages and families to avoid being so general that it loses descriptive and prescriptive utility. The model will be further restricted to clinical approaches which are behaviorally or systems oriented. Despite numerous differences in technique and orientation, specific behavioral and systems oriented programs generally share important assumptions about the "cause" and "meaning" of behavior, as well as sharing many assumptions about how behavior should be changed.

Table 2 contains a summary of the Anatomy of Intervention Model. The model identifies five major dimensions of intervention, which include the *phases of intervention,* the *goals* of each phase, *therapist functions* necessary to attain the goals, *therapist skill* classes that are necessary to attain the functions of each phase, and *representative activities* involved in each phase. The phases of intervention can be considered sequential, although the phases are not necessarily mutually exclusive or fixed in order or time. Specific intervention models will place different emphasis on different phases, may undertake two or more phases simultaneously, and may reverse the order of some phases. However, the sequence of phases as described should not be considered arbitrary. It is based not only on the principles underlying many intervention models, but also on a considerable body of "nonclinical" psychological literature on relationship development and the change process. It is beyond the scope or purpose of this chapter to review that literature, but the interested reader may consult representative literature in the areas of the acquaintance process and relationship formation (Johnson & Matross, 1977; Morton, Alexander, & Altman, 1976), attribution theory (Valins & Nisbett, 1972), interpersonal relationships (Kelley & Thibaut, 1978), interpersonal influence (Safilios-Rothschild, 1970), and attitude acquisition and change (Watson & Johnson, 1972).

Each phase of clinical intervention involves a particular set of goals, therapist functions, and activities required to attain these goals. While different intervention approaches may use different technologies to attain a goal, the goals are relatively invariate across approaches. In the assessment phase, for example, some approaches may use behavioral observation, some use self-report, some measure motivation, attributions and desires, some identify in-session transactions, and some use personality measures. All approaches, however, share a common goal of understanding the family dynamics, estimating the most likely avenues of change, and identifying potential or actual sources of resistance. All do assessment, though different approaches may use different techniques which are more or less formal, and may differ in terms of when the assessment is accomplished.

It is not the goal of this chapter to identify the myriad technologies

TABLE 2
The Anatomy of Intervention Model

Phase of Intervention	Introduction/ Impression	Assessment/ Understanding	Induction/ Therapy	Treatment/ Education	Generalization/ Termination
Goal(s)	Expectations of change	Understand family and change parameters	Create context for change	Produce change	Maintain change; produce independence
Therapist Functions	Credibility	Elicit, structure, and analyze information	Contingent directiveness; interpersonal sensitivity	Linear directiveness; performance sensitivity	Same as Assessment, Induction, Treatment
Therapist Skills	Expertness; appropriateness; resources	Intelligence; perceptiveness; conceptual model	Relationship skills	Structuring skills	Same as Assessment, Induction, Treatment

Representative Activities	Set stage/tone of intervention via referral process and professional trappings (e.g., type and location of treatment center, clothing, degrees, secretaries, furniture arrangement). Present stimulus qualities clients see as facilitating change.	Map behaviors, cognitions, and affect. Identify the context and functions of problematic and adaptive patterns. Identify extrafamily and intrafamily stressors, support, and constraints. Evaluate resistant and cooperative response patterns to therapist. Identify family value and language systems.	Modify adverse reactions to therapist's stimulus properties. Change meaning and attributions, emphasizing positive. Define problems and establish a language system so that the family sees change as desirable and possible. Motivate *all* relevant members to change, or establish considerable control over those who are not motivated. Provide rationale for treatment techniques.	Apply change techniques to intrafamily processes (e.g., communication training/contracting, modify behavioral antecedents and consequences, modify cognitive and affective reactions, model and prompt, etc.) Identify and modify resistant behavior, cognition, and affect.	Insure attainment of adaptive family process and problem-solving styles. Insure problem cessation. Anticipate future stresses within and without the family. If necessary intervene directly with extrafamily systems. Look for or create spontaneity of adaptive styles and independence from therapist. Structure follow-up (if any).

that are used by the various clinical approaches to families in assessment or any of the other phases. These technologies and the rationale for their use have already been described in the literature. As emphasized at length above, however, the therapist characteristics required to apply them successfully are not as well described.

Prior to discussing specifics of the Anatomy of Intervention model, we must note that therapist goals, functions, and skills cannot be thought of solely in strict behavioral terms independent of the client. That is, they often represent relationship states or conditions as *experienced by the client(s)*, rather than behavioral properties of the therapist per se. While certain specific behaviors or therapist characteristics may produce a certain desired function with most clients, we cannot assume that those behaviors will always do so. For example, in the introduction/impression phase (see Table 2), the AIM approach argues that *credibility* represents an essential therapist function. With many clients, it may be that being a middle-aged white male in a three-piece suit (with Mercedes keys prominently displayed on the oak desk) will function to create a sense that the therapist is credible in the eyes of the client(s). Stereotypically this would be the case in a Beverly Hills private practice. However, the very same therapist characteristics could create anything but a sense of credibility in a different client context. For example, a welfare mother being seen in an urban storefront crisis clinic may experience a totally different set of therapist characteristics (e.g., a female therapist who gives cues of being a mother herself, who is more casually dressed, etc.) as credible. For this welfare mother, the nattily dressed male therapist could be experienced as inappropriate by virtue of gender, socioeconomic status, values, and the like.

Thus, as behaviorists we must ultimately strive to specifically define and operationalize the behaviors that represent therapist functions, skills, and activities. However, we must constantly remember that these behaviors can be defined only in the context of particular clients and only in terms of their function with the particular clients. Effectiveness of therapist behavior is determined by the client context rather than by their independently defined topographical characteristics.

Introduction/Impression

The major *goal* of the introduction/impression phase of intervention is the creation of expectations for change in the family. This phase can be seen as relatively transitory, since it ends at the point when therapists begin to engage in the processes of assessment, therapy, and education (see below). Thus the introduction/impression phase essentially refers to expectations that are created prior to therapeutic interaction, up to and including the client's response to the superficial stimulus qualities of the therapist and the service delivery system as a whole.

The introduction/impression phase has received considerably less attention than the other phases of intervention which are described below. Oftentimes this phase is simply taken for granted, particularly when clients are seen as "motivated." In such cases the clients' motivation is often seen as a function of successful therapeutic interventions, and it is not considered that some or all of this positive motivational state may have resulted from expectations created in the introduction/impression phase. To the contrary, when clients fail to follow through after initial contacts, this failure is often ascribed to a deficiency in the client (usually again in motivational terms). However, the failure of clients to engage successfully in later intervention phases may be a function of less than optimal activities and expectations that are created during the introduction/impression phase.

During this phase, the major *therapist function* (and here therapist also includes the larger service delivery system) is credibility. The general *therapist skill classes* required to establish credibility are appropriateness, resources, and expertise. Prior to and during the initial stages of therapeutic contact, the therapists must create the impression that their skills, training, values, and personal characteristics are appropriate for the client. Therapists must create the impression that they possess the resources to deal successfully with what the clients experience as being the problem, and they must create the impression that they have the necessary expertise to do so.

In what some see as crass terms, the introduction/impression phase is more of a marketing issue than a performance issue. The clients' belief that the "product" will be useful will alone not make it so. Subsequent intervention procedures must in truth involve expertness, appropriateness, and resources. However, the clients' *belief* in their utility and *expectation* for positive change prior to the actual application of intervention procedures will considerably enhance their positive impact.

The activities that affect credibility and the expectation for change can vary greatly. The therapist can set the stage or tone of intervention by manipulating the referral process, the type and location of the treatment center, the ways in which furniture is arranged, the types of clothing worn and other stimulus cues present, the behavior of "front-end" personnel such as secretaries and intake workers, and even the type and number of forms the client is required to complete prior to the beginning of therapy. The example of the welfare mother's perception of the Beverly Hills therapist demonstrates how stimulus properties of the therapist himself could have negative impact on the establishment of credibility in this phase. As proposed above, any activity having negative impact on the establishment of credibility could, in turn, influence the client's decision to return and participate in subsequent sessions.

A number of authors have directly discussed or alluded to this phase in terms such as "expectations," "self-fulfilling prophecy," "trust," and "interpersonal attraction" (Sheras & Worchel, 1979). These authors cite considerable literature which suggests the general conclusion that therapy process and outcome are enhanced by client and therapist similarity. They emphasize that interpersonal attraction must be high for successful intervention and suggest that one specific mechanism for enhancing interpersonal attractiveness is through client-therapist similarity on as many dimensions as possible. In a similar vein, Goldstein (1971) emphasizes that when working with patients of a different social class, therapists must be responsive to the assumptions of the clients and must treat clients in accordance with their lifestyle. He cites the emphasis on using paraprofessionals, nonprofessionals, and indigenous therapists as providing "discrepancy reduction" between clients and therapists.

Though not restricted to the introduction-impression phase, these conclusions imply that systematic manipulation of therapist and service delivery characteristics, in light of the expectations and characteristics of clients, can enhance the intervention process. Of course, many important therapist characteristics (e.g., gender and race) cannot be manipulated. When this is the case, we should at least know if the expectations we are creating serve to enhance or impede our subsequent interventions.

In conjoint marriage and family therapy it is impossible to match a single therapist to all the clients on one crucial dimension, that of gender. Though a therapist may be androgynous or otherwise have flexible attitudes, during the initial introduction/impression phase she or he presents stimulus qualities of a particular gender which cannot match both the male and the female adults in the couple or family. In a direct study of the impact of gender on intervention process in families, Warburton, Alexander, and Barton (Note 1) found a strong interaction between therapist gender and parent sex on coalition formation in the first session of family therapy. Specifically, Warburton found that mothers coalesce strongly with female therapists but not with male therapists. In contrast, fathers coalesce strongly with male therapists but not with female therapists. These data suggest that therapist gender as a stimulus property may powerfully influence family members' behavior in the early phases of intervention, so that therapists of different sexes will face very different family behavior patterns solely as a function of gender. It is fair to assume these different patterns will also vary as a function of many other dimensions of therapists' characteristics.

Taking the idea of pre-intervention manipulation one step further, Goldstein et al. (1966) discuss the potential advantage of using "plants" to influence client behavior. Specifically, they cite considerable research evidence which suggests that positive therapeutic involvement will be enhanced even prior to intervention if prospective clients either directly or indirectly overhear people they believe are successfully treated clients providing information that is dissonant with resistant behavior.

Taken together, this literature suggests what most behavior change agents already know, but which many intervention models fail to formalize: Initial impression formation can powerfully influence the beginning, if not the entire course, of intervention. As mentioned above, the private practitioner in Beverly Hills would be wise to have a well appointed office, as well as dress and behave in ways that are consistent with the expectations and values of the Beverly Hills client population. Such behaviors and stimulus properties might include a professional receptionist, a MUZAK system, and a well developed referral system from other professionals. In contrast, a therapist in a relatively depressed urban area or in a poor rural setting would be wise to dress modestly, to have less expensive office furniture, and to not have an ostentatious car, thereby better matching the dress standards and expectations of the clients. When these manipulations are impossible or unpalatable, therapists must at least be aware of the client expectations created by therapist stimulus properties, since they are important parts of the introduction/impression phase. Therapists should be prepared to either modify adverse reactions (this process is discussed in more detail in the induction/therapy portion of the chapter) to their stimulus properties, or recognize alternatives to cope with clients' less than complete participation in intervention.

As a final note, it must be remembered that in this phase (and this phase only) the "therapist skills" category refers less to what therapists can do and more to what they *look like they can do from the clients' perspective*. Similarly, the question is not if and how the clients can change, but whether *they expect they can change*. The question of what the clients actually do, and what needs to be changed, is addressed in the assessment/understanding phase to be discussed next. That phase involves a very different set of goals, functions, therapist skills, and activities.

Assessment/Understanding

The goals of the assessment/understanding phase are to understand the behavior, affect, and cognition of the family. In addition, the therapist needs to understand what needs to be changed and what intrafamilial and extrafamilial family variables will enhance and impede positive change. Though the more strictly behaviorally oriented models engage in the process throughout intervention, most formal emphasis on information-gathering is done prior to any change attempts.

Patterson (1976) and Weiss and his associates (Weiss & Margolin, 1977; Weiss & Cerreto, Note 2; Margolin & Weiss, 1978), for example, make extensive use of a wide variety of assessment instruments, many of which must be completed before an initial therapy appointment will even be scheduled. Such pretherapy assessment usually includes self-report questionnaires, spouse observation checklists, laboratory and in-home observations of client interactions, and in-session observation of interview or first-session behavior. Using the therapist, the clients, and raters or coders of observations as sources of information, these devices and techniques are designed to yield both subjective and objective information about the behavior, affect, and cognitions of clients. From this information the therapist develops a sense of the client's strengths and a plan for behavior change.

In the systems oriented models, assessment is not seen as a distinct or separate phase. In these models, assessment activities and goals are intermingled with induction/therapy (see below). For example, Haley (1976) presumes that the problem descriptions that families present are not accurate and that these descriptions interfere with the process of intervention. Therefore, Haley generates a whole new description of the family's problem, one that fits his behavioral change purposes rather than reflecting a family's reports. Minuchin (1974) actually creates family interaction processes (enactments) which represent or mimic families' problem behavior, structuring and intervening the process immediately. All these models presume that therapists cannot passively document problem behavior in assessment, but must actively respond to the assessment information they create.

Models also differ in the relative emphasis they place on behavioral vs. cognitive vs. affective modes of expression. Recent marriage and family literature has acknowledged the importance of eliciting and assessing information in more than one mode. Jacobson (1981) describes the importance of assessing partners' interactional behavior, their cognitions concerning their spouse's behavior, and their feelings about the relationship in behavioral marital therapy. Haley (1976) advocates gathering family members' opinions and behavioral descriptors concerning the problem, but not collecting affective information in the first interview. The functional family therapy model describes family members' affective, behavioral, or cognitive modes as irrelevant when taken out of the family context (Alexander & Parsons, 1982). The relevance lies in what mode or modes the family members use when describing their interactions with each other.

Despite the differences in timing, focus, and specific activities reflected in the different intervention models, the therapist's *functions* and general *skill classes* are remarkably similar across models. The therapist or therapy delivery system must structure the situation in which information can be elicited, usually through some combination of observation of interactive behavior in the treatment context and the natural context, formal tests and inventories, and direct verbal interview.

In addition to adhering to a conceptual model, the therapists must have the skills of perceptiveness and intelligence to accomplish these functions. That is, the therapist structures and elicits the desired information based on a particular therapy model, integrates the information and makes decisions about the direction of the intervention process. In terms of what is usually considered to be therapeutic skill, in this phase (and this phase alone) it is more appropriate to think of the therapist as a computer rather than as a therapist. A self-paced on-line computer has the capability to present a structured information-eliciting context, score it, and generate a profile and even treatment recommendations based on a preprogrammed model. This preprogrammed conceptual model essentially tells the computer how to structure and elicit the information, what it means, and (in later phases) what needs to be changed. Of course, at this point in time computers alone cannot assess the entire range of information necessary to make all treatment decisions. And because computers may present undesirable stimulus qualities (see previous introduction/impression phase), we would perhaps not rely on them as the primary vehicle for assessment/understanding in terms of skill classes if they could assess all the relevant information. Nonetheless, a computer reflects the information-processing dimensions that are most relevant for therapists in this early phase.

In addition to the types of skills that are involved, a major difference between the introduction/impression phase and the assessment-understanding phase is the *actual* level of competence. In the introduction/impression phase therapists need not actually be competent, but rather must create that impression in the client's frame of reference.

In the assessment phase the therapist must actually be competent. While it is also helpful for the clients to perceive the therapist as competent, subsequent treatment activities will be inappropriate or ineffective if therapists are actually not sufficiently perceptive, intelligent, or steeped in an adequate conceptual model. Positive expectations and good initial impressions, although extremely important in setting the stage for successful intervention, can be disconfirmed by subsequent behavior which is not professionally competent.

Therapists will develop a set of subjective impressions of the clients, created by the analytic focus of assessment. However, during this assessment/understanding phase it is very important for therapists to identify and conceptualize clients' resistant and cooperative response patterns from the objective framework of an intervention model. Therapists should be able to identify resistant patterns early in the intervention process. Patterns of resistance (e.g., arguing with the therapist, arguing with other family members, persisting in blaming, not wanting to come in as a family) are typically patterns which will consistently reemerge over the course of therapy until they are changed. These patterns prevent the family from benefiting from therapy, compromise a therapist's credibility, and render therapy a "problem by problem" series of technical operations with no generalization or maintenance. It is therefore essential that intervention models specify assessment techniques to recognize these patterns and put them in a useful context, as well as specify therapeutic techniques to neutralize these patterns early on in the course of therapy.

Induction/Therapy

The primary goal of the induction/therapy phase is the creation of a context for change. Unlike the introduction/impression phase, this context is not based on superficial stimulus qualities of the therapist, but instead on specific attributional and motivational processes brought about by specific therapist interventions. For most behaviorally and systems oriented family therapy models, this process involves changing the meaning of family members' behavior, with particular emphasis on positive attributions. Again, specific therapies differ in particular techniques and philosophies. Minuchin (1974), for example, describes the need to "change the family's reality." More behaviorally oriented approaches describe the importance of inducing positive expectancies and creating a collaborative set in the early stages of therapy (Jacobson, 1981).

Despite their particular differences, all of these approaches emphasize the need for the family members to consider their behavior as being motivated and maintained by variables other than individual "badness," predisposition, or malevolence. In the process of accomplishing this goal, Alexander and his colleagues (Alexander & Parsons, 1982; Barton & Alexander, 1980) describe the tactics of nonblaming family members and relabeling their behavior to make it seem more logical, adaptive, and legitimate. They posit that family members are then more likely to appreciate the orderly interdependence of their behavior. This appreciation can, in turn, produce a nonthreatening environment for change. Patterson and colleagues use the context of the language system to modify family members' attributions about one another. For example, they often have family members read books which explain behavior according to social learning principles (Patterson, 1971; Patterson & Gullion, 1968).

Other approaches also stress the importance of the language system in therapy. Minuchin (1974), for example, emphasizes the process of "joining" the family. This process includes adopting, to a certain degree, the perspective and language system of the family. The functional family model (Alexander & Parsons, 1982; Barton & Alexander, 1980) emphasizes the need to understand the family's mode of expression, whether it be affective, cognitive, or behavioral. Still others create new language systems and an in vivo family process by having family members play games, which in turn metaphorically serve as adaptive family processes (Blechman, 1980; Blechman & Olson, 1976; Robin, 1980). In any event, most authors emphasize that the family and therapist must share a language and value system for intervention to be successful. This emphasis is consistent with the research discussed earlier, which concludes that the more similar the client and therapist are the more successful the intervention will be. Unlike the introduction/impression phase, however, during the induction/therapy phase therapists actually create this similarity, rather than creating the *impression* of similarity.

During induction/therapy therapists also modify adverse reactions to therapists' stimulus properties, provide a rationale for subsequent treatment techniques, and develop techniques for establishing control over relevant people who are not being directly seen in therapy. For example, in families with delinquent teenagers, peers may play an important role in maladaptive behavior. Since it is often difficult or impossible to directly engage these peers in the intervention process, the therapist begins to develop techniques through which their maladaptive influence is modified. Such techniques may include changing family members' attributions about the peers through previously described techniques of nonblaming and relabeling, as well as enhancing the positive valence of family members (vs. peers) for the delinquent, also through the use of such techniques as relabeling and nonblaming. If extrafamilial influences are not identified during the assessment phase or dealt with during the therapy and later education phases, positive treatment effects and/or long-term follow-up effects are unlikely.

The therapist *functions* necessary to create a context for change are contingent directiveness and interpersonal sensitivity. The general *therapist skill classes* necessary are best described as relationship skills (Alexander et al., 1976). Contingent directiveness is defined as therapist behaviors such as relabeling that influence family members' cognitions and affect. These behaviors are based on, and represent contingent responses to, the behavior, affect, and cognitions of those family members. In a lag-analysis sense, contingent directiveness reflects a stronger lag-one rather than lag-two association. That is, if family members and therapist alternate speeches, what the therapist says and does is determined more by what the family says and does than by what the therapist previously said or did. Of course, for therapists' behavior to be sensitive to the family, they must possess the interpersonal sensitivity to what family members think, do, and feel.

Relationship skills have received considerable emphasis in the literature, though more so in the traditional individual psychotherapy literature than in the behavioral or systems literature. Descriptive labels in the literature include such words as "warmth," "concern," and "empathy." Though not emphasized in the behavioral literature, they are recently being seen as more and more important (as discussed earlier in this paper). These skills, at least in preliminary research, seem to have important impact in the conjoint therapies as well (Alexander et al., 1976). Intuitions about these skills nonetheless eclipse the sparse descriptiveness of the data, and researchers must struggle more to understand why therapists' skills seem to predict substantial variance in the qualities of therapeutic outcomes (Stuart & Lott, 1972).

Treatment/Education

The major goal of treatment/education is to produce long-term change in the family. During the previously described induction/therapy phase, techniques are designed to change the meaning of behavior, the attributions family members have about one another, and family members' motivations. While most models assume such changes are important precursors to long-term change, it is felt that by themselves such changes will not be maintained unless carefully planned interactive pattern changes also occur. Treatment/education is designed to implement these latter changes, and involves the application of most of the change techniques we think of as behavior modification. Representative activities include communication training, contracting, modeling, and the manipulation of environmental events for the purpose of stimulus control and appropriate consequation. Which activities or techniques are used and how they are applied depend on the particular therapy approach. Stuart (1976), for example, applies techniques in a consistent level structure across dysfunctional couples. He introduces "curing days" designed for an immediate positive behavior change in the relationship, then moves to communication training activities, then contracting procedures and so on. Couples must succeed at one level before going to the next, but the total program is designed to terminate within 12 weeks. Weiss (1978) tailors the use of the various techniques to particular couples in terms of skills deficits in different content areas, taking time of life cycle into consideration. Alexander and Parsons (1982) also tailor their application of techniques to particular families, doing so in terms of a functional analysis of each family member's behavior. Haley (1963) includes a paradoxical intervention technique to encourage behavior such that the family member cannot continue to perform it, based on theories of family resistance to the therapist. He might, for example, instruct an overinvolved mother to be more protective of her child.

In contrast to the induction/therapy phase, the therapist functions in treatment/education primarily include linear directiveness and performance sensitivity. Linear directiveness differs from contingent directiveness in that the therapist's behavior is (relatively speaking) sequential and programmed. Therapists behave much more as if they are following "scripts," as particularly emphasized in educating family members in communication skills, contracting, and the like. In the lagged sense described previously, a stronger association exists at lag two than at lag one (assuming therapists reflect every other lag).

Of course, therapists must be sufficiently sensitive to clients to insure that the clients are understanding and performing as desired. This performance of sensitivity, however, is only deviation focused. That is, as long as clients "follow the program," therapists do not interrupt the progression of educational technologies. Because of this, therapists' criteria for family members' performance are best operationalized as learning or acquisition criteria.

The therapist skills required in this phase have been identified as structuring skills (Alexander et al., 1976). They include clarity, nonverbal and verbal control and pacing of information and activities, and often

the utilization of props such as charts, graphs, and other carefully structured materials which constrain and/or direct client's behavior. In general, these are the types of skills which are included in good teaching,
and guide family clients along a narrower path at a faster pace. It is
presumed these skills are appropriate because the more difficult tasks
of identifying what family members should do differently and why have
been resolved in the induction/therapy phase.

However, during the treatment/education phase therapists must also
be particularly sensitive to behavior, affect, and cognitions that can be
categorized as resistance. Specific behavioral and systems models differ
in how they conceptualize resistance. Some see it as an inevitable reaction
to systems change (Haley, 1963; Watzlawick, Weakland & Fisch, 1974).
Others see it as a failure on the therapist's part of providing the appropriate educational structure (Christophersen, Arnold, Hill, & Quilitch,
1972; Patterson, 1973; Stuart, 1971). Yet others see it as a failure to "fit"
the nature and goals of the specific change techniques to the information
developed during assessment (Barton & Alexander, 1980). That is, the
specific changes that the therapist attempts to develop are inconsistent
with the value system and/or functions of the family.

When resistance occurs, therapists must "recycle" back to the assess-
ment/understanding and induction/therapy phases. No matter how they
conceptualize resistance, almost all models require that the therapists
identify the family parameters that produce and/or maintain the resistance. Most models also exhort the therapist to provide additional rationales for treatment techniques, motivate all relevant family members,
and change the attributions that underlie or covary with the resistance.
In other words, when serious resistance to educational technology is
encountered, therapists must change their orientation and once again
utilize their intelligence, perceptiveness, conceptual model, contingent
directiveness, and interpersonal sensitivity. When that is done successfully, they can again move back into the treatment/education phase.

Generalization/Termination

The goals of the generalization/termination phase are to maintain the
changes previously initiated and at the same time produce independence
from the treatment context. It could be argued that in a private practice
context therapists may not want to produce independence and have the
changes maintained in the natural environment. However, the history
of behavioral interventions has included a strong emphasis on temporal
and, if possible, setting generalizability (Wahler, Berland, & Coe, 1979).

To accomplish this, therapists must insure not only that the "referral problems" have terminated, but also that family interaction patterns and problem-solving styles are now adaptive. In addition, these interaction processes and problem-solving styles must be spontaneous and operate independent of the therapist's constant monitoring and prompting. If such spontaneity and independence are not apparent, therapists must apply specific educational techniques which insure generalization. This goal can be attained through such procedures as overlearning, anticipating and role playing future crises and stresses within the family, and evaluating and sometimes directly intervening with extrafamilial systems.

Further, therapists can initiate long-term programs which will increase the probability of maintenance, but which do not require or involve constant therapist monitoring. For example, in dealing with the family of a delinquent teenager the therapist may directly work with the family and a vocational training program to initiate vocational training for the teenager. Since some of these programs last up to two years, the therapist need not consider that the vocational training is a direct part of the intervention process per se. However, the therapist can insure that the program has been successfully initiated and that the family is spontaneously behaving in ways which are consistent with the teenager's maintenance in the program.

In fact, it can often be argued that much of what family therapists do represents nothing more than an extremely effective referral process. We do not produce *all* the changes that are necessary for families to maintain adaptive behaviors, but we accomplish the intrafamilial changes that are necessary for family members to respond in adaptive ways to other opportunities. Additional examples of this philosophy include helping unemployed adults get into alternative employment training opportunities, helping mates become involved in new social activities (such as clubs), "mainstreaming" children back into educational programs, and the like.

SUMMARY AND CONCLUSIONS

The Anatomy of Intervention Model described above is aptly named. For example, it does not contain prescriptions about how activities should be performed, skills manifested, and goals attained. As such, it is not the "physiology" of intervention, but its anatomy. Descriptions of how the various activities should be accomplished must be left to specific therapeutic approaches. How these activities will be accomplished depends on the particular philosophies of behavior and the relative emphasis that is placed on different activities and phases in each approach. However, we argue that all behavioral and systems oriented family and marriage intervention models include each of the phases described above. As mentioned, they are formalized to a different extent in each of the models, but every instance of intervention must include each of those phases, with their attendant goals, functions, and therapist skill classes. The primary contribution of the model is contained in its identification of and emphasis on the relatively unique therapist skills that are required in each phase. The implications of these differences are that therapists cannot successfully assume that a particular style or set of skills will be effective across the entire intervention process. Yet, while we recognize that families in different developmental stages require quite different technologies, we rarely consider that these differences are also required of therapists. Hopefully, the Anatomy of Intervention Model will not only serve as an heuristic reminder to therapists that very different skills are required at different phases of intervention, but also help therapists identify a critical set of variables that may be operating when an apparently successful intervention suddenly (or not so suddenly) goes awry.

As mentioned in the introduction to this chapter, some of the prescriptions and conclusions drawn in this paper are based on reasonable theory and at least some degree of empirical support. However, since therapist's qualities have received relatively little attention, many of the conclusions are based to some extent on intuition and clinical experience, which are sources of information which we decried at the beginning of this paper. Thus, it is important to consider the specifics of the Anatomy of Intervention Model as suggestions rather than as guidelines, and as appeals for empirical investigation rather than statements of dogma. Nevertheless, the fact that such a model exists should help clarify the intervention process and enhance both the efficiency and effectiveness of our interventions.

REFERENCES

ALEXANDER, J.F., & BARTON, C. In J.P. Vincent (Ed.), *Advances in family intervention, assessment, and theory: Volume I.* Greenwich: JAI Press, 1980.

ALEXANDER, J.F., BARTON, C., SCHIAVO, R.S., & PARSONS, B.V. Systems-behavioral intervention with families of delinquents: Therapist characteristics, family behavior, and outcome. *Journal of Consulting and Clinical Psychology,* 1976, *44*(4), 656-664.

ALEXANDER, J.A., & PARSONS, B.V. *Functional family therapy.* Monterey: Brooks/Cole, 1982.

BARTON, C., & ALEXANDER, J.F. Functional family therapy. In A.S. Gurman & D.P. Kniskern (Eds.), *Handbook of family therapy.* New York: Brunner/Mazel, 1980.

BERZINS, J.I. Therapist-patient matching. In A.S. Gurman & A.M. Razin (Eds.), *Effective psychotherapy: A handbook of research.* Oxford, England: Pergamon Press, 1977.

BLECHMAN, E.A. Family problem-solving training. *American Journal of Family Therapy,* 1980, *8,* 3-22.

BLECHMAN, E.A., & OLSON, D.H.L. The family contact game: Description and effectiveness. In D.H.L. Olson (Ed.), *Treating relationships.* Lake Mills, Iowa: Graphic Publishing Company, 1976.

CASTELLAN, N.J. The analysis of behavior sequences. In R.B. Cairns (Ed.), *The analysis of social interactions: Methods, issues, and illustrations.* Hillside, N.J.: Erlbaum, 1979.

CHRISTOPHERSEN, E., ARNOLD, C.M., HILL, D.W., & QUILITCH, H.R. The home point system: Token reinforcement procedures for application by parents of children with behavior problem. *Journal of Applied Behavior Analysis,* 1972, *5,* 485-497.

FRANK, J.D. The present status of outcome studies. *Journal of Consulting and Clinical Psychology,* 1979, *47*(2), 310-316.

GARFIELD, S.L. Research on client variables in psychotherapy. In S.L. Garfield & A.E. Bergin (Eds.), *Handbook of psychotherapy and behavior change: An empirical analysis* (2nd ed.). New York: Pergamon Press, 1978.

GELDER, M.G., MARKS, I.M., & WOLFF, H.N. Desensitization and psychotherapy in the treatment of phobic states: A controlled inquiry. *British Journal of Psychiatry,* 1967, *113,* 53-75.

GOLDSTEIN, A.P. *Psychotherapeutic attraction.* New York: Pergamon Press, 1971.

GOLDSTEIN, A.P., HELLER, K., & SECHREST, L.B. *Psychotherapy and the psychology of behavior change.* New York: Wiley & Sons, 1966.

HALEY, J. *Strategies of psychotherapy.* New York: Grune and Stratton, 1963.

HALEY, J. *Problem-solving therapy.* San Francisco: Jossey-Bass, 1976.

JACOBSON, N.S. Behavioral marital therapy. In A.S. Gurman & D.P. Kniskern (Eds.), *Handbook of Family Therapy.* New York: Brunner/Mazel, 1981.

JACOBSON, N.S., & MARGOLIN, G. *Marital therapy.* New York: Brunner/Mazel, 1979.

JOHNSON, D.W., & MATROSS, R. Interpersonal influence in psychotherapy: A social psychological view. In A.S. Gurman & A.M. Razin (Eds.), *Effective psychotherapy: A handbook of research.* Oxford, England: Pergamon Press, 1977.

KANFER, F.H., & GOLDSTEIN, A.P. *Helping people change.* New York: Pergamon Press, 1980.

KELLEY, H.H., & THIBAUT, J.W. *A theory of interdependence.* New York: Wiley, 1978.

MARGOLIN, G., & WEISS, R.L. Communication training and assessment: A case of behavioral marital enrichment. *Behavior Therapy,* 1978, *9,* 508-520.

McCLEARY, R., & HAY, R.S. *Applied time series analysis for the social sciences.* Beverly Hills: Sage, 1980.

MINUCHIN, S. *Families and family therapy.* Cambridge, Mass.: Harvard University Press, 1974.

MORTON, T.L., ALEXANDER, J.F., & ALTMAN, I. Communication and relationship definition. In G.L. Miller (Ed.), *Explorations in interpersonal communication.* Beverly Hills: Sage, 1976.

PARLOFF, M.B., Waskow, J.E., & WOLFE, B.E. Research on therapist variables in relation to process and outcome. In S.L. Garfield & A.E. Bergin (Eds.), *Handbook of psychotherapy and behavior change: An empirical analysis* (2nd ed.). New York: Pergamon Press, 1978.

PATTERSON, G.R. *Families: Applications of social learning to family life.* Champaign, Ill.: Research Press, 1971).

PATTERSON, G.R. Changes in status of family members as controlling stimuli: A basis for describing treatment process. In L.A. Hamerlynck, L.C. Handy, and E. Mash (Eds.), *Behavior change: Methodology, concepts, and practice.* Champaign, Ill.: Research Press, 1973.

PATTERSON, G.R. Some procedures for assessing changes in marital interaction patterns.

Oregon Research Institute Research Bulletin, 1976, *16,* No. 7.

PATTERSON, G.R. & COBB, J.A. Stimulus control for classes of noxious behaviors. In J.F. Knutson (Ed.), *The control of aggression: Implications from basic research.* Chicago: Aldine, 1973.

PATTERSON, G.R., & GULLION, M.E. *Living with children: New methods for parents and teachers.* Champaign, Ill.: Research Press, 1968.

PINSOF, W.M. Family therapy process research. In A.S. Gurman & D.P. Kniskern (Eds.), *Handbook of family therapy.* New York: Brunner/Mazel, 1981.

POPE, B. Research on therapeutic style. In A.S. Gurman & A.M. Razin (Eds.), *Effective psychotherapy: A handbook of research.* Oxford, England: Pergamon Press, 1977.

ROBIN, A.L. Parent-adolescent conflict: A skill training approach. In D.P. Rathjen & J.P. Foreyt (Eds.), *Social competence: Interventions for children and adults.* New York: Pergamon, 1980.

REID, J.B., PATTERSON, G.R., & LORBER, R. The treatment of multiple-offending young adolescents using family treatment based on social learning principles. *Proceedings of the Juvenile Justice System Conference Commemorating the International Year of the Child,* University of New Mexico, Albuquerque, New Mexico, 1980.

SACKETT, G.P. The lag sequential analysis of contingency and cyclicity in behavioral interaction research. In J. Osofsky (Ed.). *Handbook of human infant development.* New York: Wiley, 1977.

SAFILIOS-ROTHSCHILD, C. The study of family power structure: A review 1959-1966. *Journal of Marriage and the Family,* 1970, *32,* 359-552.

SHERAS, P.L., & WORCHEL, S. *Clinical psychology: A social psychological approach.* New York: Van Nostrand Co., 1979.

SHOBEN, E.J. Psychotherapy as a problem of learning theory. *Psychological Bulletin,* 1949, *46,* 366-392.

STRUPP, H.H. Psychotherapy research and practice: An overview. In S.L. Garfield & A.E. Bergin (Eds.), *Handbook of Psychotherapy and Behavior Change: An empirical analysis* (2nd ed.). New York: Pergamon Press, 1978.

STRUPP, H.H., & BERGIN, A.E. Some empirical and conceptual bases for coordinated research in psychotherapy: A critical review of issues, trends, and evidence. *International Journal of Psychiatry,* 1969, *7,* 18-90.

STRUPP, H.H. HADLEY, S.W., & GOMES-SCHWARTZ, B. *Psychotherapy for better or worse.* New York: Jason Aronson, Inc., 1977.

STUART, R.B. Behavioral contracting with families of delinquents. *Journal of Behavior Therapy and Experimental Psychiatry,* 1971, *2,* 1-11.

STUART, R.B. An operant interpersonal program for couples. In D.H.L. Olson (Ed.), *Treating Relationships.* Lake Mills, Iowa: Graphic Publishing, 1976.

STUART, R.B. & LOTT, L.A., Jr. Behavioral contracting with delinquents: A cautionary note. *Journal of Behavior Therapy and Experimental Psychiatry,* 1972, *3,* 161-169.

TRUAX, C.B., & CARKHUFF, R.R. *Toward effective counseling and psychotherapy: Training and practice.* Chicago: Aldine, 1967.

VALINS, S., & NISBETT, R.E. Attribution processes in the development and treatment of emotional disorders. In E.E. Jones, D.E. Kanouse, H.H. Kelley, R.E. Nisbett, S. Valins, and B. Weiner (Eds.). *Attribution: Perceiving the causes of behavior.* Morristown, N.J.: General Learning Press, 1972.

WACHTEL, P.L. *Psychoanalysis and behavior therapy.* New York: Basic Books, 1977.

WAHLER, R.G., BERLAND, R.M., & COE, T.D. Generalization processes in child behavior change. In B.B. Lahey & A.E. Kazdin (Eds.), *Advances in clinical child psychology* (Vol. II). New York: Plenum Press, 1979.

WATSON, R.E., & JOHNSON, D.W. *Social psychology: Issues and insights.* Philadelphia: Lippincott, 1972.

WATZLAWICK, P., WEAKLAND, J., & FISCH, R. *Change: Principles of problem formation and problem resolution.* New York: W.W. Norton, 1974.

WEISS, R.L. The conceptualization of marriage from a behavioral perspective. In T.J. Paolino and B.S. McCrady (Eds.), *Marriage and marital therapy: Psychoanalytic behavioral and systems theory perspectives.* New York: Brunner/Mazel, 1978.

WEISS, R.L., & MARGOLIN, G. Marital conflict and accord. In A.R. Ciminero, K.S. Calhoun, and H.E. Adams (Eds.), *Handbook for behavioral assessment.* New York: Wiley, 1977.

WILSON, G.T., & EVANS, I.M. The therapist-client relationship in behavior therapy. In A.S. Gurman & A.M. Razin (Eds.), *Effective Psychotherapy: A Handbook of Research.* Oxford, England: Pergamon Press, 1977.

WILSON, G.T., HANNON, A.E., & EVANS, I.M. Behavior therapy and the therapist-patient relationship. *Journal of Consulting and Clinical Psychology*, 1968, *32*, 103-109.

WOLPE, J. *Psychotherapy by reciprocal inhibition.* Stanford, California: Stanford University Press, 1958.

REFERENCE NOTES

1. WARBURTON, J., ALEXANDER, J.F., & BARTON, C. *Sex of client, sex of therapist: A family process study.* Unpublished paper presented at American Psychological Association Convention, Montreal, 1980.

2. WEISS, R.L., & CERRETO, M. *Marital Status Inventory.* Unpublished manuscript, University of Oregon, 1975.

4

Clinical Innovations in Behavioral Marital Therapy

NEIL S. JACOBSON

Among the consumers and contributors to the behavior therapy literature, the attempt to transform the field of psychotherapy from art to science has generally been viewed as a noble aspiration. With unparalleled pioneering zeal, and with a degree of optimism that has been described as "unbridled," behavior therapists have sought to technologize the practice of psychotherapy over the past 25 years. More than any other paradigm in the history of psychotherapy, behavior therapy has emphasized detailed specification of treatment procedures and committed itself to rigorous self-scrutiny in the form of outcome studies where null hypotheses must be rejected before truth be declared. By the middle of the last decade, the achievements had been notable, the idealism appeared to be justified, and the promise for the future appeared limitless. Everywhere one looked, evidence was proliferating: Fear and anxiety were being eradicated, aggressive preadolescents were smiling sweetly and compliantly, young children were being toilet trained in less than a day, shy adults were asserting themselves, and mute children were being taught to speak. Tempers were being controlled, stress was becoming manageable, and hospitalized schizophrenics were being discharged.

Yet it seems to be in the nature of the psychotherapy beast that things are always more complicated than they seem. As our research has improved and our capacity for self-criticism has been enhanced, sobering reappraisals have gradually replaced unbridled optimism. It has turned out to be easier to eradicate fear in mildly fearful college students than to perform similar feats with severely dysfunctional agoraphobics. It is one thing to help obese people lose 20 pounds; it is quite another to help them lose 50—and maintain that loss. Hospitalized schizophrenics can be trained to make their beds and keep their delusions to themselves, but whether or not they can be helped to lead happy and productive lives is another matter. Problems of generalization and maintenance are frequently alluded to in discussion sections and mentioned in review articles as important foci for future research. Unfortunately, the future is seldom now, and the clinically meaningful issues rarely fall within the purview of the "present study."

In addition to the decline in unbridled optimism, there seems to be a growing recognition that the therapy setting is invariably more complicated than our technology would wish it to be and that the attempt to capture this complexity in writing continues to elude us. Despite our attempts to specify in detail what we as therapists actually do, we cannot manage to eliminate "nuisance" variables such as clinical skill and individual differences among our clients.

Marital therapy has escaped neither the unbridled optimism phase nor the sobering reappraisal phase. When controlled outcome studies began to appear in the literature (Jacobson, 1977, 1978a; Liberman, Levine, Wheeler, Saunders, & Wallace, 1976; Margolin & Weiss, 1978; O'Leary & Turkewitz, 1978), much was made of the significant treatment effects of behavioral marital therapy (BMT) relative to control groups—both waiting-list and placebo. Even as recent outcome studies continue to confirm these treatment effects (Azrin, Besalel, Bechtel, Michalicek, Mancera, Carroll, Shuford, & Cox, 1980; Baucom, 1982; Emmelkamp, van der Helm, MacGillavry, & Van Zanten, 1981; Hahlweg, Schindler, Revenstorf, & Brengelmann, 1981; Turkewitz & O'Leary, 1981), we have begun to look at our data more critically (Baucom, in press; Jacobson, Berley, Melman, Elwood, & Phelps, in press; Weiss, 1980). It is true that BMT appears to be better than no treatment for most couples and that many treated couples leave therapy with more satisfying relationships. Some even leave therapy with relationships that are markedly more satisfying. However, some relationships are in no better shape subsequent to therapy than they were upon entering—a greater number than our misleading group means would imply. Others improve on our measures yet leave therapy with relationships of dubious quality. In short, our outcome research has obfuscated as much as it has illuminated.

Moreover, in marital therapy there continues to exist that additional troublesome phenomenon, articulated in detail elsewhere (Jacobson, Berley et al., in press), that the direction to follow does not define itself as it does with other forms of therapy. The final destiny of a relationship can be either perpetuation or termination, and it is not always clear, even to the couple, which would be the more desirable outcome of therapy. At times the interests of one or both spouses is contrary to the interests of the continuation of the relationship. For example, at the time the couple enters therapy, the husband might be quite satisfied with the status quo, whereas the wife may be extremely unhappy and desirous of numerous changes. To carry this hypothetical example further, if the wife is oppressed by the current structure of the relationship and her continuance in the relationship is based primarily on a fear of being alone or economic dependency, it may very well be that her interests are best served by a treatment plan facilitating her disengagement from the marriage. The husband, on the other hand, has a clear interest in maintaining the relationship with as little change as possible; therefore, disengagement would not be a suitable treatment plan. To say that the client is the relationship in this situation simply begs the question. How is the therapist to satisfy these competing interests? This is but one example of many possible ambiguities in treating relationships, which defy the behavior therapist's efforts to set umambiguous treatment goals as well as criteria for success and failure.

Finally, in BMT as in other areas of behavior therapy there continues to exist an elusive gap between theory and practice which defies even our best efforts toward specifying what the therapist actually does. When Gayla Margolin and I decided to write our marital therapy book (Jacobson & Margolin, 1979), our goal was a detailed specification of therapist behavior that was not possible in journal articles. Indeed, our hope was that the book would serve as a self-contained treatment manual. The book does contain a detailed discussion of the clinical practice of marital therapy. Yet, as soon as we began to use the book in training our own students, its inadequacies became shockingly apparent. Even after reading the book, students who attend our courses and workshops ask, "But what do you do when. . . .?"

In short, despite the notable advances in the theory and practice of BMT, the field must contend with a number of limitations and shortcomings. This chapter provides a selective summary of recent efforts to deal with them. Most of these efforts constitute attempts to refine the clinical practice of BMT. The first section discusses the decline of contingency control as a primary emphasis in behavioral technology. The second reviews efforts to incorporate cognitive procedures into BMT. The third reviews our recent attempts to specify classes of therapist behavior which are hypothesized to be most critical in producing positive outcomes.

The chapter concludes with a section on future directions. In this section I begin what will hopefully prove to be a fruitful dialogue regarding issues in the clinical practice of BMT which are not easily subsumed under the category of empirical questions. Implicit in this concluding discussion are some rather fundamental reservations about the research strategies commonly adopted in studying BMT, and a plea for creative and innovative conceptualizations of marital distress and therapy.

THE DECLINE OF CONTINGENCY MANAGEMENT

BMT began as the application of learning principles to the problems of distressed relationships (Azrin, Naster, & Jones, 1973; Liberman, 1970; Patterson & Hops, 1972; Stuart, 1969; Weiss, Hops, & Patterson, 1973). With the aforementioned faith in operant psychology serving as a backdrop, it hardly seemed controversial to focus therapeutic efforts on teaching spouses to use positive control rather than aversive control in their attempts to modify the behavior of one another. If positive behaviors were occurring with insufficient frequency, spouses were taught to reinforce such behaviors, with the expectation that their frequency would increase. Contingency contracting epitomized these early applications (Stuart, 1969; Weiss, Birchler, & Vincent, 1974). For example, in the "quid pro quo" contract, each spouse agrees to a behavior change desired by the partner, and these changes are cross-linked such that each change is made contingent upon the other. More generally, traditional BMT teaches spouses to utilize their reinforcement power to systematically and immediately reward desired or highly valued behaviors from the partner (Azrin et al., 1973; Liberman, 1970; Stuart, 1969).

However, in recent years there has been a growing tendency to be critical of contingency management procedures in general, and contingency contracting procedures in particular. Critiques have emerged from clinical observations as well as from research findings. Clinical observations have suggested that the explicit specification of contingencies may be both fruitless and self-defeating: fruitless because the real reinforcers in most intimate relationships are very difficult to specify discreetly and provide on demand; self-defeating because the act of contingency specification may serve to neutralize the reinforcing properties of both targeted behaviors and alleged reinforcers. In short, contingency specification may be either superfluous, at best, or clinically destructive, at worst (Jacobson, 1978b; Jacobson & Margolin, 1979). Consider physical affection, a response class which is an important source of gratification in marriage. The reinforcing power of affection usually stems not simply from its intrinsic properties, but also because it represents a statement of love and caring to the receiver. Once affection from spouse A is designated as a reinforcer in a contingency contract and presented contingently following the occurrence of some desired behavior on the part of spouse B, there is a significant risk that affection will cease to be reinforcing when it occurs according to contractual stipulations. Rather than being perceived as an act of caring or love, it is likely to be interpreted as an act performed for extrinsic reasons, because the contract dictated that it occur. In other words, spouse A is likely to attribute spouse B's behavior to external factors, whereas the reinforcing impact of affection depends upon the receiver's casual attributions being internal, i.e., "My partner is hugging me out of a spontaneous and internally-motivated desire to express love." Given the growing body of evidence suggesting that distressed couples tend to neutralize the impact of rewarding behaviors from the partner by attributing them to extrinsic factors, this tendency is particularly likely among couples in therapy (Jacobson, McDonald, & Follette, 1981).

Findings from recent research investigations also point to the dangers in using marital therapy to promote the use of positive control strategies (Gottman, 1979; Jacobson, Follette, & McDonald, 1982; Jacobson, Waldron, & Moore, 1980.) The use of immediate contingency control to maintain behavior in relationships seems to be uniquely characteristic of unhappy couples. Although the evidence in support of this proposition is stronger for punishing than for rewarding behavior, there is evidence that distressed couples are particularly sensitive to immediate or recent relationship events. In happy relationships, on the other hand, immediate contingency control appears to be a less viable explanation for why positive behaviors occur at a high rate. The subjective satisfaction of generally happy couples is relatively independent of recent or immediate relationship events. Moreover, there is little evidence that positive behaviors in generally happy relationships are immediately reinforced. Rather, there is a growing consensus among research investigators that happy couples exchange high rates of noncontingent positive behavior.

The abundance of gratifying transactions appears to be under the control of a long history of stable and frequently provided rewards. As a consequence of their learning history with one another, immediate reciprocity is unnecessary to maintain positive behavior. Certainly external control is not absent in such relationships. If spouse A suddenly reduced his/her rate of rewards delivered to spouse B, eventually spouse B's rate would decline as well. The point is that a point-for-point exchange model based on the simplistic application of operant conditioning principles does not seem relevant to most satisfying marital relationships.

The clinical implications of these observations and research findings are far-reaching. To the extent that distressed couples are taught in therapy to use contingency management strategies to generate positive changes in the relationship, we may simply be teaching them more of the same (cf. Gurman & Knudson, 1978). The task of the therapist is to promote high rates of positive exchanges that are not linked by an immediate contingency. Marital therapy should be structured in such a way that rewarding behaviors are perceived by the spouses as internally motivated; even as the therapist utilizes contingency control, s/he must attend to how these changes are perceived by spouses so that relationship-enhancing attributions accompany behavior change. The necessity of promoting behavior change without relying on explicit contingency management greatly complicates the task of therapy. Let us now examine how BMT has changed to accommodate this reconceptualization of the change process.

First, contingency contracting is on the wane. When written change agreements are used, the therapist specifically avoids the use of explicit reinforcers and punishers. This does not mean, of course, that contingencies are absent. On the contrary, when both spouses are generating positive changes in response to their commitment to therapy, it is likely that implicit contingencies *are* operating. But the emphasis is on directives which instigate simultaneous, parallel changes.

Second, there has been a trend toward therapeutic tasks and directives which maximize the number of options that clients have in fulfilling the assignment (cf. Weiss, 1978, 1980; Weiss, Hops, & Patterson, 1973). For example, Stuart (1980) utilizes large-scale holistic contracts where spouses can fulfill contractual obligations by implementing any one of a number of desired behavior changes. Each spouse agrees simultaneously to implement the contract, but the commitments are viewed as independent rather than linked by a contingency. In our work, during the early stages of therapy homework assignments are stated rather generally, and we avoid prescribing specific behavior changes. For example, the therapist might direct each spouse to "devote the next week to increasing your partner's overall satisfaction with the relationship," while leaving the specific mode of implementation to each spouse. Usually, such a directive follows training in pinpointing important reinforcers in the marriage. Here spouses are taught to examine empirically the relationship between their own behavior and the partner's relationship satisfaction and to generate hypotheses regarding which behaviors on their part, if delivered more often, would produce a happier partner. Thus, by the time the directive to change is delivered, each spouse has a large pool of potentially reinforcing behaviors to choose from. The directive simply requires that they deliver some of the items from that pool at an increased rate, without requiring them to deliver any particular behavior.

Although this trend toward more general and less specific assignments runs counter to the traditional emphasis in behavior therapy on specificity, it is, in my view, a better strategy for promoting changes that will persist subsequent to the termination of therapy. As task directives become less specific and client options become broader, the likelihood that subsequent changes will be well received is maximized. Consider a husband who chooses to fulfill the assignment by being more affectionate. The wife leaves the previous therapy session without knowing what to expect from him during the coming week. He has not been asked to be more affectionate, nor has he committed himself in advance to increased affection. Rather, both from the perspective of the wife and in reality, he is choosing to be affectionate. An external attribution which would neutralize the reinforcing impact of his behavior is unlikely. Despite the directive to change, the particular behavior changes that do occur are less likely to be attributed to the assignment per se and more likely to be perceived as internally motivated.

One might add that this type of general assignment carries with it an additional fringe benefit, not directly related to the discussion at hand but vitally important to the ultimate success of therapy. From the perspective of the spouse who is changing his behavior, the more options he has, the less likely he will be to resist the therapist's directive (cf. Jacobson, 1981; Weiss, 1980). This is not an empirically tested hypothesis, but it is consistent with social-psychological research on the phenomenon of reactance. This research would predict that when a therapist provides directives which are perceived by clients as restricting their freedom of choice, they are likely to resist them. This prediction is consistent with my clinical experience. The more behavioral flexibility that is allowed in the implementation of a directive, the more options clients have in complying with a homework assignment, the more likely they are to comply.

Third, in our behavior change directives, we avoid situations where one spouse is requesting behavior change from the other, particularly during the early treatment sessions. Instead, we leave the initiative in the hands of the spouse whose behavior is changing. This tactic is illustrated in the assignment presented above. By training each spouse to pinpoint behaviors on their part which would enhance the partner's relationship satisfaction, and then directing spouses to provide some of these behaviors, we circumvent the need for direct requests from the potential recipient. Although this tactic runs counter to the more widely used strategy of having each spouse ask for what he/she wants (cf. Stuart, 1980), I believe that when the provider of rewards is in charge of determining which reward to deliver, rather than responding to a request from the receiver, the behavior changes are more likely to occur and more likely to be reinforcing when they do occur. The rationale here is the same as that provided for the use of generalized rather than highly specific directives. However, even when the behavior change directives are specific, the provider can still be responsible for deciding what to provide. The therapist can ask, "What are you willing to commit yourself to this next week?", rather than asking the partner, "What would you like this week?" When the provider decides what to provide, he/she perceives himself/herself as being in control of the change process and will therefore be less likely to feel coerced and constrained. Moreover, the changes that are forthcoming are more likely to be highly valued by the receiver because they occur at the provider's initiative.

I am not recommending the exclusive use of provider-initiated behavior change directives. Input as well as requests for change from the receiver are still included in our marital therapy program during later phases. But during the early treatment sessions we leave the decision-making power almost entirely in the hands of the provider.

All of the principles mentioned in this section represent departures from standard clinical practice of BMT. The deemphasis on contingency contracting, the use of general rather than specific directives, and the avoidance of requests for change from the partner during early treatment sessions are all designed to facilitate change as well as ensure that the changes will be reinforcing when they occur. They are all based in part on the belief that cognitive processes play an important role in marital conflict and its resolution. In the next section, the cognitive emphasis will be extended to some guidelines for the more direct modification of cognitive processes in BMT.

TOWARD THE MODIFICATION OF DYSFUNCTIONAL COGNITIONS

BMT, in its early years, focused almost exclusively on altering the overt behavior of distressed spouses (Liberman, 1970; Stuart, 1969; Patterson & Hops, 1972; Weiss et al., 1973). It was assumed that dysfunctional attitudes, cognitions, and affective states would change automatically if therapy was successful in generating increases in positive behavior and teaching couples behavior change skills. Although there has been no direct test of this assumption, it is our belief, based on clinical experience, that behavior change does not always lead to the desired or predicted cognitive, attitudinal, and affective changes. When behavior changes occur in the absence of desired internal changes, the former are likely to be temporary and marital therapy ultimately fails to significantly improve the relationship. In the previous section I suggested some alterations in behavioral interventions which are more conducive to promoting desirable internal changes. In addition, a number of clinical innovations have been suggested in recent years which focus more directly on cognitive change (Baucom, 1981; Epstein, 1982; Jacobson, in press; Schindler & Vollmer, 1981).

Baucom (1981) has developed a brief (six session) cognitive restructuring format designed to precede behavioral procedures. The cognitive treatment focuses both on attributional processes and on unrealistic expectations held by spouses. During the cognitive restructuring sessions, no attempt is made to generate behavior changes in the relationship. Each session focuses on a particular type of cognitive distortion thought to be prevalent in the repertoires of distressed couples. For example, one session focuses on the distinction between internal and external causal attributions. Another focuses on unrealistic expectations that each spouse has for himself/herself and the partner. The format of each session includes the following components: an explanation of the concept, along with examples; an analysis of one or more problems from the couple's own relationship in terms of the particular cognitive concept in question; and a homework assignment involving practice in the types of analyses and skills discussed during the session. Following completion of the cognitive restructuring format, BMT is provided.

Hopefully, by the end of the cognitive restructuring period, spouses are more likely to recognize that each person's interpretation of a relationship problem mediates his/her emotional response to that problem, and that certain types of causal attributions (external, specific, unstable) regarding the partner's negative behavior are both more benign and more adaptive for the relationship than others (internal, global, stable attributions). Presumably, they should also be more inclined once they have completed this program to have realistic expectations about their partner and the relationship and to interpret the partner's behavior in such a way that the impact of negative behavior is minimized and the responsiveness to positive behavior is enhanced. It is expected that these cognitive changes should then facilitate the process of behavior change as treatment shifts to the latter focus.

Baucom (1981) argues for the separation of the cognitive restructuring component from the behavior change component, with the cognitive component presented first. The primary rationale for this sequencing of treatment modules is that dysfunctional cognitions often interfere with and preclude behavior change; therefore, it makes sense to begin by changing cognitions first. Weiss (1980) has approached the cognitive/behavioral interface somewhat differently, by developing an integrative approach where both cognitive and behavior changes are targeted concurrently. Jacobson (in press) describes an effort, still in its exploratory stages, to integrate cognitive restructuring procedures directly into formats focusing on behavior change. Specifically, a cognitive exploration component has been proposed to accompany the communication training module known as problem-solving training (Jacobson & Margolin, 1979). Problem-solving training is a structured set of techniques designed to teach couples skills to help them resolve conflicts in their relationship. The content of the training program is elaborated in a manual, which specifies rules that spouses must follow when they discuss conflict situations. In therapy sessions, the instructions are augmented by behavior rehearsal, performance-based feedback from the therapist, and homework assignments designed to foster generalization of these skills to the home environment.

Problem-solving training has typically emphasized behavior change and accommodation, to the relative exclusion of explorations of cognitions which accompany the problematic behaviors in the relationship. The format does not include discussions of such issues as "Why is that a problem for you?" or "What does it mean to you when he does that?" In the new cognitive component to problem-solving training, the definition of a problem includes an effort to poinpoint the cognitions which follow the targeted behavior. For example, Frank would become furious at Mabel when she neglected her household tasks. When he broached this problem during a problem-solving session, the therapist stopped the action to engage in a dialogue with Frank regarding the inferences he drew from Mabel's neglect: To what does he attribute her neglect? What does her neglect mean to him? What is it about the neglect that makes it upsetting? Often, such dialogues elicit irrational ideas, catastrophic or unrealistic expectations, or unwarranted causal attributions. In this case, Frank interpreted Mabel's neglect as evidence of not caring about the family, placing the family at the bottom of her list of priorities.

Once these accompanying cognitions are verbalized and clarified, actual restructuring becomes possible. The restructuring process can take many forms. The therapist might call in the partner to counter the irrational beliefs. Mabel, when called upon, explained that her neglect was indicative of her forgetfulness, nothing more. The therapist supported this more benign interpretation, thereby lending the weight of his credibility to the interpretation which was more likely to generate collaboration between the spouses. At times calling on the partner to do the debunking can be risky, since spouses cannot always be relied upon to respond therapeutically: The optimal strategy is often for the therapist to offer an alternative interpretation. The therapist might have suggested to Frank, for example, that "We have lots of evidence that she does care about the family, including her commitment to working on the relationship; I think that there are other explanations for her neglect of household tasks which make more sense." Or the therapist might adopt a more Socratic style of cognitive restructuring, asking questions which lead to the adoption, or at least the consideration, of alternative interpretations of the same behavior. Some commitment on the part of the complainant to considering these alternative interpretations is necessary prior to the resumption of problem-solving.

There are many potential benefits to be derived from this type of cognitive exploration. First, whether or not the spouses actually give up their dysfunctional cognitions, their cognitive repertoires are at least expanded in the sense that they are made aware of more benign interpretive options. With the therapist lending his/her credibility to the more benign interpretations, the emotional impact of problem behaviors is attenuated. At times the need for behavior change is greatly reduced or obviated as a result. More commonly, the behavior change process continues but with a reduction in the degree of emotional intensity such that a collaborative solution is more easily attained. Second, once the inferences which the spouse draws from a particular behavior are made explicit, greater empathy is often fostered in the partner. The basis for behavioral complaints which had formerly been viewed outside of their cognitive context now becomes clearer to the object of the complaint, and, regardless of the validity of the cognitions, the negative emotional impact becomes comprehensible. The therapist can facilitate an empathic response by punctuating the cognitions of the spouse with whom the exploration is occuring and at critical points inviting the partner's participation.

Cognitive restructuring interventions can be used in other ways to foster relationship improvement. I have been discussing cognitive exploration which focuses on the spouse who is complaining about a particular partner-initiated behavior. But these procedures are also applicable to the spouse who is the object of the complaint, particularly in reference to the inhibitions or unrealistic expectations that might help to explain why this partner engages in the behavior in question. At times, behavior change is inhibited by fear and mistrust; these factors can be undercut or otherwise dealt with if the therapist encourages the spouse to verbalize them.

Finally, spouses can be taught to explore the cognitive concomitants of their relationship problems independent of the therapist, as part of the problem-solving process. To the extent that such training is possible, generalization and maintenance of therapeutic gains will be more likely.

Thus far, I have discussed two strategies for incorporating cognitive interventions into BMT, one involving a purely cognitive component which precedes behavioral training and the other integrating cognitive interventions into a standard behavioral treatment. Ultimately, the relative merits of these two strategies constitute empirical questions. My clinical impression thus far is that the integrative approach with which we have been experimenting is more promising. My impression stems from two concerns regarding the sequential option, both of which are mitigated by the integrative approach. First, when dysfunctional relationship cognitions are discussed as general principles apart from specific issues that the spouses in question face in their own relationship, the training procedures are less salient for the couple, and therefore unlikely to transfer to cognitive changes when dealing with major relationship problems. Although Baucom's program does utilize illustrative examples from the couple's own relationship, the description implies that the program remains fundamentally focused on teaching general principles. In the integrative approach, principles emerge from discussion of particular relationship issues and are thereby more likely to be relevant to that particular couple. Under those conditions, I believe that the relevant principles will be more easily learned, as well as applied to the issues of concern in a particular relationship.

Second, when marital therapy begins with a purely cognitive module which does not require either spouse to consider enacting behavior changes, a precedent of inertia is established. Successful BMT is predicated on each spouse assuming responsibility for improving the marriage, and much of the therapist's work is focused on generating action. Given the prevalent tendency toward blaming the partner and wanting the partner to change unilaterally, those efforts toward collaborative change must be harnessed early in therapy. Once a precedent for passivity in regard to behavior change is set, it will be difficult to overcome. Moreover, if behavior change instigations are avoided for six therapy sessions, the couple will experience little or no subjective relief from the problems plaguing their marriage. Yet, I have argued elsewhere that immediate changes are necessary to foster collaboration and maintain positive expectancies. One has to wonder about the potential dropout rate in an approach which responds to spouses' emotional anguish with general discussions of dysfunctional cognitive processes, relevant illustrative examples notwithstanding.

In addition to the innovations suggested by Baucom (1981) and Jacobson (in press), a number of other theorists have proposed that cognitive procedures be incorporated into BMT. Weiss (1980), in an important paper, has outlined a conceptual model for determining when cognitive interventions are indicated in lieu of or as a supplement to behavioral interventions. Epstein (1982) has specified a number of cognitive distortions common among distressed couples, and has recommended treatment strategies derived from the work of Beck, Rush, Shaw, & Emery (1979) with individual clients. For modifying unrealistic expectations regarding either the partner or the relationship, Epstein recommends strategies such as "reality testing," which involves examining the expectation in light of the couple's past and present life experiences, and the "behavioral experiment," prescribed to test the hypotheses implied by the expectation. Epstein also suggests using self-instructional training (Meichenbaum, 1977) to aid couples in the task of deescalating quarrels. Schindler and Vollmer (1981) recommend a similar procedure termed "crisis management." Finally, Abrams (1980), like Baucom (1981), recommends the therapy begin with cognitive interventions; unlike Baucom, she suggests that at least some of these sessions should be held with each spouse separately. Interestingly, other advocates of cognitive strategies also suggest a partial return to a concurrent therapy model for cognitive interventions (Epstein, 1982; Schindler & Vollmer, 1981). For Abrams, individual sessions are more likely to foster unilateral acceptance of responsibility for cognitive change. In addition, Schindler and Vollmer (1981) suggest that without the partner present individual spouses may be less afraid to test new responses. Epstein (1982) adds that individual sessions may be necessary to provide sufficient help for those whose self-regulatory capacities are severely impaired.

Let us conclude this section on a note of caution. I have mentioned a number of innovations aimed at modifying cognitive processes. To describe a procedure for modifying internal states is not the same as demonstrating that these procedures successfully accomplish that task. Whether or not the exploration and relabeling strategies described above actually alter spouse cognitions remains an untested assumption. In general, there is very little evidence in the cognitive therapy literature that standard "cognitive interventions" actually modify internal states (cf. Wilson & O'Leary, 1980). Even in those instances where the effectiveness of cognitive therapy seems evident, such as Beck's cognitive treatment for depression (Rush, Beck, Kovacs, & Hollon, 1977), the treatment package includes multiple components and the power of the specific cognitive restructuring interventions has not been isolated. In fact, there is considerable evidence in the behavior therapy literature that performance-based treatments are more effective than those which involve purely verbal or symbolic operations (Wilson & O'Leary, 1980). In short, it might turn out that in BMT, the most effective way to promote cognitive changes is through carefully designed performance-based interventions such as those described in the previous section. Although it seems clear that relationship improvement usually requires covert as well as overt changes, it is by no means clear at this stage of our knowledge how to best facilitate changes in these two response systems.

As a final note to this section, let us beware of throwing out the proverbial baby with the bath water in our zeal for incorporating cognitive procedures into BMT. Behavioral technology has been carefully constructed to overcome the reluctance on the part of distressed spouses to commit themselves to changing their behavior. It seems apparent that the efficacy of BMT is based at least in part on strategies which counter spouses' efforts to find reasons not to change. As cognitive procedures are added to BMT technology, we run the risk of diluting this message. To the extent that the focus of therapy shifts from undesirable behavior to irrational cognitions and unrealistic expectations, we may be unwittingly providing spouses with ammunition which will support their reluctance to enact behavioral compromises. Indeed, this may be exactly what is needed to balance the heretofore exclusive emphasis on behavior change which permeates the BMT literature. But it is important that we not take these risks lightly. If cognitive interventions are to be incorporated into behavoral procedures, the mixture should not result in contradictory messages presented to distressed couples.

THE BEHAVIOR OF THE THERAPIST

A third area in which behavioral technology is expanding focuses on the behavior of the therapist. Over the past two years, we have identified a number of therapist response classes which play an important role in facilitating positive outcomes in BMT. Although the clinical skills required of a good marital therapist are exceedingly complex and subtle, our intensive analyses of ongoing cases has revealed a number of specifiable dimensions (Jacobson, Berley et al., in press). Ultimately, the goal is to investigate the predictive power of these dimensions empirically. In addition, to the extent that relevant therapist behaviors can be specified, they can be built into the technology of BMT so that the proportion of outcome variance attributable to therapist characteristics is reduced. In the paragraphs below, I will list and describe five dimensions of therapist behavior which are hypothesized to be predictive of positive outcome in BMT.

Structuring Skills

BMT is a highly structured, brief treatment requiring an active, directive therapist. Structuring skills refer to the capacity for setting and implementing agendas so that the goals of a particular therapy session are met. They also refer to intersession pacing, the ability to effectively integrate therapy sessions so that the ultimate goals of therapy are attained.

To a certain extent structure can be built into the format of treatment sessions by the inclusion of rules and guidelines which determine both the therapists' and the clients' behavior during treatment sessions. But therapists vary in the extent to which they effectively adhere to format and structure; they also vary in their ability to enforce rule violations on the part of spouses. Variability in the former type of behavior has to do with pacing during a treatment session. The regulation of client behavior involves a wide range of skills which fall into the category of prompting and shaping adherence to an agenda. Therapists with adequate structuring skills respond consistently to rule violations on the part of spouses: For example, if a rule states that "no blaming statements are allowed," the therapist must consistently interrupt and redirect all blaming statements. Moreover, good therapists involve the spouses themselves in a critique of their own rule violations and aid them in the self-monitoring and self-regulation of their own performance.

Instigation Skills

BMT places a heavy emphasis on instigating behavior change in the home environment. Effective instigation involves the induction and maintenance of a collaborative set, the ability to induce compliance with homework assignments, and the ability to produce changes which maintain themselves subsequent to the termination of active treatment. The establishment and maintenance of a *collaborative set* require the following: providing spouses with a convincing theoretical rationale for the problems in the marriage, a rationale emphasizing mutual responsibility for relationship problems and requiring a collaborative effort to bring about improvement; inducing a commitment on the part of both spouses to engage in collaborative behavior despite ambivalent or even hostile reactions to the therapist's model of the relationship; and structuring therapy so that some positive changes occur very quickly, in order that the commitment to collaboration is reinforced (Jacobson & Margolin, 1979). *Compliance* with homework assignments depends on how the assignment is presented (stimulus control) and how the therapist responds to noncompliance, should it occur despite the effective use of stimulus control (Jacobson, 1981a; Jacobson, Berley et al., in press). Stimulus control strategies include emphasizing the importance of the task, gaining prior commitment from the spouses, anticipating and repudiating potential excuses for noncompliance, and the provision of adequate prompts in the home environment. Noncompliance must not be reinforced either by continuation of "business as usual" or by support and understanding when clients explain why they were "unable" to comply. Effective *generalization* and *maintenance* of skills acquired during therapy sessions require that the therapist's role evolve from that of teacher to a much less active monitoring of spouse performance. The therapist must know when and how to step back so that the clients learn to function on their own.

Teaching Skills

A good behavioral marital therapist is a good teacher. In explaining principles and guidelines to clients, therapists frequently overestimate the capacity of their clients for processing information. Clients, even highly educated ones, are not colleagues, and information needs to be transmitted simply and clearly, in the clients' language. Frequent repetition is required, along with inquiries to make sure that therapist communications are being accurately decoded by spouses. In addition, the therapist must make sure that clients are learning "principles" rather than simply enacting new behaviors in response to therapist prompts. Principles can and should be conveyed in a variety of ways: explaining the rationale for new behaviors suggested by the therapist; eliciting active involvement on the part of clients in critiquing their own performance; and debriefing various treatment exercises to ensure that clients understand what has just transpired.

Fostering Positive Expectancies

To the extent that couples expect therapy to lead to a significantly improved relationship, they are more likely to persist in the behaviors which are necessary to ensure a positive outcome. Both collaboration during sessions and compliance with assignments between sessions are more likely if spouses remain optimistic that their efforts will bear fruit. Frequently verbalized optimism on the part of the therapist, along with both verbal and nonverbal enthusiasm for the treatment program, is critical to client perseverance. What might not be quite so obvious is that positive expectancies are more likely to be maintained if the therapist's optimism is tempered by the frequent acknowledgment of both the reality constraints and the difficulties of marital therapy. Since even successful therapy is often punctuated by alternating periods of progress and relapse, it is necessary for the therapist to anticipate and prepare couples for the valleys as well as the peaks. Without such preparation, spouses may become demoralized during typical midtherapy crises. Paradoxically, positive expectancies are fostered by sobering reminders from the therapist: Relapses are likely to occur; the tasks are difficult and often seem mechanical; during certain phases of therapy, such as pretreatment assessment or early stages of problem-solving training, no change is expected; and ultimately, despite the presence of a highly potent technology, a positive response to treatment is the responsibility of the couple. Thus, the maintenance of positive expectancies in the couple requires finely-tuned balance of optimism and realism from the therapist.

Providing Emotional Nurturance

A number of discrete types of intervention are required of the appropriately nurturant therapist. *First*, spouses must have the opportunity to express negative feelings during the course of therapy. If the therapist simply cuts off negative affect in the service of structure and collaboration, spouses may become frustrated, feel misunderstood, and disengage themselves from the therapy process. Anger expression often produces defensiveness in the partner, but as long as the therapist prevents the anger from dictating the course of therapy, its expression is not contraindicated. For example, spouses often use anger as an excuse for failing to collaborate either at home or in session. The therapist must oppose such strategies, while at the same time acknowledging and validating the partner's feelings. Often such acknowledgment from the therapist is sufficient; spouses want to make sure that therapists "really understand" how they feel, and if the therapist stays on course even after listening to the spouse's affective expression, that course is likely to attain greater credibility for the angry spouse.

Second, the nurturant therapist frequently probes spouses to elicit feelings about therapy and about the spouse. Elsewhere, we have referred to such probes as "taking the couple's affective temperature" (Jacobson, Berley et al., in press). One can not assume that negative feelings or reservations about therapy will emerge spontaneously, and in order to effectively cope with these feelings the therapist often must elicit them. Moreover, therapists must not become so enamored of their technology that they fail to track the nonverbal cues emanating from spouses. Couples may be compliant and collaborative but at the same time feel negatively about the events of therapy. These inconsistencies are often revealed by subtle facial expressions, paralinguistic cues, and body language.

More generally, the nurturant therapist is gentle and supportive despite the directive, firm, and sometimes confronting style required of the behavioral marital therapist. The ability to combine these "soft" clinical skills with the role of highly structured, effectively instigative teacher can make the difference between successful and unsuccessful marital therapy.

In conclusion, this section has focused on dimensions of therapist behavior which we have identified as central to the outcome of therapy. There is no claim to comprehensiveness in the presentation of this list.

Indeed, these areas of clinical skill are put forth tentatively awaiting more systematic documentation as to their salience. The important point is that behavioral technology is always delivered in some context, and it is up to the therapist to provide a context which supports meaningful relationship change. Despite the emphasis in the BMT literature on technology, it has long been recognized that technology comprises only one source of outcome variance in psychotherapy (Garfield & Bergin, 1978). Therapist variables comprise a second source, and it is toward an understanding of this second major source of variance that much of our current effort is directed.

FUTURE DIRECTIONS: EMPIRICAL AND NONEMPIRICAL QUESTIONS

Toward an Integrated Relationship Therapy

Research on BMT provides a glaring example of the costs inherent in surrendering to the constraints imposed by the rigid application of scientific methodology in the narrowest sense of the term. In an attempt to adhere to the requirements of between-groups designs, we have developed standardized outcome measures, all of which imply that marital therapy is always directed toward an improved and sustained relationship. Similarly, despite using terms such as "functional analysis" and "idiographic," both research investigations and extended clinical treatises describe standardized techniques without identifying limitations in the applicability of those techniques. Our model of marital distress, steeped in the inductive tradition of behavioral science, prematurely invokes the principle of parsimony by describing what marital distress is, as if marital distress has only one, or at most a few, causes. Our research tradition divorces our work from the realities of clinical practice, and our glib insistence on the efficacy of these procedures frustrates those who endeavor to be consumers of our research.

The "secret" is that we have not as yet developed a complete approach to treating relationships, but instead have focused our attention on the development and refinement of very specific techniques of limited scope and limited applicability. BMT in its present form is just what the doctor ordered for some couples, somewhat useful for many others, but for still other couples misses the point. The literature virtually ignores the incredible heterogeneity in our distressed couples by attempting to subsume them all under generic rubrics such as "problem-solving deficits" or "reinforcement erosion." The problem is that the struggle to maintain an intimate relationship can go awry for a vast number of reasons, and our attempts to modify faulty communication or increase reinforcement skills are largely irrelevant for some couples. A truly comprehensive and integrated approach to treating relationships will be impossible unless we expand our vision and broaden our focus. Two brief examples are provided both to illustrate the problem and chart future directions.

The Artificial Dichotomy Between Marital and Sexual Problems

One of the peculiar idiosyncracies of our field is that marital therapy and sex therapy form two distinct literatures. There is very little in the BMT literature on the treatment of sexual problems, and the sex therapy literature is similarly devoid of insight into the treatment of nonsexual marital problems (Heiman, LoPiccolo, & LoPiccolo, 1981; Masters & Johnson, 1970). Yet, in clinical practice, most distressed couples report sex as a problem area, and it is the exception rather than the rule when couples enter therapy with a dissatisfying sex life in an otherwise satisfying relationship (Melman & Jacobson, in press). Although with some couples sexual problems can be overcome using standard behavioral interventions, special procedures commonly associated with sex therapy are often necessary as an adjunct to BMT. There has been almost nothing written in the literature on integrating these two technologies. Relevant issues include the sequencing of sexual and nonsexual interventions; the potency of BMT for helping couples overcome sexual difficulties when those difficulties are primarily effects rather than causes of marital problems in nonsexual domains; the effects of BMT or modified sex therapy techniques on sexual problems where no clear-cut dysfunction exists, such as loss of interest, reduced frequency, and the like. A truly integrative relationship therapy avoids artificial dichotomies. Clearly, marital and sex therapy investigators must combine their efforts, so that the treatments described and evaluated in the literature correspond more closely to the complexities and realities of clinical practice.

The Idiographic Determination of Treatment Goals

In my view, the most fundamental challenge to behavioral research on marital therapy in the coming years involves paying adequate attention to the heterogeneity of distressed couples' presenting complaints and treatment goals. Flexible, multifaceted, treatment interventions must replace standardized techniques which falsely imply that marital distress comprises a monolithic entity. More importantly, the emphasis

on relationship as client must be tempered by a recognition that relationships are comprised of two individuals who often enter therapy with
competing interests, with different amounts and types of individual distress, and with differing levels of commitment toward improving the
present relationship. Traditional BMT literature has devoted little attention to safeguarding the interests of the two individuals comprising
the marital dyad: The outcomes of marital therapy are measured solely
in terms of relationship improvement (with individual spouse scores
summed to create a dyadic measure); BMT emphasizes and promotes
collaboration, accommodation, and behavior change without explicitly
taking into account the costs of such a focus to the individuals involved;
and BMT *assumes* that the two spouses are equally to blame and equally
in need of behavior change.

Unfortunately, there are some relationships where the personal costs
resulting from the collaborative effort required in BMT are extremely
high. Oppression and abuse are at times skewed and imbalanced, so that
equal amounts of behavior change on the part of each spouse would not
eradicate the problem. Moreover, there are times when a relationship
is so opresive to one spouse that the therapist's directives toward mutual
responsibility and change serve to reinforce the existing oppression.

BMT offers little by way of explicit theory regarding what constitutes
a good relationship. However, as it currently stands, BMT is implicitly
pro-relationship and anti-divorce. By emphasizing the need for a collaborative effort toward relationship enhancement, BMT implies that
it is good to subordinate one's peronal goals toward the improvement
of a relationship. By designing interventions which attempt to counter
spouses' reluctance to collaborate, BMT implies that it is bad to refuse
to collaborate. Although this emphasis is appropriate for some couples,
it can in some cases offer support to an exploitative relationship and
punish healthy independent strivings toward disengagement.

A brief example will illustrate these points. Recently, a couple married
for 20 years sought therapy. The husband was a very successful, wealthy
professional who was seriously considering divorce. He was good-look-
ing, flirtatious with other women, and was in various ways gradually
disengaging from the relationship. The wife, although quite attractive
and intelligent, was very dependent on her husband both economically
and psychologically. He was very much the more powerful person in the
relationship, not only because of his control over finances but because
his options were considerably broader than hers. She had no career,
little confidence in herself, and was terribly frightened by the prospect
of the marriage terminating. She was also quite jealous and suspected

him of engaging in extramarital affairs, a charge which he denied. In order to remain in the relationship, he demanded that she stop challenging his efforts to control the finances, accept his devotion to his career, and cease her expressions of mistrust and jealousy. This case, by no means extraordinary, illustrates the dangers of applying a standard BMT format to certain couples. The premise that spouses must be equally willing to change and the notion that each spouse's stated treatment goals are a priori valid would lead in this case to the therapist's validating the current oppression in the relationship. One could argue that the wife's interests in this case would be safeguarded only by helping her overcome her dependency and develop her capacities to function as a single person. To maintain that she is freely choosing to stay with him runs contrary to the obvious constraints which their relationship history and, to some extent, our culture have imposed on her. On the other hand, the ethical dilemmas inherent in leading her on a path which runs contrary to her stated wishes must also be recognized.

Dilemmas such as these have no easy solutions. I raise them simply because they require attention. Thus far, BMT has failed to provide a basis for promoting individual well-being while at the same time fostering relationship change. BMT has little to say to those spouses whose problems seem better suited to a focus on disengagement than to increased intimacy. Perhaps the addition of cognitive interventions will help restore some balance to the excessive dyadic emphasis of BMT. But clearly something more is needed in order to ensure that the relationship that emerges at the conclusion of therapy is a relationship which better serves its individual members.

SUMMARY AND CONCLUSIONS

In this chapter recent clinical innovations in the behavioral treatment of marital distress are reviewed. The need for clinical innovation is suggested by the limitations of current behavioral technology; the new developments parallel a great deal of clinical expansion and conceptual reappraisal in the behavior therapy field as a whole. Discussion focused on three types of clinical innovations: alternatives to contingency control; cognitive interventions; and the delineation of critical dimensions of therapist behavior. Future directions for further clinical innovations are suggested, with the ultimate goal being a more comprehensive, integrated method of treating relationships.

These are both exciting and challenging times for BMT. The primary challenge is implicit in the tension between empirical and nonempirical questions. This chapter reflects the divergence in the directions suggested by the empirical and nonempirical domains of inquiry. Empirical questions direct our efforts toward improving our technology for helping couples improve their relationships. Nonempirical questions challenge these goals by casting doubt on the desirability of our single-minded pursuit of relationship-enhancing technology. Let us hope that as scientists and clinicians we can find a way to resolve the inconsistencies and progress along both fronts, so that our efforts will better benefit both relationships and the individuals involved in those relationships.

REFERENCES

ABRAMS, J.L. *Cognitive-behavioral strategies to induce and enhance a collaborative set in the treatment of distressed couples.* Unpublished manuscript, 1980.

AZRIN, N.H., BESALEL, V.A., BECHTEL, R., MICHALICEK, A., MANCERA, M., CARROLL, D., SHUFORD, D., & COX, J. Comparison of reciprocity and discussion—type of counseling for marital problems. *American Journal of Family Therapy*, 1980, *8*, 21-28.

AZRIN, N.H., NASTER, B.J., & JONES, R. Reciprocity counseling: A rapid learning-based procedure for marital counseling. *Behavior Research and Therapy*, 1973, *211*, 365-382.

BAUCOM, D.H. *Cognitive behavioral strategies in the treatment of marital discord.* Paper presented at the Annual meeting of the Association for the Advancement of Behavior Therapy, November, 1981, Toronto.

BAUCOM, D.H. The relative utility of behavioral contracting and problem-solving/communications training in behavioral marital therapy: A controlled outcome study. *Behavior Therapy*, 1982, *13*, 162-174.

BAUCOM, D.H. Conceptual and psychometric issues in evaluating the effectiveness of behavioral marital therapy. In J.P. Vincent (Ed.), *Advances in family intervention, assessment, and theory* (Vol. 3). Greenwich, CT: JAI, Inc, in press.

BECK, A.T., RUSH, A.J., SHAW, B.F., & EMERY, G. *Cognitive therapy of depression.* New York: Guilford Press, 1979.

EMMELKAMP, P., VAN DER HELM, M., MACGILLAVRY, D., & VAN ZANTEN, B. *Marital therapy with clinically distressed couples: A comparative evaluation of systems-theoretic, contingency contracting and communication skills approaches.* Paper presented at the Symposium "Marital interaction: Analysis and modification," July, 1981, Munich, West Germany.

EPSTEIN, N. Cognitive therapy with couples. *American Journal of Family Therapy*, 1982, *10*, 5-16.

GARFIELD, S.L., & BERGIN, A.E. (Eds.), *Handbook of psychotherapy and behavior change.* New York: Wiley, 1978.

GOTTMAN, J.M., *Marital interaction: Experimental investigations.* New York: Academic Press, 1979.

GURMAN, A.S., & KNUDSON, R.M. Behavioral marriage therapy: I. A psychodynamic systems analysis and critique. *Family Process*, 1978, *17*, 121-138.

HAHLWEG, K., SCHINDLER, L., REVENSTORF, D., & BRENGELMANN, J.C. *The Munich marital therapy study.* Paper presented at the Symposium "Marital Interaction: Analysis and modification," July, 1981, Munich, West Germany.

HEIMAN, J.R., LOPICCOLO, L., & LOPICCOLO, J. The treatment of sexual dysfunction. In A.S. Gurman & D.P. Kniskern (Eds.), *Handbook of family therapy*. New York: Brunner/Mazel, 1981.

JACOBSON, N.S. Problem solving and contingency contracting in the treatment of marital discord. *Journal of Consulting and Clinical Psychology*, 1977, *45*, 92-100.

JACOBSON, N.S. Specific and nonspecific factors in the effectiveness of a behavioral approach to the treatment of marital discord. *Journal of Consulting and Clinical Psychology*, 1978, *46*, 442-452. (a)

JACOBSON, N.S. A stimulus control model of change in behavioral marital therapy: Implications for contingency contracting. *Journal of Marriage and Family Counseling*, 1978, *4*, 29-35. (b)

JACOBSON, N.S. Marital problems. In J.L. Shelton and R.L. Levy (Eds.), *Behavioral assignments and treatment compliance: A handbook of clinical strategies*. Champaign, IL: Research Press, 1981. (a)

JACOBSON, N.S. *The modification of cognitive processes in behavioral marital therapy: Integrating cognitive and behavioral intervention strategies*. Paper presented at the Symposium "Marital Interaction: Analysis and modification," July, 1981, Munich, West Germany. (b)

JACOBSON, N.S. The modification of cognitive processes in behavioral marital therapy: Integration of cognitive and behavioral intervention strategies. In K. Hahlweg and N.S. Jacobson (Eds.), *Marital interaction: Analysis and modification*. New York: Guilford Press, in press.

JACOBSON, N.S., BERLEY, R., MELMAN, K., ELWOOD, R., & PHELPS, C. Failure in behavioral marital therapy. In S. Coleman (Ed.), *Failure in family therapy*. New York: Guilford Press, in press.

JACOBSON, N.S. FOLLETTE, W.C., & MCDONALD, D.W. Reactivity to positive and negative behavior in distressed and nondistressed married couples. *Journal of Consulting and Clinical Psychology*, 1982, *50*, 706-714.

JACOBSON, N.S., & MARGOLIN, G. *Marital therapy: Strategies based on social learning and behavior exchange principles*. New York: Brunner/Mazel, 1979.

JACOBSON, N.S., MCDONALD, D.W., & FOLLETTE, W.C. *Attributional differences between distressed and nondistressed married couples*. Paper presented at the annual meeting of the Association for the Advancement of Behavior Therapy, November 13, 1981, Toronto.

JACOBSON, N.S., WALDRON, H., & MOORE, D. Toward a behavioral profile of marital distress. *Journal of Consulting and Clinical Psychology*, 1980, *48*, 696-703.

LIBERMAN, R.P. Behavioral approaches to family and couple therapy. *American Journal of Orthopsychiatry*, 1970, *40*, 106-118.

LIBERMAN, R.P., LEVINE, J., WHEELER, E., SANDERS, N., & WALLACE, C. Experimental evaluation of marital group therapy: Behavioral vs. interaction-insight formats. *Acta Psychiatrica Scandinavia*, 1976, *Supplement*.

MARGOLIN, G., & WEISS, R.L. A comparative evaluation of therapeutic components associated with behavioral marital treatment. *Journal of Consulting and Clinical Psychology*, 1978, *46*, 1476-1486.

MASTERS, W.H., & JOHNSON, V.E. *Human sexual inadequacy*. Boston: Little, Brown, 1970.

MEICHENBAUM, D.H. *Cognitive-behavior modification: An integrative approach*. New York: Plenum, 1977.

MELMAN, K.N., & JACOBSON, N.S. The integration of behavioral marital therapy and sex therapy. In M.L. Aronson and L.R. Wolberg, (Eds.), *Group and family therapy 1983—an overview*. New York: Brunner/Mazel, in press.

O'LEARY, K.D., & TURKEWITZ, H. The treatment of marital disorders from a behavioral perspective. In T.J. Paolino & B.S. McGrady (Eds.), *Marriage and marital therapy: Psychoanalytic, behavioral, and systems theory perspectives*. New York: Brunner/Mazel, 1978.

PATTERSON, G.R., & HOPS, H. Coersion, a game for two: Intervention techniques for marital conflict. In R.E. Ulrich & P. Montjoy (Eds.), *The experimental analysis of social behavior.* New York: Appleton-Century-Crofts, 1972.

RUSH, A.J., BECK, A.T., KOVACS, M., & HOLLON, S. Comparative efficacy of cognitive therapy and pharmacotherapy in the treatment of depressed outpatients. *Cognitive Therapy and Research,* 1977, *1,* 17-37.

SCHINDLER, L., & VOLLMER, M. *Cognitive perspectives in behavioral marital therapy: Some proposals for bridging theory, research, and practice.* Paper presented at the Symposium "Marital Interaction: Analysis and modification," July, 1981, Munich, West Germany.

STUART, R.B. Operant interpersonal treatment of marital discord. *Journal of Consulting and Clinical Psychology,* 1969, *33,* 657-682.

STUART, R.B. *Helping couples change.* New York: The Guilford Press, 1980.

TURKEWITZ, H., & O'LEARY, K.D. A comparative outcome study of behavioral marital therapy and communication therapy. *Journal of Marital and Family Therapy,* 1981, *7,* 159-170.

WEISS, R.L. The conceptualization of marriage from a behavioral perspective. In T.J. Paolino and B.S. McGrady (Eds.), *Marriage and marital therapy: Psychoanalytic, behavioral, and systems perspectives.* New York: Brunner/Mazel, 1978.

WEISS, R.L. Strategic behavioral marital therapy. In J.P. Vincent (Ed.), *Advances in family intervention, assessment and theory.* Volume I. Greenwich, CT: JAI Press, 1980.

WEISS, R.L., BIRCHLER, G.R., & VINCENT, J.P. Contractual models for negotiation training in marital dyads. *Journal of Marriage and the Family,* 1974, *36,* 321-331.

WEISS, R.L., HOPS, H., & PATTERSON, G.R. A framework for conceptualizing marital conflict, a technology for altering it, some data for evaluating it. In L.A. Hamerlynck, L.C. Handy, & E.J. Mash (Eds.), *Behavior change: Methodology, concepts & practice.* Champaign, IL: Research Press, 1973.

WILSON, G.T., & O'LEARY, K.D. *Principles of behavior therapy.* Englewood Cliffs, NJ: Prentice-Hall, 1980.

5
Couples Treatment of Agoraphobia: Initial Outcome

DAVID H. BARLOW, GERALD T. O'BRIEN, CYNTHIA G. LAST, and ARTHUR E. HOLDEN

Agoraphobia is a relatively rare condition when compared to the more prevalent anxiety disorders, particularly generalized anxiety disorder, but it is an important problem to study because agoraphobia is the one anxiety disorder that subsumes all of the important clinical features associated with the remaining anxiety disorders and with anxiety in general. For example, almost all agoraphobics are generally anxious. That is, they are nervous, apprehensive, vigilant, and complain of a variety of somatic symptoms often associated with anxiety. For this reason, if they did not avoid a variety of situations they could easily be classified in the category of generalized anxiety disorder. For this reason, also, the majority of agoraphobics first visit their primary care physician's office, where they are administered thorough physicals and, unless the physician is well informed about anxiety disorders, minor tranquilizers. In addition to being generally anxious, agoraphobics almost always have discrete and acute episodes of anxiety that we have come to refer to as panic. If the somatic symptoms associated with generalized anxiety dis-

This research was supported by National Institute of Mental Health Grant MH34176.

order have not brought them to their physician's office, then almost certainly the panic will, for it is most often attributed by clients to heart attacks or other cardiovascular disturbances that will surely result in death. Many agoraphobics have seen the inside of emergency rooms.

Since agoraphobics are often traumatized by the first panic experience, it is very common to see them reliving this nightmare symbolically in their dreams. In addition, they often anticipate and dread a recurrence of the initial panic in a variety of situations that are similar to or on a generalization gradient with the situation in which the first panic occurred. These phenomena resemble post-traumatic stress disorder. Any clinician who has dealt with agoraphobics has also observed occasional intrusive, unwanted thoughts which could be categorized as obsessional. Often these thoughts are associated with the catastrophic consequences of panic, but equally often they may be quite independent of the central features of agoraphobia. For example in our clinic we find that a large majority of our agoraphobic women with children have mild to moderate obsessive thoughts of harming or killing their children, particularly if left alone with them for a long period of time. This is often one of the last clinical features to emerge during the treatment of female agoraphobics, since it is virtually impossible for them to admit to anyone that they are entertaining these horrific and frightening thoughts—a state of affairs that, of course, is probably responsible for their becoming obsessive thoughts in the first place (Rachman & Hodgson, 1980).

Finally, almost all agoraphobics have a variety of social or evaluative and specific fears embedded within the broad range of avoidance patterns and general fear of fear that characterize agoraphobia. Thus, the successful treatment of agoraphobia and the process by which this occurs not only is interesting and important from a clinical point of view, but also may inform our research and treatment of the whole gamut of anxiety disorders, an area in which everyone has opinions but surprisingly little is known (Barlow & Wolfe, 1981).

During the 1960s, the clinical entity of agoraphobia became well delineated as a syndrome in its own right (Marks, 1969; Mavissakalian & Barlow, 1981; Snaith, 1968) and by the beginning of the next decade an exciting sequence of research had isolated prolonged in vivo exposure as the treatment for choice for agoraphobia (Mavissakalian & Barlow, 1980; O'Brien & Barlow, in press). In vivo exposure, it turned out, was better than any alternative treatment and far better than no treatment at all in alleviating the distress of agoraphobia (Marks, 1978; Mavissakalian & Barlow, 1980).

Now, almost anyone can treat agoraphobia and almost everyone is doing it. Much like the growth of sex therapy after Masters and Johnson, phobia clinics are springing up in every section of North America—and, we suspect, the rest of the world as well. People professing expertise in the treatment of agoraphobia, using supervised in vivo exposure and some cognitive restructuring, are multiplying even faster than sex therapists it would seem; treating agoraphobia even has the added advantage of not requiring a two-week stay in St. Louis to learn the essentials of the program. On the contrary, one major qualification seems to be having once suffered from and conquered a phobia. Another would be buying Claire Weekes' book, *Peace From Nervous Suffering* (1972), that through 1977 had been through 13 printings and sold over 350,000 copies. The number of agoraphobics, as well as therapists, buying this book has stimulated a trade in the mail-order treatment of agoraphobia that is becoming increasingly competitive. It would seem at the very least that this method of delivering treatment has reached hundreds of thousands of people. In our own city, Albany, New York, at present there are two "self-help" groups for agoraphobics that are dealing with from 40 to 50 agoraphobics each at any one time. These programs are led for the most part by ex-agoraphobics, with occasional consultation from professionals, and although they bill themselves as *phobia* self-help clinics, in fact the ratio of agoraphobics to specific phobics is on the order of five-to-one. This kind of response evident around the country makes one wonder if the estimated prevalence rate of agoraphobia of 6:1000 population mentioned by Agras, Sylvester, and Oliveau (1969) wasn't far too conservative.

Furthermore, who is to say these programs aren't effective? Although the various clinics and self-help groups around the country and around the world have not been evaluated in any formal way, informally their clinical results seem satisfactory. In addition, Marks (Marks, 1981; Marks, Bird, & Lindley, 1978) has shown that nurses are at least as good as psychologists and psychiatrists in delivering these kinds of treatments. Benjamin and Kincey (1981) also demonstrated marked improvement in agoraphobic patients treated by staff with minimal training.

OUTCOME OF TREATMENT

Thus, we have a rather standard treatment for agoraphobia being delivered increasingly in specialty clinics, sometimes by nonprofessionals, that seems to be developing an existence that is largely autonomous from current and probably future research developments. But how effective is it? As we have pointed out before (Barlow, 1980; Mavissakalian & Barlow, 1981), the clinical outcome, while better than alternative treatments, is still not particularly good, based on current estimates, since there are many examples of failures, relapses, and limited clinical improvement. Estimates of long-term outcome are difficult to make since there are many issues involved in determining outcome, such as definitions of "improvement"; length and type of follow-up, which is complicated, of course, by experimental designs that preclude follow-up; dropouts; and relapses. Nevertheless, as data accumulate, it is possible to examine this issue more closely.

Considering the problem of dropouts first, in a review of some early studies (Mavissakalian & Barlow, 1981), we estimated the median dropout rate at approximately 22%. A more updated review of a larger number of studies, or reports of series of cases, indicates the dropout rate averages around 10%, with the highest rate by far those in which drugs are administered, where dropout rates in the range of 40% are not uncommon (e.g., Jansson & Ost, 1982; Zitrin, Klein, & Woerner, 1978). Dropouts, of course, are a problem for any therapeutic modality, and the wide range of dropouts among behavioral approaches to therapy indicates that perhaps we should examine more closely those programs with low dropout rates. Within the drug-free behavioral treatments, for example, preliminary indications are that a more graduated exposure strategy produces much lower dropout rates than the prolonged, therapist-assisted in vivo exposure treatments characteristic of many of the outcome studies to date (Barlow & Wolfe, 1981; Jansson & Ost, in press; O'Brien & Barlow, in press). This seems to be one disadvantage of prolonged exposure in vivo.

A more important issue for our purposes is the outcome from treatment of those who do not drop out. The best estimates from a number of follow-up studies are that 60% to 75% of those agoraphobics completing treatment will show some noticeable clinical benefit as a result of treatment and that these effects will be maintained, on the average, without either further improvement or deterioration for periods of four or more years (e.g., Emmelkamp & Kuipers, 1979; Munby & Johnston, 1980; McPherson, Brougham, & McLaren, 1980). This seems a very good outcome, particularly with a disorder as difficult as agoraphobia. Nevertheless, the negative side of this is that at least 25% of all agoraphobics fail to benefit from these treatments and of the remaining 75% a substantial percentage may not reach truly clinically useful levels of functioning. For example, Marks (1971) reported that only three of 65 clients (4.6%) were completely symptom-free at follow-up, as determined by assessors' clinical ratings, in the study of an early group of mixed phobics. McPherson et al. (1980) reported that among clients who showed some improvement following behavioral treatment, only 18% who were reached at follow-up rated themselves as being completely free of agoraphobic symptoms. Finally, Munby and Johnston (1980) observed relapses occurring in as many as 50% of patients who had benefited clinically, although in most cases these patients were evidently able to return to a level of clinical improvement previously reached in treatment. This kind of outcome is very consistent with our own experiences.

Thus, it would seem premature at least to say that we have a truly effective treatment for agoraphobia; it would be even more dangerous to stop systematic investigation and analysis of treatments on the assumption that we have such a treatment. This situation, of course, has occurred in the field of sex therapy, although every study yet conducted has failed to show the superiority of a Masters and Johnson type, direct behavioral approach over some alternative in the treatment of sexual dysfunction (e.g., Marks, 1981).

ACTIVE INGREDIENTS IN TREATMENT

In the 1970s, therapist-assisted, prolonged exposure in vivo was settled upon as the treatment of choice for agoraphobia. A more recent development is that, in the long run, therapist-assisted, prolonged exposure in vivo may be less effective than alternative treatments and might even be detrimental if looked at in a broader context. We have already discussed the possibility of greatly increased dropouts from this rather drastic treatment, but other equally important issues include the desirability of continuing improvement after the end of treatment and the effects on the patient's interpersonal relationships. As noted above, when long-term follow-up has been assessed, improvement does not continue beyond the point achieved during the in vivo exposure treatment period itself. Since improvement in the situation where the patient is dysfunctional, that is the home environment, is the criterion by which all therapy should be judged, and since improvement is often of marginal clinical significance after supervised exposure, this is seen as a serious shortcoming of these treatments. An intriguing exception occurred in an early report of group therapy of agoraphobics who seemed to form an extremely cohesive group (Hand, Lamontagne, & Marks, 1974). What seems to have happened is that these new friends stayed in contact with one another and reinforced (motivated) continued practice and progress after the formal sessions ended. But this does not always happen and the results from Hand et al. (1974) were not replicated in subsequent attempts (e.g., Teasdale, Walsh, Lancashire, & Mathews, 1976). Nevertheless, these data indicate that the problem of no further progress might be overcome by the recruitment of co-therapists in the home environment, as was seemingly evident in the cohesive group. These co-therapists, who might be friends, relatives, etc., could then continue to motivate the client to engage in exposure after formal treatment has terminated.

What makes this notion particularly intriguing is the finding, observed with increasing frequency, that while in vivo exposure may be superior to alternative treatments at outcome, almost any other good treatment, including systematic desensitization in imagination, will catch up to in vivo exposure in terms of effectiveness at a follow-up of six months or more (Barlow & Mavissakalian, 1981; Emmelkamp, 1977; Mathews, 1978; Mathews, Johnston, Lancashire, Munby, Shaw, & Gelder, 1976). Several investigators have concluded that the operative factor here is continued practice in the home environment either between sessions or after the termination of treatment. Thus, it seems the most important part of treatment may be arranging for the client to practice between sessions and gradually expose himself/herself to feared situations, something that is easier said than done. If this is true, then even supportive psychotherapy may produce results that, after a sufficient period of time, such as six months, equal those of supervised exposure, as was reported by Klein (e.g., Klein & Rabkin, 1981; Zitrin, 1981). Klein (Klein & Rabkin, 1981) has speculated that the induction of an atmosphere encouraging practice is why supportive psychotherapy did so well when compared to other more direct treatments in their controlled outcome study (Zitrin, Klein, & Woerner, 1978; see also, Sheehan, Ballenger, & Jacobsen, 1980).

If practice between sessions is the major active ingredient in any direct treatment of agoraphobia and everything else we do is effective only to the extent that it facilitates this practice, then it seems logical to assume that having a motivating agent close by to assist and reinforce practice will produce a superior outcome with continuing improvement after formal treatment. And, indeed, there are now some additional data supporting the usefulness of this notion. For example, Munby and Johnston (1980), in following up three controlled studies conducted in the middle '70s, noted that the home-based treatment (Mathews, Teasdale, Munby, Johnston, & Shaw, 1977) in which spouses were directly included in treatment produced continuing improvement after the end of treatment and that these results were superior at a four-to-nine-year follow-up to those from agoraphobics treated without this advantage. Sinnott, Jones, Scott-Fordham, and Woodward (1981) noted that agoraphobics treated as a group, who all lived in the same neighborhood, were superior on many outcome measures to a group composed of agoraphobics from diverse geographical regions who presumably did not meet, socialize, or generally support each other during or after therapy.

If practice between sessions is important, then it may be helpful if another agoraphobic lives nearby, but the most logical motivating agent is the spouse, where one is available, who is of course most intimately involved with the problem and often in the best position to be a motivating agent. Other advantages of this arrangement have been noted by several investigators. Among them are avoiding the dependence that the agoraphobic may form on the therapist which would preclude further improvement once the therapist left, as well as the cost efficiency of this approach (Jannoun, Munby, Catalan, & Gelder, 1980).

INTERPERSONAL CONTEXT OF TREATMENT

The growing evidence supporting practice between sessions as the critical therapeutic ingredient, no matter what one does during sessions, is paralleled by a growing research emphasis on the social context of agoraphobia and, in particular, the relation of agoraphobia to marital adjustment. Evidence from this area also suggests possible detrimental effects of prolonged in vivo exposure.

For many years, of course, interpersonal relations and particularly marital relationships have been considered important in the development and maintenance of agoraphobia (Agulnik, 1970; Andrews, 1966; Fry, 1962; Goldstein, 1970; Goldstein & Chambless, 1978; Lazarus, 1966; Webster, 1953; Wolpe, 1970). Goldstein and Chambless' (1978) well-known conceptualization that "complex agoraphobia" (agoraphobia that is not secondary to a drug experience or physical disorder) virtually always develops in a climate of marked interpersonal conflict has received wide attention. Individuals with low levels of self-sufficiency experience conflict concerning a desire to escape from an unsatisfactory marriage on the one hand, and fears of independence on the other. This produces anxiety and panic. Although this reanalysis has not yet been empirically validated, it does seem to be consistent with the clinical picture of many female agoraphobics.

Some clinicians and researchers have also suggested that interpersonal factors, particularly the quality and pattern of the client's marriage, may have an important influence on the client's response to treatment and that, conversely, treatment-produced change in phobic symptomatology may significantly affect the client's marriage and other interpersonal relationships. For example, many clinicians report that husbands and/or marriages deteriorate with increased independence of the agoraphobic wife, resulting in problems such as suicidal attempts by husbands and extreme pressure on wives to return to their dependent role (Hafner, 1977; Hudson, 1974). In an interesting paper by Hafner (1979), seven cases of agoraphobic women married to abnormally jealous men are described. Such men equate improvement of their wife with sexual infidelity (since they are now able to go out alone, they must be having affairs with other men). In these cases, also, improvement on the part of the wives was associated with increased morbidity in husbands. Bland and Hallam (1981), however, reported that treating agoraphobia has little effect on marital adjustment per se, but Milton and Hafner (1979), looking at the effects of treatment on marital relationships, found that couples who were initially satisfied reported improvement in their relationships, whereas couples who were initially maritally dissatisfied did not improve in these areas. Thus, the picture is mixed when one examines the effects of treatment on marriages, although there are many concrete examples of harmful effects.

In examining the other side of this coin, Hafner (1977, 1979; Milton & Hafner, 1979) has presented evidence of the deleterious effect of marital problems on the response to behavioral treatments of agoraphobia. For example, Milton and Hafner (1979) reported that agoraphobics with unsatisfactory marriages, defined as those couples in the lower half of a median split on a measure of overall marital adjustment, were less likely than patients with satisfactory marriages to improve following intensive, prolonged, in vivo exposure treatment. Patients with unsatisfactory marriages were also more likely to relapse during the six-month follow-up period. Similar results were reported by Bland and Hallam (1981), although Emmelkamp (1980) reported that levels of marital satisfaction did not seem to predict outcome. The implication here, of course, as noted by Bland and Hallam (1981) is that poor marriages may be associated with less favorable outcome, since spouses may be less likely to provide spontaneous support and encouragement to their partners during treatment and follow-up and that clients may be less likely to accept such support even if offered.

What is common about the Bland and Hallam and Hafner studies, as well as other clinical studies where marked deterioration in marriages and spouses' mental health have been noted after changes in agoraphobia (Hafner, 1977; Hudson, 1974), is that treatment was therapist-supervised, prolonged exposure in vivo, usually taking no more than two weeks' time. Spouses were not involved in any way. This intensive intervention, particularly when completed in as little as two weeks, would seem inevitably to impact on any social system, particularly a marriage, and it is only common sense that this influence would be negative, since major changes in the spouse's role, to which he has presumably become adapted, are occurring beyond his control. One possibility is that including spouses actively in treatment and spreading out treatment over a longer period of time to allow practice to occur between sessions not only may result in more substantial improvement in a greater number of clients, with further continuation of this improvement beyond therapy, but might also avoid resulting marital dissatisfaction so often observed previously. The feasibility of including spouses, particularly husbands, in the treatment of agoraphobia has been demonstrated previously (e.g., Jannoun, et al. 1980; Jones, Sinnott, & Scott-Fordham, 1980; Mathews et al., 1977). Several years ago we began a project experimentally evaluating the usefulness of including the husband directly in the treatment of agoraphobic women without the use of therapist-supervised, prolonged, in vivo exposure.

EXPERIMENTAL PLAN

As originally conceived, the purpose of this trial was to test the contribution that cooperative husbands make to the treatment of their agoraphobic wives by actually attending all treatment sessions, learning about agoraphobia, listening to treatment rationales, participating in group discussions of agoraphobia with other similar couples, and directly assisting their wives in practice between sessions. To analyze the contribution of this participation, a second group of agoraphobic women were treated without their spouses present, although these husbands had also indicated during a pretreatment screening that they would be willing to accompany their wives to treatment. This was designed to control for the actual presence of the husbands, since presumably husbands in these two groups were equally cooperative.

In our original plans, yet a third group of agoraphobic women would be treated whose husbands would indicate at a prescreening interview that they were not interested in accompanying their wives to treatment.

Presumably these husbands would have been noncooperative. In fact, unlike some other large agoraphobia clinics, we could not find enough noncooperative husbands, by this definition, to constitute this group. Of the 31 married agoraphobic women who met our rather rigorous screening procedures, only three husbands indicated an unwillingness to come. In at least one case, this noncooperativeness was due to conflicting work hours and, in fact, it was later learned that the husband was quite supportive of his wife and would have been willing to come but for this conflict.

Client Selection and Screening

Both the Phobia and Anxiety Disorders Clinic at the State University of New York at Albany and this clinical trial began in the fall of 1979. After some initial publicity, a large number of referrals from professionals, as well as self-referred individuals, began the screening process. The first contact included a lengthy, structured screening interview conducted by one of the investigators for purposes of classification. All prospective clients met DSM-III criteria for agoraphobia. In addition, the interviewer and a second clinician reviewing the data independently rated clients on a scale of agoraphobic symptomatology, including both anxiety and avoidance, that ranged from zero to eight. Each client had to be rated 4.0 or higher to qualify. This is the standard zero to eight clinical rating scale introduced by Watson and Marks (1971) and used in most phobia clinics around the world (e.g., Agras & Jacob, 1981) as one method of standardizing clinical improvement. If scores of the two raters were one point apart, for example a 6 and a 7, a rating of 6.5 was given. If ratings were two points apart—and this has been the maximum divergence during the past two years—the individual was interviewed by another staff member and the mean of the subsequent ratings, which may or may not have changed from the original ratings, was used as the pretreatment rating.

A similar procedure produced posttreatment ratings. A number of clients otherwise meeting DSM-III criteria for agoraphobia scored less than four on this scale and therefore were excluded from the trial. Since most agoraphobics are women, only married female agoraphobics were included to insure a greater homogeneity within groups. Other exclusion criteria included positive diagnosis of primary affective illness, schizophrenia, or organic brain syndrome, or a classification within one of the other anxiety disorders, such as social phobia, generalized anxiety disorder, or obsessive-compulsive disorder. Finally, initiation of antidepressant medications within three months of the start of treatment excluded clients, due to the well-known impact of such medications on panic (Zitrin, 1981).

MEASURES

Behavioral Measures

Once a woman qualified for the trial, a number of behavioral, physiological and subjective measures were administered to her. Many of these have been described before (Barlow, Mavissakalian, & Hay, 1981; Barlow, Mavissakalian, & Schofield, 1980). Briefly, two behavioral measures were employed. The first measure was a standardized walk first used by Agras, Leitenberg, and Barlow (1968). This consists of a standard, one-mile course divided into 20 approximately equal segments or "stations." Clients are alone on the course, which leads from the front door of the Clinic to an increasingly crowded area of downtown Albany. Each client walks this course before treatment and also after six sessions (midtreatment), and at posttreatment. The behavioral measure, of course, is the number of stations completed. In addition, clients report current level of anxiety on a zero to eight scale at each station by reporting their rating into a lapel microphone that attaches to a concealed miniature cassette recorder, usually placed in the purse or the pocket of a coat. Finally, a physiological measure, specifically heart rate, is monitored through a portable pulsemeter consisting of an electrode belt attached directly to the upper abdominal area. This pulsemeter has been wired so that the voltage signal is diverted from a speaker that would normally emit an audible tone with each heartbeat directly to a microcassette recorder. These physiological data will be the subject of another paper.

A second behavioral measure is modeled after Mathews et al. (1977) and involves constructing a hierarchy of 10 idiosyncratic situations in the client's home environment, such as going to the local grocery store or drugstore or walking down to the end of the block. Five of these items are then directly assessed during a home visit conducted by a doctoral student in clinical psychology. Specifically, the client is asked to do each of these five hierarchy items in ascending order of difficulty. The client may either refuse to do so, attempt an item but not complete it, or complete the item. During any completions, subjective estimates of anxiety on the same zero to eight scale are also recorded.

Self-report Measures

The full 10-item hierarchy constructed before treatment begins also was rated by the client before each session on the same zero to eight scale reflecting a combination of anxiety and avoidance. If the husband attended, he also rated the hierarchy, based on his perceptions of his wife's behavior. In fact, over the years this has proved to be a very useful measure, probably due to its individualized nature. Before treatment began, clients were also instructed in a detailed fashion on the use of a weekly record form on which they self-monitored behavior such as total amount of time spent out of the house each day, destination of any trips, distance from home, method and time of travel, amount of time spent alone, as well as frequency of practice sessions between treatments.

Finally, other periodic self-report measures in the form of questionnaires administered before treatment, as well as at midtreatment and posttreatment, include the Fear Questionnaire developed by Marks and Mathews (1979), the Beck Depression Inventory, and the Symptom Rating Scale introduced by Marks (e.g., Hafner & Marks, 1976) and Mathews et al. (1976), where clients rate on zero to eight scales the severity of such symptoms as panic attacks, depersonalization, etc., as well as the relative interference of their agoraphobia with work, social, and leisure time functioning. When clients completed the interview, the battery of questionnaires, the standardized walk, and the home visit, they were then assigned to a treatment group.

TREATMENT PROGRAM

Treatment consisted of 12 weekly, 60-to-90-minute group discussion sessions. As noted above, two groups eventually completed treatment. In one group, the husband attended all sessions while in the other the husband indicated he was willing to attend but was not invited to do so. These will be termed spouse and non-spouse groups. The first three sessions were devoted to explaining the nature of agoraphobia, a rationale for the treatment to be used, instructions for coping with anxiety and panic and, if the husbands attended, ways in which they could assist their wives in subsequent practice sessions. Thus, the treatment could be best characterized as a self-initiated, graduated, exposure treatment combined with instruction in panic management procedures, as well as cognitive restructuring combining the use of coping self-statement (Meichenbaum, 1977), paradoxical intention (Ascher, 1980), and, in general, methods that obviated cognitive avoidance of fear. Following the third treatment session, clients were given individualized homework assignments to practice. Typically, these assignments were derived from the clients' individualized fear and avoidance hierarchies that they rated each session. The least difficult item was chosen initially, followed by more difficult times, and clients were instructed to practice this item at least three times between sessions. Naturally they could attempt other situations not on their hierarchies as well. For clients in the spouse group, the husband was instructed to accompany his wife at least once, but no more than twice, during the week on the assigned practice. An upper limit was put on this practice since, of course, most of these husbands were "safe" people, which would presumably negate the point of practicing in the first place. Nevertheless, when he did accompany, he was instructed to coach his wife in the application of therapeutic coping procedures, etc., not only during practice but in any other situations in which his wife might experience anxiety or panic. In addition, each couple was encouraged to communicate more often with one another concerning phobic situations.

INITIAL OUTCOME OF COUPLES TREATMENT: AGORAPHOBIA MEASURES

During the past several years there have been three spouse and three non-spouse groups consisting of from three to six agoraphobics, with or without their husbands, for a total of 14 agoraphobics seen in each condition. Two of these women met a more liberalized criteria in that they were not actually married, but had been seriously involved and/or living with their partner for a year or more and were planning marriage. One of these women was assigned to the spouse group and another to the non-spouse group. This trial has only recently been completed, and data are now available for analyses of results at posttest, although follow-ups are not yet complete. In view of the non-therapist-supervised nature of the treatment and the graduated rather than prolonged pattern of in vivo exposure, it is interesting to compare overall outcome from this group with other published outcomes in the behavioral treatment of agoraphobia, almost all of which relied on therapist-assisted, prolonged exposure. On the 9-point rating scale, the mean improvement for the 28 patients, based on an average of the therapist and independent assessor's clinical ratings, was 2.36. This represents the usual and customary range of clinical improvement from behavioral treatment of agoraphobia and thus it is significant that this was accomplished without supervised practice. When one looks at individual data, the improvement is also substantial. Of the 28 clients, 23 (or 82%) showed some improvement; that is, improved one point or more on the global clinical rating scale. This leaves five clients who could be considered failures; that is, improved 0.5 points on the rating scale or less. One client actually deteriorated during treatment. If one takes the customary criterion of substantial clinical improvement, specifically improvement of two points or more on the scale, then 19 (or 68%) of the 28 clients met this criterion. This also compares favorably with the 60 to 75% success rates cited in alternative studies using therapist-assisted exposure.

Therapist-assisted exposure, of course, is conducted differently in almost every clinic or research center around the world. In most clinics and research centers it means having a therapist, either professional or nonprofessional, actually accompany the agoraphobic for long periods of time to various feared situations. But for someone like Emmelkamp (1980), therapist-assisted exposure may mean sending a therapist to the home who then outlines and supervises formal practice sessions.

At least two studies, however, did not use therapist-assisted exposure. Using only instructions without therapist supervision, as we did, McDonald, Sartory, Grey, Cobb, Stern, and Marks (1979) told a group of agoraphobics to practice and compared this to the more usual supervised exposure. Instructions alone resulted in substantially less improvement. In the one series comparable to ours (Mathews et al., 1977), therapists visited the home a total of eight times, but essentially remained out of the practice sessions, confining their participation to discussion of a detailed manual describing how practice should be conducted with the assistance of the spouse. This procedure also did not produce as much improvement on the clinical rating scale immediately after treatment, when compared to therapist-supervised flooding, but improvement was approximately equal for both treatments at a six-month follow-up (1.6 points improvement on a 5-point scale). As noted above, this is one of the few studies that demonstrated continued improvement past the point of treatment, presumably due to continued practice, although this was not tested.

The one difference between our procedures and the McDonald et al. (1979) study, and even the Mathews et al. (1977) study, is that we met with our clients for a total of 12 sessions, eight of which were devoted to discussing the experience of prior practice and strategies for further practice. McDonald et al. (1979) met with their clients only four times, while Mathews et al. (1977) met eight times with their clients. Thus, it seems that improvement comparable to therapist-supervised massed exposure can be produced even at posttreatment using only instructions by the therapist to practice. Of course, spouses were directly involved in assisting 14 of the 28 clients.

Of more interest here, however, are differences between the spouse and non-spouse groups. Continuing with results of the clinicians' ratings, Table 1 demonstrates marked improvement, as well as an advantage to the spouse group, at posttest. The spouse group improved from an average pretest rating of 5.82 to 3.0, while the non-spouse group improved from 5.61 to 3.71. These changes are highly significant ($p<.001$) based on a repeated measures ANOVA, but the group × sessions (between groups) interaction does not reach statistical significance ($p<.16$). Nevertheless, there are some marked differences between groups if one examines the individual data. For example, if one looks at the distribution of clients improving less than two points on the clinical rating scale, six of the nine are to be found in the non-spouse group, while only three are included in the spouse group. However, one client in the spouse group actually deteriorated by one full point during treatment, which, of course, increases the intersubject variability within this group. On the other hand, examining those clients who improved three points or more, which would translate into very substantial clinical benefit, nine of the 12 are to be found in the spouse group and only three in the non-

TABLE 1

Improvement Scores on Clinician's Ratings for
Spouse and Non-Spouse Groups

Spouse	Non-Spouse
4.5	0.0
2.0	3.5
3.5	2.5
3.5	3.0
0.5	2.5
3.0	0.0
3.5	2.0
1.5	0.5
− 1.0	2.0
3.0	1.0
4.0	2.5
6.0	1.0
3.5	1.5
2.0	4.5

spouse group. Thus, there appears to be an advantage for the spouse
group if one examines these individual data.

Repeated measures analysis of variance demonstrates consistent, positive, therapeutic changes across the variety of measures of agoraphobia
from pre to posttest for both groups. These analyses also indicate a trend
in favor of the spouse group that reaches statistical significance on a
number of measures at posttest. On the behavioral walk, both groups
showed significant improvement in number of steps completed, with no
differences between groups, but ratings of anxiety at each station on the
zero to eight scale improved significantly more for the spouse group
when compared to the non-spouse group (p<.05). If one looks at these
Subjective Units of Disturbance (SUDs) ratings only for steps actually
completed at the initial walk, which we refer to as indexed SUDs, then
the ratings for these items at subsequent walks also demonstrate a strong
trend toward improvement for the spouse group when compared to the
non-spouse group (p<.07). Similar patterns of improvement were noted
on both number of items completed and SUDs scores during the home
behavioral approach test; this did not reach significance between groups
but reflected highly significant positive changes pre to post. This pattern
was also noted on the clients' ratings of the idiosyncratic fear and avoid-

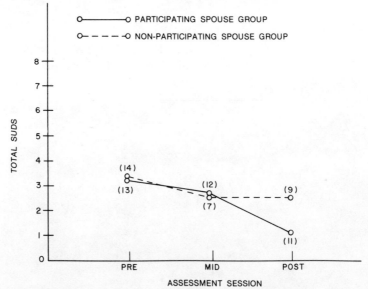

FIGURE 1. Changes in total SUDs during behavioral walk for each group at pre-, mid-, and
posttreatment assessment points. Number completing test in parenthesis.

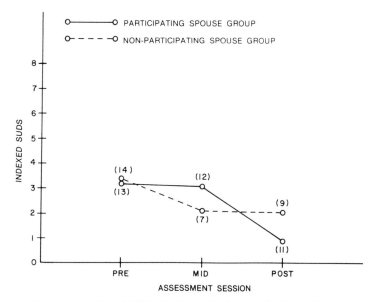

FIGURE 2. Changes in indexed SUDs during behavioral walk for each group at pre-, mid-, and posttreatment assessment points. Number completing test in parenthesis.

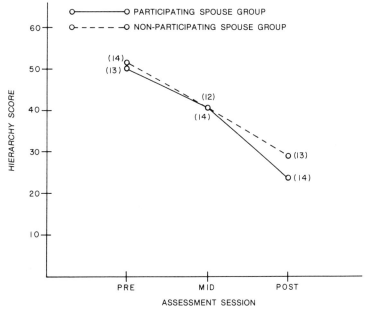

FIGURE 3. Change in fear and avoidance hierarchy scores for each group at pre-, mid-, and posttreatment assessment points. Number completing test in parenthesis.

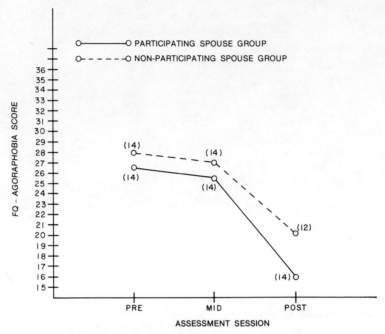

FIGURE 4. Changes in the agoraphobia subscale of the Fear Questionnaire for each group at pre-, mid-, and posttreatment assessment points. Number completing test in parenthesis.

ance hierarchies and the agoraphobia subscale, as well as the total score of the Fear Questionnaire, with the spouse group trending toward greater improvement on each measure. Some other interesting findings from the Fear Questionnaire are reflected in the increase in scores on the blood and injury subscale of this questionnaire at midtest. This seemed to reflect the recognition by many of our clients, in both groups, of a strong blood and injury component to their fears as the sessions progressed. In several subjects this emerged as a major problem needing specific attention at the end of the treatment program. A similar phenomenon was noted in the social phobia subscale, which also reflected a marked increase at mid-treatment, followed by a substantial decrease.

A common finding in the treatment of agoraphobics is a marked decrease in severity of accompanying depression; our results are no exception. Scores on the Beck Depressive Inventory, although somewhat lower for the spouse group at pretreatment, improved significantly for both spouse and non-spouse groups with no differential pattern of change.

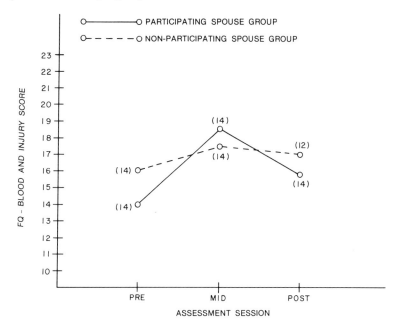

FIGURE 5. Changes in the blood and injury subscale of the Fear Questionnaire for each group at pre-, mid-, and posttreatment assessment points. Number completing test in parenthesis.

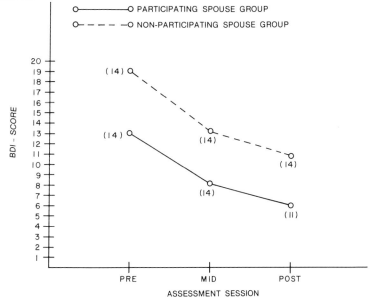

FIGURE 6. Changes in the Beck Depression Inventory scores for each group at pre-, mid-, and posttreatment assessment points. Number completing test in parenthesis.

SOCIAL AND MARITAL FUNCTIONING

Another interesting pattern of results emerged on clients' ratings of the effect of their agoraphobia on their family and social functioning. For example, spouse groups reported early and significantly greater changes in their ability to function in their work setting, which included completing necessary functions around the house (p<.01), compared to non-spouse groups. A somewhat different pattern of change, also statistically significant, was noted on ratings of the effects of agoraphobia on social leisure, which refers to socializing with friends or other groups of people, with the spouse group improving significantly at midtest compared to the non-spouse group (p<.05). However, the non-spouse group also improved significantly on this measure by the end of treatment, matching the gains of the spouse group. A similar pattern, also statistically significant, was observed for ratings of family functioning. Private leisure, which refers to participation in individually enjoyable activities, showed a similar trend. These data reflect one direct, although temporary, benefit of including the spouse in treatment.

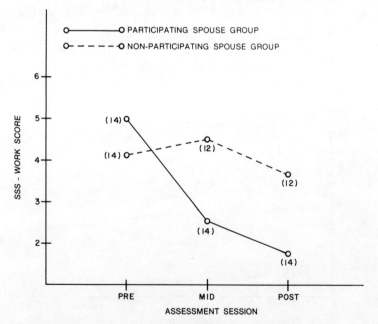

FIGURE 7. Changes in self-rated ability to work scores for each group at pre-, mid-, and posttreatment assessment points. Number completing test in parenthesis.

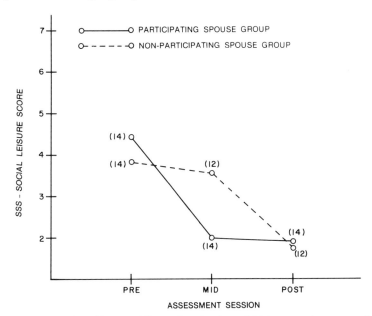

FIGURE 8. Changes in self-rated ability to function in social leisure settings scores for each group at pre-, mid-, and posttreatment assessment points. Number completing test in parenthesis.

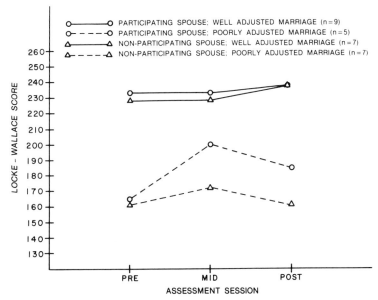

FIGURE 9. Changes in self-ratings of family functioning scores for each group at pre-, mid-, and posttreatment assessment points. Number completing test in parenthesis.

A preliminary analysis of the effect of treatment on marital adjustment reveals some interesting differences from previous findings. In this figure, the combined scores of client and spouse on the Locke Wallace Marital Adjustment Inventory are plotted at pre-, mid-, and posttest for both well adjusted and poorly adjusted marriages in each treatment group. The recommended score of 100 was used to define a well-adjusted marriage, which resulted in a slightly different number of subjects in each group (16 well adjusted and 12 poorly adjusted marriages). These scores demonstrate little change, or perhaps slight improvement, in well adjusted marriages, something that Milton and Hafner (1979) also found, but marked increases in marital satisfaction in the spouse group if the marriages were poorly adjusted to begin with, compared to the non-spouse group, a finding quite at variance with Hafner's (Milton & Hafner, 1979).

In what is perhaps the most interesting finding of these initial results, improvement as reflected by clinicians' ratings was plotted by well adjusted and poorly adjusted marriages in each group. In the non-spouse group, seven well adjusted and seven poorly adjusted marriages participated. In the spouse group, nine marriages were well adjusted and five

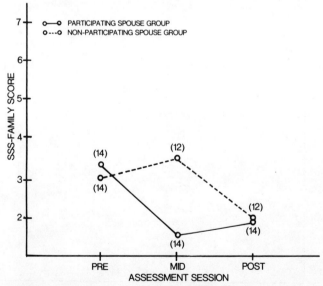

FIGURE 10. Changes in combined client and spouse Locke Wallace scores of marital adjustment for well adjusted and poorly adjusted marriages for each group at pre-, mid-, and posttreatment assessment points.

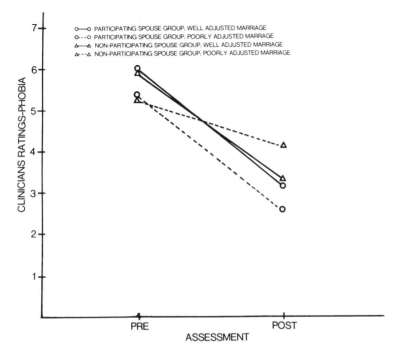

FIGURE 11. Changes in clinicians' ratings of agoraphobia for both well adjusted and poorly adjusted marriages in each group at pre- and posttreatment assessment points.

poorly adjusted. These data demonstrate identical patterns of improvement in agoraphobia within well adjusted marriages, but significantly different improvement in poorly adjusted marriages. Including the husband in treatment overcame the negative effect of these marriages observed in other studies (e.g., Milton & Hafner, 1979) by producing improvement similar to that observed in the well adjusted marriages. If husbands did not attend, however, then agoraphobic wives improved significantly less (p<.05).

SUMMARY AND CONCLUSIONS

In summary, a pattern of results is emerging supporting the effectiveness of couples treatment of agoraphobia on the agoraphobia itself. This is somewhat surprising to us at posttreatment since we had surmised, along with Mathews et al. (1977), that the major benefit of spouse involvement in therapy would not occur during the treatment itself, but rather after treatment, in that husbands would facilitate continued improvement during follow-up periods. Thus, if any differences were to emerge, they were expected at six-month follow-up or beyond. The fact that a trend seems to be emerging at posttreatment lends some support to the usefulness of including spouses, although the critical six-month and one-year follow-ups will be necessary to confirm this. Particularly important is the finding that the deleterious effect of a bad marriage on treatment outcome can be overcome with couples treatment, although follow-up will be critical here also since we would have every reason to expect relapse in the absence of permanent improvement in marital functioning. Nevertheless, it is possible that this "bad marriage" phenomenon accounts for most of the advantage of our treatment.

The remaining pattern of initial results, demonstrating a differential response among groups, is the rather strong trend for major improvements in social and marital adjustment during treatment itself. But this difference does not continue at posttest (with the exception of functioning in work related situations and marital adjustment), since non-spouse groups also report substantial positive changes in many of these areas.

Assuming that these trends in phobic improvement are maintained, and perhaps even strengthened at follow-up, it will be important to determine why. It seems probable that changes in social and marital functioning may well be due to increased communication and joint participation in an important activity, as required by the spouse group. A more important issue will be determining factors that account for the seeming superiority of the couples treatment on the agoraphobia itself, particularly if it holds up or even increases at follow-up. The most likely candidate, mentioned by Mathews et al. (1976) and hypothesized by us earlier, is the increased quantity and quality of self-initiated practice between sessions and after treatment as facilitated by a cooperative husband, or at least the absence of counterproductive husbands as suggested by substantial changes in the poorly adjusted group. A detailed analysis of weekly records will shed some light on our understanding of this explanation of differential success.

Another possibility, of course, is that including the spouse in treatment improves the marriage in such a way that daily stress and conflicts are lessened, allowing progress to be made on agoraphobia. It does indeed seem, from our preliminary data, that marriages are improved in the spouse group somewhat more than in the non-spouse group, particularly marriages that are distressed or maladjusted to begin with. Of course, Cobb, McDonald, Marks, and Stern (1980), although noting some beneficial effects on marital relationships of treating agoraphobia, reported that treating marital disturbance itself did not seem to affect agoraphobia. However, their results should be interpreted cautiously. The sample was very small, not all clients were agoraphobics, neither exposure nor marital treatment produced significant improvement on two structured marital adjustment questionnaires, and the crossover design precluded follow-up of either individual treatment. Perhaps more importantly, there is no information on whether these were good or bad marriages to begin with. Finally, as with most studies, no information is provided on the type of change in marriage patterns and relationships that may be produced by exposure treatment.

Since it seems that couples treatment provides an advantage, particularly with poorly adjusted marriages, detailed analyses of actual behavioral changes within the marital dyad are very important in order to determine what spouses of successful and unsuccessful outcomes are actually doing. Simply asking spouses if they will come to a group or not is a very insensitive measure of cooperativeness and support, since husbands in both good and bad marriages volunteered to attend treatment. For example, in both groups there were many husbands who were sarcastic, critical, unable to understand why their wives could not move about freely, and generally very nonsupportive, as well as many supportive, understanding husbands who went out of their way to assist their wives at every turn.

Our data suggest that including the husbands in treatment may facilitate the usefulness of the husband when marriages are good to begin with and precludes counter-productive criticism, bullying, or other efforts to sabotage treatment when marriages are not that good to begin with. But additional behaviors associated with successful outcomes may be much more specific than simply the presence of a well or poorly adjusted marriage. If differences are discovered in the actual behavior of spouses in couples with successful outcome, then the possibility remains that future spouses can be trained to participate in the kinds of activity and behavior found most effective in overcoming agoraphobia of the partner, behaviors that may go beyond simply attending 12 sessions of group therapy and receiving instructions in "coaching." For example, spouses in well adjusted marriages could carry out treatment themselves, with the help of "self-help" manuals, once these critical behaviors were identified, since there seems no advantage to having them come to sessions. On the other hand, poorly adjusted couples might need specific training in these therapeutic behaviors that could only occur in the context of a therapeutic group. Perhaps marital therapy would also be necessary to insure long-term success. Answers to these questions await further analyses of these data, as well as data from the more fine-grained analysis of the effects of this treatment now ongoing.

REFERENCES

AGRAS, W.S. & JACOB, R. Phobia: Nature and measurement. In M.R. Mavissakalian & D.H. Barlow (eds.), *Phobia: Psychological and pharmacological treatment*. New York: Guilford Press, 1981.

AGRAS, W.S., LEITENBERG, H. & BARLOW, D.H. Social reinforcement in the modification of agoraphobia. *Archives of General Psychiatry*, 1968, *19*, 423-427.

AGRAS, S., SYLVESTER, D., & OLIVEAU, D. The epidemiology of common fears and phobia. *Comprehensive Psychiatry*, 1969, *10*, 151-156.

AGULNIK, P.L. The spouse of the phobic patient. *British Journal of Psychiatry*, 1970, *117*, 59-67.

ANDREWS, J.D.W. Psychotherapy of phobias. *Psychological Bulletin*, 1966, *66*, 455-480.

ASCHER, L.M. Paradoxical intention. In A. Goldstein & E.B. Foa (eds.), *Handbook of behavioral interventions: A clinical guide*. New York: John Wiley, 1980.

BARLOW, D.H. Behavior therapy: The next decade. *Behavior Therapy*, 1980, *11*, 315-328.

BARLOW, D.H. & MAVISSAKALIAN, M.R. Directions in the assessment and treatment of phobia: The next decade. In M.R. Mavissakalian & D.H. Barlow (eds.), *Phobia: Psychological and pharmacological treatment*. New York: Guilford Press, 1981.

BARLOW, D.H., MAVISSAKALIAN, M., & HAY, L.R. Couples treatment of agoraphobia: Changes in marital satisfaction. *Behaviour Research and Therapy*, 1981, *19*, 345-357.

BARLOW, D.H., MAVISSAKALIAN, M.R., & SCHOFIELD, L.D. Patterns of desynchrony in agoraphobia: A preliminary report. *Behaviour Research and Therapy*, 1980, *18*, 441-448.

BARLOW, D.H. & WOLFE, B.E. Behavioral approaches to anxiety disorders: A report on the NIMH-SUNY, Albany, research conference. *Journal of Consulting and Clinical Psychology*, 1981, *49*, 448-454.

BENJAMIN, S. & KINCEY, J. Evaluation of standardized behavioural treatment for agoraphobic in-patients administered by untrained therapists. *British Journal of Psychiatry*, 1981, *138*, 423-428.

BLAND, K. & HALLAM, R.S. Relationship between response to graded exposure and marital satisfaction in agoraphobics. *Behaviour Research and Therapy*, 1981, *19*, 335-338.

COBB, J., McDONALD, R., MARKS, I., & STERN, R. Marital versus exposure therapy: Psychological treatments of co-existing marital and phobic-obsessive problems. *Behavioural Analysis and Modification*, 1980, *4*, 3-16.

EMMELKAMP, P.M.G. Phobias—theoretical and behavioural treatment considerations. In J.C. Boulougouris & A. Rabavilas (eds.), *Phobic and obsessive-compulsive disorders*. London: Pergamon Press, 1977.

EMMELKAMP, P.M.G. Agoraphobics' interpersonal problems: Their role in the effects of exposure in vivo therapy. *Archives of General Psychiatry*, 1980, *37*, 1303-1306.

EMMELKAMP, P.M.G. & KUIPERS, A.C.M. Agoraphobia: A follow-up study four years after treatment. *British Journal of Psychiatry*, 1979, *134*, 352-355.

FRY, W.F. The marital context of an anxiety syndrome. *Family Process*, 1962, *1*, 245-252.

GOLDSTEIN, A.J. Case conference: Some aspects of agoraphobia. *Journal of Behavior Therapy and Experimental Psychiatry*, 1970, *1*, 305-313.

GOLDSTEIN, A.J. & CHAMBLESS, D.L. A reanalysis of agoraphobia. *Behavior Therapy*, 1978, *9*, 47-59.

HAFNER, R.J. The husbands of agoraphobic women and their influence on treatment outcome. *British Journal of Psychiatry*, 1977, *131*, 289-294.

HAFNER, R.J. Agoraphobic women married to abnormally jealous men. *British Journal of Medical Psychology*, 1979, *52*, 99-104.

HAFNER, R.J. & MARKS, I.M. Exposure in vivo of agoraphobics: Contribution of diazepam, group exposure, and anxiety evocation. *Psychological Medicine*, 1976, *6*, 71-88.

HAND, I., LAMONTAGNE, Y., & MARKS, I.M. Group exposure (flooding) in vivo for agoraphobics. *British Journal of Psychiatry*, 1974, *124*, 588-602.

HUDSON, B. The families of agoraphobics treatment by behaviour therapy. *British Journal of Social Work*, 1974, *4*, 51-59.

JANNOUN, L., MUNBY, M., CATALAN, J., & GELDER, M. A home-based treatment programme for agoraphobia: Replication and controlled evaluation. *Behavior Therapy*, 1980, *11*, 294-305.

JANSSON, L., & OST, L. Behavioral treatments for agoraphobia: An evaluative review. *Clinical Psychology Review*, 1982, *2*, 311-337.

JONES, R.B., SINNOTT, A., & SCOTT-FORDHAM, A. Group in vivo exposure augmented by the counselling of significant others in the treatment of agoraphobia. *Behavioral Psychotherapy*, 1980, *8*, 31-35.

KLEIN, D.F. & RABKIN, J. (eds.), *Anxiety: New research and changing concepts*. New York: Raven Press, 1981.

LAZARUS, A.A. Behavior rehearsal vs. non-directive therapy vs advice in effecting behavior change. *Behaviour Research and Therapy*, 1966, *4*, 209-212.

MCDONALD, R., SARTORY, G., GREY, S.J., COBB, J., STERN, R., & MARKS, I.M. The effects of self exposure instructions on agoraphobic outpatients. *Behaviour Research and Therapy*, 1979, *17*, 1183-1185.

MCPHERSON, F.M., BROUGHAM, L., & MCLAREN, S. Maintenance of improvement in agoraphobic patients treated by behavioural methods—a four-year follow-up. *Behaviour Research and Therapy*, 1980, *18*, 150-152.

MARKS, I.M. *Fears and phobias*. London: Heinemann, 1969.

MARKS, I. Phobic disorders four years after treatment: A prospective follow-up. *British Journal of Psychiatry*, 1971, *118*, 683-688.

MARKS, I.M. Exposure treatments: Clinical applications. In W.S. Agras (ed.), *Behavior modification: Principles and clinical applications*. Second Edition. Boston: Little Brown, 1978.

MARKS, I. *Cure and care of neuroses: Theory and practice of behavioral psychotherapy*. New York: John Wiley, 1981.

MARKS, I.M., BIRD, J., & LINDLEY, P. Behavioral nurse therapists 1978: Developments and implications. *Behavioral Psychotherapy*, 1978, *6*, 25-36.

MARK, I.M. & MATHEWS, A.M. Brief standard self-rating for phobic patients. *Behaviour Research and Therapy*, 1979, *17*, 263-267.

MATHEWS, A. Fear-reduction research and clinical phobias. *Psychological Bulletin*, 1978, *85*, 390-404.

MATHEWS, A.M., JOHNSTON, D.W., LANCASHIRE, M., MUNBY, M., SHAW, P.M., & GELDER, M.G. Imaginal flooding and exposure to real phobic situations: Treatment outcome with agoraphobic patients. *British Journal of Psychiatry*, 1976, *129*, 362-371.

MATHEWS, A.M. TEASDALE, J., MUNBY, M., JOHNSTON, D., & SHAW, P.S. A home-based treatment program for agoraphobia. *Behavior Therapy*, 1977, *8*, 915-924.

MAVISSAKALIAN, M.R. & BARLOW, D.H. (eds.) *Phobia: Psychological and pharmacological treatment*. New York: Guilford Press, 1981.

MEICHENBAUM, D. *Cognitive behavior modification: An integrative approach*. New York: Plenum, 1977.

MILTON, F. & HAFNER, J. The outcome of behavior therapy for agoraphobia in relation to marital adjustment. *Archives of General Psychiatry*, 1979, *36*, 807-811.

MUNBY, J. & JOHNSTON, D.W. Agoraphobia: The long-term follow-up of behavioural treatment. *British Journal of Psychiatry*, 1980, *137*, 418-427.

O'BRIEN, G.T. & BARLOW, D.H. Agoraphobia. In S.M. Turner (ed.), *Behavioral treatment of anxiety disorders.* New York: Plenum, in press.

RACHMAN, S. & HODGSON, R. *Obsessions and compulsions.* Englewood Cliffs, NJ: Prentice-Hall, 1980.

SHEEHAN, D.V., BALLENGER, J., & JACOBSEN, G. Treatment for agoraphobia with group exposure in vivo and imipramine. *Archives of General Psychiatry,* 1980, *37,* 51-62.

SINNOTT, A., JONES, R.B., SCOTT-FORDHAM, A., & WOODWARD, R. Augmentation of in vivo exposure treatment for agoraphobia by the formation of neighborhood self-help groups. *Behaviour Research and Therapy,* 1981, *19,* 339-347.

SNAITH, R.P. A clinical investigation of phobias. *British Journal of Psychiatry,* 1968, *114,* 673-697.

TEASDALE, J., WALSH, P., LANCASHIRE, M., & MATHEWS, A. Group exposure for agoraphobics: A replication study. *British Journal of Psychiatry,* 1976, *130,* 186-193.

WATSON, J.P. & MARKS, I.M. Relevant and irrelevant fear in flooding: A crossover study of phobic patients. *Behaviour Therapy,* 1971, *2,* 275-395.

WEBSTER, A. The development of phobias in married women. *Psychological Monographs,* 1953, *67,* 1-18.

WEEKES, C. *Peace from nervous suffering.* New York: Hawthorne Books, 1972.

WOLPE, J. Identifying the antecedents of an agoraphobic reaction: A transcript. *Journal of Behavior Therapy and Experimental Psychiatry,* 1970, *1,* 299-304.

ZITRIN, C.M. Combined pharmacologic and psychotherapeutic treatment of phobia. In M.R. Mavissakalian & D.H. Barlow (eds.), *Phobia: Psychological and pharmacological treatment.* New York: Guilford Press, 1981.

ZITRIN, C.M., KLEIN, D.F., & WOERNER, M.G. Behavior therapy, supportive psychotherapy, imipramine, and phobias. *Archives of General Psychiatry,* 1978, *35,* 307-321.

6

The Modification of
Obsessions and Compulsions

STANLEY J. RACHMAN

During the 1960s, the growing confidence of behavior therapists who were called upon to help people with excessive fear or anxiety was almost palpable. At that time, however, it was not possible to provide reliable and effective help for those unfortunate people who were spending a great deal of their energy and time carrying out senseless and repetitive compulsions or who were repeatedly distressed by intrusive unwanted thoughts of a repugnant quality. More often than not, the arrival of one of these disabled people reinforced the behavior therapist's feelings of incompetence and helplessness. There was no shortage of attempts to explain puzzling obsessional-compulsive behavior (e.g., Eysenck & Rachman, 1965; Metzner, 1963; Mowrer, 1960), but the gap between the intellectual challenge and the provision of effective help was embarrassingly large.

Against this historical note, it now is possible to state that important progress has been made and we are in a position to give effective advice and assistance to a majority of those people who are entangled and tormented by compulsions and obsessions. When staleness threatens to permeate behavior therapy, it is as well to be reminded of such milestones.

In most cases a significant reduction in compulsive activities can be achieved within a reasonably short time by the institution of a systematic program of exposure and response prevention. The reduction in this behavior usually is accompanied or followed by a small but nevertheless significant reduction in associated discomfort and distress. When it comes to the tormenting, unwanted intrusive thoughts that qualify for the term "obsessions," especially if these are not accompanied by compulsive behavior that we can get a grip on, we are on less firm ground. As far as the rare variant of obsessional-compulsive disorders, primary obsessional slowness, is concerned, we have yet to develop methods for ensuring long-term improvement beyond the more readily achieved short-lived improvements.

DEFINITIONS

In this chapter I will discuss the nature of obsessions and of compulsions, their common and distinguishing features, the conditions that are thought to maintain them, and current techniques for modifying these disorders.

Obsessions are defined as repetitive, intrusive and unwanted thoughts, images or impulses; their recurrence is resisted and they are difficult to remove. The ideas and impulses are generally of an abhorrent nature, frequently involving the possibility of harm coming to oneself or other people. Compulsions are repetitive, stereotyped patterns of behavior and, like obsessions, usually are resisted by the person executing them. People complaining of these problems generally recognize that they have an irrational basis; indeed, for many of them the strength and persistence of the compulsive acts or intrusive thoughts are distressing precisely because they are felt to be irrational. Although obsessions and compulsions occur independently, most often the two types of problem arise in association.

Obsessional-compulsive disorders are not unduly common, but can be extremely distressing and disabling. They account for about 0.5% of psychiatric outpatient samples but nearly 2% of the inpatient population. Even though this self-defeating persistent behavior is recognized by the actor to be irrational, it nevertheless remains beyond the affected person's voluntary control for much of the time. It is an easily recognized disorder and intimately related to depression. In many ways obsessions and compulsions are ideal examples of abnormal behavior: They are irrational and/or exaggerated, are recognized to be so, but nevertheless remain relatively uncontrolled. A full discussion of the definitions and phenomenology of the disorders is given in Rachman and Hodgson (1980).

For a considerable time, obsessions and compulsions were regarded as neurotic illnesses. In keeping with the move away from the medical approach to problems of this kind, many psychologists, myself among them, now are of the opinion that obsessions and compulsions are not profitably regarded as illnesses. These difficulties are better construed as emotional or behavioral problems. Although this change of view is enlightening, the satisfactory development of the consequences of adopting this change of perspective is hampered by our failure to produce a new and more appropriate vocabulary to match the new perspective. For want of better terms and because most of the people who participated in the research which I shall be describing were in fact registered patients at one or another clinic or hospital, I shall continue to use the older terminology in this chapter.

TREATMENT EFFORTS

As noted, the early successes in the treatment of phobias and anxiety were not accompanied by similar progress in dealing with obsessional disorders. The position prevailing at the end of the 1960s was summarized in a review by Meyer, Levy, and Schnurer. Writing in 1974, they concluded that the success rates reported by behavior therapists dealing with obsessional-compulsive problems were significantly lower than those achieved in handling other disorders. From a variety of sources they collected clinical reports on 61 patients who had received behavioral treatment. The results were not encouraging. A surprisingly large number of treatment variations had been attempted—too great a diversity of treatment options for the same problem is seldom a good sign.

Prompted by the encouraging developments in the research on therapeutic applications of modeling and flooding, and partly encouraged by the success reported by Meyer (1966) in treating two severely disabled patients, a number of psychologists began experimenting with in vivo procedures. Meyer himself, in collaboration with Levy and Schnurer, has continued to chalk up clinical successes, which were reported in his 1973 and 1974 series (Meyer et al., 1974). According to their figures on 15 severely disabled people, their success rate is in excess of 80%. The treatment procedure includes response prevention and in vivo exposure, with the greatest emphasis placed on the response prevention element.

In many cases, the patient is placed under 24-hour supervision by nursing staff, who attempt to ensure that no compulsive activities whatsoever are carried out. After a comparatively long period of such intensive supervision and response prevention, the patient is increasingly exposed to stimuli that provoke the urge to carry out the compulsive activity.

Using methods which have at least some common features (e.g., exposure), Boulougouris (1976) in Athens reported successes, as did Ramsay (1976) in Amsterdam, Wonnenberger, Henkel, Arentewicz, and Hasse (1975) in Heidelberg, Emmelkamp and von Kraanen (1977) in Groningen, and Hackmann and McClean (1975) in Oxford. During this first phase of the attack on compulsive disorders, the only discordant note was that reported by Heyse (1975), working in Munich, who reported indifferent results.

At the Institute of Psychiatry in London and at the Maudsley and Bethlem Hospital, my colleagues Hodgson, Marks, and Roper and I have for the past several years been carrying out research into the behavioral modification of these disorders. During this time we have seen more than 200 patients; many of these have participated in various control trials and/or experiments. For present purposes I will restrict my description and comments to a connected series of small controlled trials in which a total of 30 severely affected patients participated; then I will give an outline of our most recent and largest clinical trial carried out on 40 severely affected patients.

The first important question to which we addressed ourselves was whether or not in vivo methods of treatment are capable of bringing about clinically significant improvement in these handicapped patients. To this end we compared the effects of therapeutic modeling and flooding, both alone and in combination.

After some preliminary pilot work (e.g., Rachman, Hodgson, & Marzillier, 1970), we set up a series of interconnected trials, for which we selected patients whose obsessive disorders were sufficiently severe to merit admission to an inpatient unit. All of the patients had been affected for a minimum of one year and most of them for considerably longer than that period (mean: 7.5 years). All of them had received other forms of treatment before being referred to our group. During the first week of their admission to the hospital, a number of assessment procedures were carried out. They then entered two consecutive three-week periods of treatment. The treatment consisted of 15 sessions, given every weekday during this three-week period. Each patient was reassessed at the completion of each phase of treatment, at the termination of treatment, and at three follow-up points. From the start of each treatment phase the patients were asked to resist the execution of any compulsive acts either during or between treatment sessions. The experimental design was simple and is illustrated in Figure 1.

In the first study, five patients received flooding treatment while the other five received modeling treatment. In both conditions, the active treatment period was preceded by a three-week period of relaxation control treatment, which we used as a basis for comparison.

In the flooding treatment the patient was asked to come into contact with the most provoking stimulus (e.g., "diseased" contaminated specimens) as soon as possible—even in the first few minutes of the first session if he or she was able to tolerate it. The aim was to arrange for rapid and prolonged contact with the most disturbing stimulus which

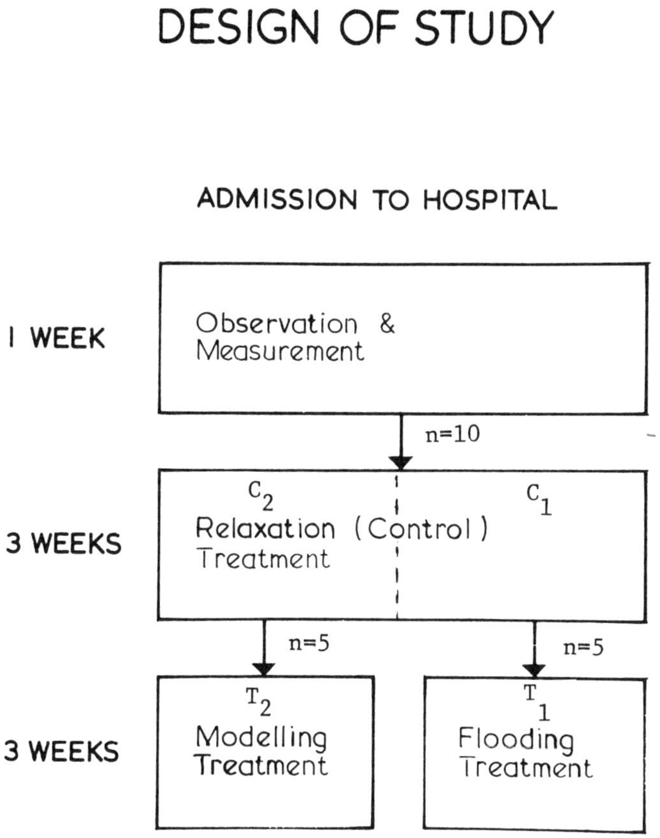

DESIGN OF STUDY

ADMISSION TO HOSPITAL

FIGURE 1. Experimental design for initial clinical trials.

the person could tolerate, rather than to proceed gradually as one might do in desensitization. Both during and after these sessions the patient was urged to refrain from carrying out his compulsive acts, i.e., response prevention instructions were instituted. The response prevention part of the program was self-regulated and was merely monitored, not supervised directly.

In the modeling treatment, directly influenced by the work of Bandura (1969), the approach was graduated and each step was first demonstrated by the therapist acting as a model. By the second or third session, the patient was encouraged to begin imitating the actions of the therapist. As in the flooding treatment, response prevention instructions were instituted at the start of the program. These brief descriptions of the methods employed should not obscure the fact that in execution the treatment generally required a delicate hand.

The flooding and modeling forms of treatment were followed by large and significant improvements, but there were no differences between the two methods. We then took the obvious step of combining the two types of treatment to see if their combined effect might exceed the effects of each method used separately.

Once again we found that the behavioral method was significantly superior to the control method, but there was no reason to conclude that the combination of modeling and flooding conferred any advantage over each method used separately. This result was then checked with a new set of five patients and the outcome was no different. As can be seen from the group results in Figure 2, substantial improvements were achieved on all measures and—what is most encouraging—these were achieved within the space of a comparatively short period. When necessary, some patients received additional treatment after the conclusion of the therapeutic trial. Hence, the results given for the follow-up period do not reflect only the therapeutic intervention provided during the experimental period. It is interesting that the improvements in obsessional-compulsive problems were accompanied by improvements in other aspects of the patient's adjustments. We have now completed a two-year follow-up on these first 20 patients and it is comforting to report that, in the main, their improvements have endured over the two-year period (Rachman & Hodgson, 1980).

Whatever the scientific interest of the results achieved with this group of 20 severe patients, clinicians are, of course, more immediately concerned with the results achieved with individuals. For this purpose a simplified table was prepared to indicate the number of patients who were substantially improved, improved, or unchanged at the end of the

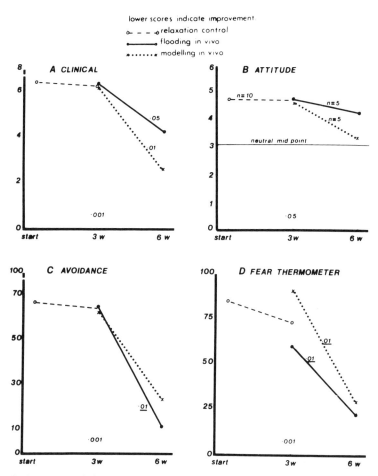

FIGURE 2. Summary of therapeutic changes, experiment no. 1, 10 patients (Rachman, Hodgson & Marks, 1971).

treatment period. For this first group of 20 patients, the failure rate was 25% and in the subsequent group of 10 patients the failure rate was only slightly smaller. Fortunately, the successfully treated patients tended to show improvements in depression, anxiety, and work adjustment (Figure 3).

This series of patients was then followed by a clinical trial in which we

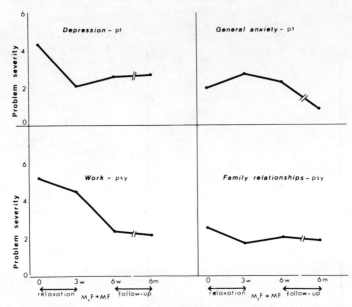

COURSE   OF   OTHER   PROBLEMS

pt = patients rating   psy = psychiatrists rating
M,F+MF= modelling, flooding or combined treatments

FIGURE 3. The longer term course of other problems reported by patients taking part in the early clinical trials (n = 20). Results show initial declines and little return of difficulties over a 6-month period.

attempted to separate out the therapeutic contributions of symbolic and participant modeling. The 10 patients who participated in this study were drawn from the same sample as the earlier patients and by the same methods. In brief, we found that while symbolic modeling (or passive modeling as it is sometimes called) is capable of achieving useful clinical improvements, the magnitude of these changes was doubled on most measures when the transition to *participant* modeling took place (Roper, Rachman, & Marks, 1975).

Encouraging though these results were, some of our patients made little or unstable progress, and clinical observations suggested that the presence of significant depression retarded their progress. In view of the acknowledged association between depression and obsessional disorders (e.g., Beech, 1974; Lewis, 1966; Rachman & Hodgson, 1980), and the therapeutic claims made on behalf of the antidepressant drug clomipramine (e.g., Capstick, 1975), it was decided to investigate the value of supplementing the behavioral treatment with this drug. Accordingly, the effects of the behavioral treatment plus clomipramine were compared with those of behavioral treatment plus placebo (Rachman, Cobb, Grey, McDonald, Mawson, Sartory, & Stern, 1979).

This study differed from the earlier ones in using a larger sample of patients, with 10 in each of four treatment conditions, and in incorporating a random allocation to the first period of the psychological treatment. Although we felt that the information available at the time and the need to answer some pertinent questions justified a project of this scale, it must be said that such large-scale trials should not be undertaken lightly—in the course of the trial over a thousand therapy hours were provided.

As can be seen from Figures 4 to 7, the behavioral treatment was followed by significant improvements on most behavioral measures. The administration of the antidepressant drug was also followed by significant improvements, but these are most noticeable on the mood scales

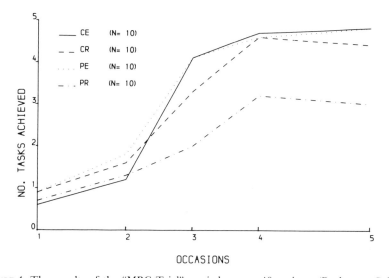

OCCASIONS

FIGURE 4. The results of the "MRC Trial" carried out on 40 patients (Rachman, Cobb, Grey, McDonald, Mawson, Sartory, & Stern, 1979). In Figures 4-7, the results are shown for five testing occasions: pretreatment (occasion 1), one week after admission to hospital (occasion 2), at the end of the first three-week treatment period (occasion 3), at the end of the second three-week treatment period (occasion 4), and at the six-month follow-up. CE = clomipramine plus behavioral treatment, CR = clomipramine plus relaxation, PE = behavioral treatment plus placebo, PR = relaxation plus placebo for three weeks, followed by PE for three weeks. Figure 4 shows the results on the Behavior Avoidance Test, in which a low score indicates avoidance.

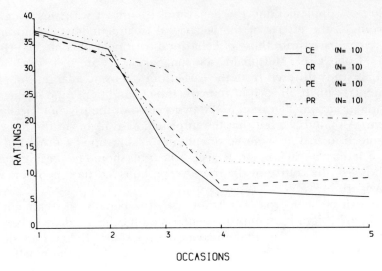

FIGURE 5. MRC Trial—patients' self-reported discomfort during the Behavioral Avoidance Tests. A high score indicates significant discomfort and/or anxiety.

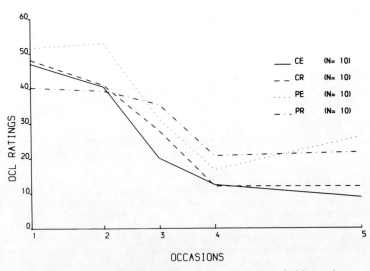

FIGURE 6. MRC Trial—Obsessional Checklist (OCL) scores recorded by patients on each of five occasions. High scores indicate excessive obsessional-compulsive activities.

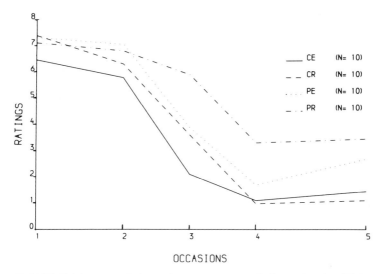

FIGURE 7. MRC Trial—assessed time taken to carry out designated tasks. High scores indicate excessive slowness.

and secondarily on some of the behavioral measures. There were no significant interactions between the two experimental conditions.

The results of the behavioral treatment were behavioral and specific. The compulsive behavior changed as predicted and was not accompanied by alterations in other aspects of the person's problems. The absence of concomitant mood or other changes emphasizes the specificity of the therapeutic changes observed to follow this form of treatment. Such specificity, although it is moderately disappointing for clinicians, is of theoretical significance, since it encourages the view that there is a direct connection between the treatment provided and the effects observed.

The administration of the drug was followed by broad improvements reflected in most measures of mood and some measures of compulsive activities. We obtained clear evidence of an antidepressive effect of the drug, but little sign that it had a direct *anti-obsessional* effect. It should also be noted that the withdrawal of the drug frequently was followed by a recurrence of significant depression. Moreover, the effects of the antidepressant drug were confined to those patients who had significant depression associated with their obsessional problems.

The results from this trial suggest that when a patient has both sets of problems—depressed affect and obsessional difficulties—the combined application of behavioral treatment and clomipramine may be justified, but care has to be taken to reduce the likelihood of a recurrence of the depressive disturbance when the drug is gradually withdrawn. The behavioral treatment can be expected to produce specific behavioral effects, while the drug can be expected to improve the patient's affective state. The results also suggest that significant depression probably helps to maintain compulsive behavior, but clarification of the close and interesting connection between depression and compulsions will need tighter experimental control of the timing of interventions and assessments.

No matter how encouraging the results of one's own clinical trials may appear to be, the need for independent confirmation cannot be avoided. Like many of the people we were studying, we found ourselves in need of reassurance. The results of small controlled trials reported by Emmelkamp and his colleagues in Holland, by Boulougouris and his colleagues in Greece, by Hackmann in Oxford, and the noncontrolled but impressive results reported by Foa and Goldstein (1978) were consistent with our own findings. Indeed, the results reported by Foa and Goldstein exceeded the best of our own success rates. The results reported by Emmelkamp and van Kraanen (1977), broadly consistent with our own, had the added merit of demonstrating the comparative robustness of the treatment technique, which appears to survive even when modified or watered down. Another encouraging sign comes from the report by Marks, Hallam, Connolly and Philpott (1976), in which it is stated that trained nurse-therapists produced clinical results that were not different from those achieved by clinical researchers who had played a part in developing the techniques. So far, the only disappointing clinical study is that carried out by Heyse (1975) on a small heterogeneous group of patients; even though this worker was trained by Meyer, who is himself responsible for what is probably the most successful outcome rates of anyone, when the method was transferred to Munich the results were poor. At present there is no satisfactory explanation of this disappointing result.

As far as drug action is concerned, it should be said that Thoren, Asberg, Cronholm, Jornestadt, and Trasuman (1980) interpreted the results of their clinical trial as providing evidence for the specific anti-obsessional effects of clomipramine. The response rate, based on some but not all of the outcome criteria, was about 50%. No prognostic indices of value were found. During the five-week treatment period, the postulated anti-obsessional effect was apparent on the blind ratings but not on measures of functioning on daily tasks or on the patients' own ratings of their symptoms. The matter is complicated by the fact that behavior therapy of an unspecified kind was also provided. Lastly, it must be remembered that, as in our own study, the withdrawal of the drug was followed by relapses occurring within a few weeks.

In our own trials, it was not apparent what factors predict therapeutic failure, except that we have some indirect evidence that patients who have adopted an obsessional lifestyle have a slightly poorer prognosis (Rachman & Hodgson, 1980). The best informed analysis of the factors that contribute to treatment failures comes from the work of Foa (1979). In a careful analysis of a small number of treatment failures, she was able to deduce that the presence of either severe depression or an overvalued idea was predictive of failure. In a later and larger study, conducted by Steketee and Foa (1981), the inhibiting influence of severe depression was once again demonstrated. Rabavilas and Boulougouris (1979) had similar results emphasizing the importance of the connection between relapses and depression.

As far as the mechanisms responsible for the therapeutic changes are concerned, the most obvious elements in the treatment procedure are in vivo exposure and the prevention of observable compulsive behaviour. Rachman and Hodgson (1980) argued that in most cases both components are necessary, but that they make relatively different contributions to treatment. They predicted that the exposure component would have its greatest effect on subjective discomfort and anxiety, while the response prevention component would have the greatest effect on inhibiting or modifying the compulsive acts themselves (see also Mills, Agras, Barlow, & Mills, 1973; Turner, Hersen, Bellack, & Wells, 1979). These expectations were broadly confirmed in a trial reported by Foa, Steketee, and Milby (1980). Regardless of whether the present interpretations are borne out in the long run, the fact remains that, when used in combination, in vivo and response prevention make a formidable contribution. Although therapeutic modeling has not been shown to be a necessary condition for change, it often is extremely useful and can be facilitative.

OBSESSIONS

All of the patients who participated in the research and clinical trials described so far complained of and demonstrated observable compulsive behavior. People who complain exclusively of obsessional ruminations are the subject of other research and progress has been slower. Rachman and Hodgson (1980) reviewed the evidence which showed that the most commonly used method, thought-stopping, was sometimes effective but was far too irregular and unpredictable in its effects to be recommended with any confidence. An alternative possibility, deduced from Rachman's (1971, 1978) construal of obsessions, is the method known as habituation training. The early use of this method produced encouraging results, and informal results reported from Sri Lanka by de Silva (1979) and from Germany by Roper (1979) combined to make an experimental trial justifiable. The results of this work produced only slight evidence to support the hope that habituation training will prove to be therapeutically effective (Likierman & Rachman, 1982), despite the fact that, in earlier research on non-psychiatric subjects, Parkinson and Rachman (1979) had shown that such training produces intra-session decrements in discomfort. The clinical problem seems to be to ensure that these within-session decreases in discomfort endure between and after the intervals between treatment sessions. The trial described by Emmelkamp and Giesselbach (1981) carried out on six patients produced promising results, but the study on five patients described by Gurnani and Vaughan (1981) "lent only partial support" to the underlying theory or its application.

The slow and often disappointing progress made in these explorations clearly indicated the need for clarification of the nature of the disorder. In an attempt to gain an improved understanding of these unwanted, intrusive cognitions, Rachman and Parkinson carried out a number of studies that had as their starting point the survey by Rachman and de Silva (1978), in which it was shown that a large majority of non-psychiatric individuals experience these phenomena, albeit at a weaker intensity and far less frequently than do obsessional patients. The research of Parkinson and Rachman (1981) showed that there is an association between the uncontrollability of these unwanted intrusive thoughts and a) their unacceptability and b) the amount of distress which they cause. Paradoxically, the more distressing and unacceptable the thought, the harder it is to remove. Obviously, this finding is connected in some way to the fact that the content of clinical obsessions is, with rare exceptions, on a theme that the person experiencing the thought regards as repugnant and objectionable. The results of this research point to the desirability of exploring the therapeutic possibility of neutralizing the repugnant aspects of the thought and/or introducing substitute cognitions. Work on these alternatives is still at a very early stage of development. The possibilities offered by indirect approaches, such as reducing stress/dysphoria or desensitizing trigger stimuli, should not be neglected. Emmelkamp and Heyden (1980) recently illustrated the value of assertiveness training in the treatment of obsessional disorders.

Primary Obsessional Slowness

The variant of obsessional disorders that is known as primary obsessional slowness is easily recognizable but rare. As a result, information about the nature and modifiability of this handicapping disorder accumulates gradually. It has been suggested that a combination of modeling, prompting, and pacing is the best way of helping people to overcome the painfully slow handicapping activities which form the basis of this problem (Rachman, 1974). Partial confirmation of the (limited) therapeutic value of this approach was provided in the case reports described by Bilsbury and Morley (1979) and by Bennun (1980).

Why Do Compulsions Persist?

It is impossible to work with obsessional patients for any length of time without becoming intrigued by the nature of the disorder itself. The extraordinary persistence of unwanted, aversive, and self-defeating obsessions and compulsions is a puzzle. The most favored answer is that compulsive behavior persists because it reduces anxiety. Although this view was proposed in one form or another before the growth of learning theory, it received powerful support from most psychologists who wrote on the subject. Mowrer's (1960) two-stage theory of fear and avoidance, stating that successful avoidance behavior paradoxically serves to preserve fear, was incorporated into many expositions of obsessional-compulsive behavior and has had a profound influence on the way in which we construe these disorders. Mowrer's conception of fear, and indirectly of compulsive rituals, served extremely well for a period, but the inadequacies of the theory are now apparent (Rachman, 1978). It cannot provide the basis for a comprehensive account of obsessions and compulsions.

In a series of connected experiments, we were able to demonstrate that compulsions most often do reduce anxiety or subjective discomfort, but there are occasions, admittedly few, when the completion of the compulsive act leaves the anxiety/discomfort level unchanged or even elevated (Rachman & Hodgson, 1980). Obsessional ruminations generally follow this latter pattern; i.e., most often they will increase discomfort. Unless the exceptions can be explained in some other, qualifying form, the anxiety-reduction theory, despite the considerable evidence in support of it, cannot aspire to be a comprehensive theory of compulsive behavior. It should perhaps be added that the exceptional findings are of greater theoretical than practical interest, because we have no reason, so far, for allowing these results to influence present therapeutic approaches.

The finding that there is a slight but significant difference in the effects observed after the execution of cleaning or checkng rituals encouraged us to explore the similarities and differences among different types of compulsions, and between compulsions and obsessions (Rachman & Hodgson, 1980). It turns out that there is a good deal of common ground between the various kinds of compulsions, but that a broad division can be drawn between checking rituals and cleaning rituals. They are precipitated in somewhat different circumstances, and the execution of cleaning compulsions more often and reliably is followed by a reduction in anxiety or discomfort. Phenomenologically, cleaning rituals appear to be restorative, while checking rituals are primarily pre-

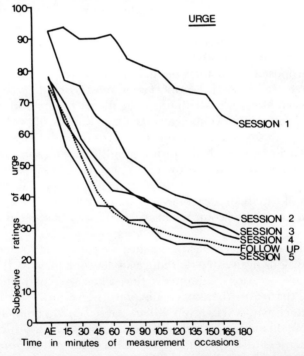

FIGURE 8. The spontaneous decay of compulsive urges (Likierman & Rachman, 1980). After exposure to a disturbing stimulus (e.g., contamination), the spontaneous decay of the urge to carry out the pertinent compulsive act is assessed by self-report at 15-minute intervals. The slow decline after test session no. 1 was followed by more rapid decreases on subsequent trials, suggesting some cumulative changes.

ventive. Investigations have also been carried out into the nature of compulsive *urges* (Likierman & Rachman, 1982; Rachman, de Silva, & Roper, 1976; Rachman & Hodgson, 1980). These compulsive urges are easy to provoke, and what is most interesting from a therapeutic point of view, they have a tendency to decay spontaneously (see Figures 8 and 9).

RESEARCH SUMMARY

In summary, a behavioral treatment that combines in vivo exposure and response prevention has proven to be moderately effective in reducing obsessional-compulsive problems. The improvements are reassuringly stable and seldom followed by the emergence of new problems. On the experimental side, it appears that most compulsive rituals are

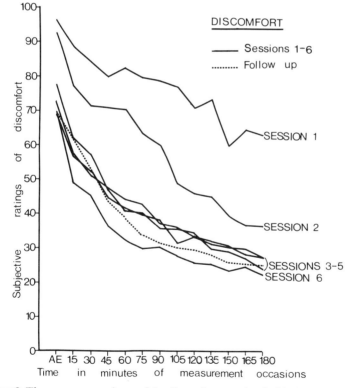

FIGURE 9. The spontaneous decay of the discomfort associated with the blocked compulsive urges follows a pattern similar to that of the urges—slow initial decline and then acceleration suggestive of cumulative tolerance (Likierman & Rachman, 1980).

followed by a reduction in anxiety/discomfort, and those exceptions that do occur are confined largely to checking rituals. The evidence is consistent, for the most part, with the anxiety-reduction theory. Although there is a good deal of common ground between various kinds of compulsions and obsessions, there is evidence which justifies a division of compulsive acts into two main categories—cleaning and checking.

Treatment Guidelines

On present knowledge, the advisable treatment for compulsive problems is a combination of exposure (graded and gradual, by preference), and response prevention. If progress is seriously impeded by depressive affect, the supplementary use of clomipramine can be considered—but great care should be taken to ensure a careful, slow (but not delayed) withdrawal of the drug because of the likely return of depression.

Obsessions associated with compulsions often abate as the manifest behavior improves, but if they do not, or if the obsessions arise in the absence of compulsions, special measures are needed. To date, no specific dependable method of treatment is available (see Rachman, 1982), but the following tactics sometimes are helpful, used alone or in combination. Because of the close connection between depression and obsessions, the relief of depression by psychological or pharmacological means often is helpful. Thought-stopping appears to be a great help to a minority of sufferers, and habituation training has a similar record—these techniques can be used in combination. A newer possibility is to help the person to adopt a more accepting attitude to his obsessions, as it has been found that difficulty in removing an unwanted intrusive thought is correlated with unacceptability (Rachman, 1981). Further, informing a sufferer that *most* people experience such thoughts, albeit less intensely and less frequently, can bring some relief and reduce the unacceptability of the obsessions. In the coming years, however, we can look forward to an improvement and refinement of our therapeutic procedures, which remain admittedly rudimentary, and to further efforts designed to improve our understanding of the mode of operation of these techniques. It is also likely that we will see an increase in experimental investigations designed to clarify the nature of obsessions and compulsions.

Finally, these useful advances in our ability to modify obsessional disorders incidentally provide the basis for a firm answer to those critics who persist in trying to reassure themselves that the methods of behavior therapy are applicable only to simple and uncomplicated problems such as the mini-phobias of university students.

REFERENCES

BANDURA, A. *The principles of behavior modification.* New York: Holt, Rinehart & Winston, 1969.

BEECH, H.R. (Ed.). *Obsessional states.* London: Methuen, 1974.

BEECH, H.R. & VAUGHAN, M. *Behavioural treatment of obsessional states.* New York: Wiley, 1978.

BENNUN, I. Obsessional slowness. *Behaviour Research and Therapy,* 1980, *18,* 595-597.

BILSBURY, A., & MORLEY, S. Obsessional slowness: a meticulous replication. *Behaviour Research and Therapy,* 1979, *17,* 405-408.

BOERSMA, D., DEN HENGST, S., DEKKER, J., & EMMELKAMP, P. Exposure and response prevention: A comparison with obsessive-compulsive patients. *Behaviour Research and Therapy,* 1976, *14,* 19-24.

BOULOUGOURIS, J. *Proceedings of the European Association of Behavior Therapy.* Spetsae, Greece, 1976.

CAPSTICK, N. Clomipramine in the treatment of true obsessional state—A report on four patients. *Psychosomatics,* 1975, *16,* 21-25.

CATTS, S., & McCONAGHY, N. Ritual prevention in the treatment of obsessive-compulsive neurosis. *Australian and New Zealand Journal of Psychiatry,* 1975, *9,* 37-41.

DE SILVA, P. Personal communication, 1979.

EMMELKAMP, P. & GIESSELBACH, P. Treatment of obsessions: Relevant vs. irrelevant exposure. *Behavioural Psychotherapy,* 1981, *9,* 322-329.

EMMELKAMP, P. & HEYDEN, H. Treatment of harming obsessions. *Behaviour Analysis and Modification,* 1980, *4,* 28-35.

EMMELKAMP, P. & VON KRAANEN, J. Therapist-controlled exposure in vivo vs. self-controlled exposure in vivo: A comparison with obsessive-compulsive patients. *Behaviour Research and Therapy,* 1977, *15,* 491-496.

EMMELKAMP, P., HELM, M., VAN ZANTEN, B. & PLOCHG, I. Treatment of obsessive-compulsive patients. *Behaviour Research and Therapy,* 1980, *18,* 61-66.

EYSENCK, H.J. & RACHMAN, S. *The causes and cures of neurosis.* London: Routledge, 1965.

FOA, E.B. Failure in treating obsessive-compulsives. *Behaviour Research and Therapy,* 1979, *17,* 169-176.

FOA, E.B. & GOLDSTEIN, A. Continuous exposure and strict response prevention in the treatment of obsessive-compulsive neurosis. *Behavior Therapy,* 1978, *17,* 169-176.

FOA, E.B., GRAYSON, J. & STEKETEE, G. Depression, habituation and treatment outcome in obsessive-compulsives. *International Symposium,* Crete, 1980, Unpublished.

FOA, E.B. & STEKETEE, G. Obsessive-compulsives. In M. Hersen, R.M. Eisler & P. Miller (Eds.) *Progress in Behavior Therapy,* Vol. 8, New York: Academic Press, 1980.

FOA, E.B., STEKETEE, G. & MILBY, J. Differential effects of exposure and response prevention in obsessive-compulsive washers. *Journal of Consulting and Clinical Psychology,* 1980, *48,* 71-79.

GURNANI, P. & VAUGHAN, M. Changes in frequency and distress during prolonged repetition of obsessional thoughts. *British Journal of Clinical Psychology,* 1981, *20,* 79-81.

HACKMANN, A., & McCLEAN, C. A comparison of flooding and thought-stopping treatment. *Behaviour Research and Therapy,* 1975, *13,* 263-269.

HEYSE, H. Response prevention and modeling in the treatment of obsessive-compulsive neurosis. In J. Brengelmann (Ed.), *Progress in Behavior Therapy.* Berlin: Springer Verlag, 1975.

HODGSON, R., RACHMAN, S., & MARKS, I. The treatment of chronic obsessive compulsive neurosis. *Behaviour Research and Therapy*, 1972, *10*, 181-189.

LIKIERMAN, H. and RACHMAN, S. Spontaneous decay of compulsive urges. *Behaviour Research and Therapy*, 1980, *18*, 387-394.

LIKIERMAN, H. & RACHMAN, S. Obsessions: An experimental investigation of thought-stopping and habituation training. *Behavioural Psychotherapy*, 1982, *10*, 324-338.

LEWIS, A. Obsessional disorder. In R. Scott (Ed.), *Price's Textbook of the Practice of Medicine*, (10th edition). London: Oxford University Press, 1966.

MARKS, I.M., HALLAM, R., CONNOLLY, J., & PHILPOTT, R. *Nursing in behavioral psychotherapy*. London: Royal College of Nursing, 1976.

METZNER, R. Some experimental analogues of obsession. *Behaviour Research and Therapy*, 1963, *1*, 231-236.

MEYER, R. Modification of expectations in cases with obsessional rituals. *Behaviour Research and Therapy*, 1966, *4*, 273-280.

MEYER, V., LEVY, R., & SCHNURER, A. The behavioral treatment of obsessive-compulsive disorder. In H.R. Beech (Ed.), *Obsessional states*. London: Methuen, 1974.

MILLS, H., AGRAS, S., BARLOW, D., & MILLS, J. Compulsive rituals treated by response prevention. *Archives of General Psychiatry*, 1973, *28*, 524-529.

MOWRER, O.H. *Learning Theory and Behavior*. New York: Wiley, 1960.

PARKINSON, L., & RACHMAN, S. Are intrusive thoughts subject to habituation? *Behaviour Research and Therapy*, 1979, *18*, 409-418.

PARKINSON, L., & RACHMAN, S. The nature of intrusive thoughts. *Advances in Behaviour Research and Therapy*, 1981, *3*, 10-110.

RABAVILAS, A., & BOULOUGOURIS, J. Mood changes and flooding outcome in obsessive-compulsive patients. *Journal of Nervous and Mental Disorders*, 1979, *167*, 495-499.

RACHMAN, S. Obsessional ruminations. *Behaviour Research and Therapy*, 1971, *9*, 229-235.

RACHMAN, S. Primary obsession slowness. *Behaviour Research and Therapy*, 1974, *11*, 463-471.

RACHMAN, S. An anatomy of obsessions. *Analysis and Modification of Behaviour*, 1978, *2*, 253-278.

RACHMAN, S. (Ed.) Unwanted intrusive cognitions. *Advances in Behaviour Research and Therapy*, 1981, *3*, 3.

RACHMAN, S. Obstacles to the successful modification of obsessions. In *Failures in Behavior Therapy*. (Ed.) P. Emmelkamp & E. Foa. New York: Wiley, 1982.

RACHMAN, S., COBB, J., GREY, S.J., McDONALD, R., MAWSON, D., SARTORY, G., & STERN, R. The behavioural treatment of obsessional-compulsive disorders, with and without clomipramine. *Behaviour Research and Therapy*, 1979, *17*, 467-478.

RACHMAN, S. & DE SILVA, P. Abnormal and normal obsessions. *Behaviour Research and Therapy*, 1978, *16*, 233-248.

RACHMAN, S., DE SILVA, P., & ROPER, G. The spontaneous decay of compulsive urges. *Behaviour Research and Therapy*, 1976, *14*, 445-453.

RACHMAN, S., & HODGSON, R. *Obsessions and compulsions*. Englewood Cliffs, N.J.: Prentice-Hall, 1980.

RACHMAN, S., HODGSON, R., & MARKS, I. The treatment of chronic obsessional neurosis. *Behaviour Research and Therapy*, 1971, *9*, 237-247.

RACHMAN, S., MARKS, I. & HODGSON, R. The treatment of chronic obsessive-compulsive neurosis by modeling and flooding in vivo. *Behaviour Research and Therapy*, 1973, *11*, 463-471.

RACHMAN, S., HODGSON, R., & MARZILLIER, J. The treatment of an obsessional-compulsive disorder by modelling. *Behaviour Research and Therapy*, 1970, *8*, 385-392.

RACHMAN, S., & PHILIPS, C. *Psychology and behavioral medicine*. New York: Cambridge University Press, 1980.

RACHMAN, S., & WILSON, G.T. *The effects of psychological therapy*. Oxford: Pergamon, 1980.

RAMSAY, R. Behavioral approaches to obsessive-compulsive neurosis. In J.C. Boulougouris

& A.D. Rabavilas (Eds.), *The treatment of phobic and obsessive-compulsive disorders.* Oxford: Pergamon, 1976.

RAMSAY, R., & SIKKEL, R. Behavior therapy and obsessive neurosis. *Proceedings of the European Conference on Behavior Therapy.* Munich, 1971.

ROPER, G. Personal communication, 1979.

ROPER, G., RACHMAN, S., & MARKS, I. Passive and participant modeling in exposure treatment of obsessive-compulsive neurotics. *Behaviour Research and Therapy,* 1975, *13,* 271-279.

STEKETEE, G., & FOA, E. Personal communication, 1981.

THOREN, P., ASBERG, M., CRONHOLM, B., JORNESTADT, L., & TRASUMAN, L. Clomipramine treatment of obsessive-compulsive disorder. *Archives of General Psychiatry,* 1980, *37,* 1281-1285.

TURNER, S., HERSEN, M., BELLACK, A., & WELLS, K. Behavioral treatment of obsessive-compulsive neurosis. *Behaviour Research and Therapy,* 1979, *17,* 95-106.

WONNENBERGER, M., HENKEL, D., ARENTEWICZ, G., & HASSE, A. Studie zu einem Selbsthilfeprogram für zwangneurotische Patienten. *Zeitschrift für Klinische Psychologie.,* 1975, *4,* 124-136.

7

A Behavioral Program for the Assessment and Treatment of Sexual Aggressors

WILLIAM L. MARSHALL, CHRISTOPHER M. EARLS,
ZINDEL SEGAL, and JULIET DARKE

We have chosen the descriptor "sexual aggressors" to characterize those men who sexually assault, rape, or molest adult females or children, because there is growing evidence that these crimes involve a far greater degree of violence than had been hitherto suspected. In our view these particular sexual offenses are quite different from those that might be described as "nuisances" (e.g., exhibitionism, obscene telephoning, etc.) specifically because they cause greater damage (psychological as well as physical) to the victim (Marshall, 1982a). Not only are sexually aggressive acts more dangerous than was once thought, but they also appear to be increasing at an alarming rate, at least over the past decade (FBI *Uniform Crime Reports*, 1980). While it is true that reporting rates appear to have increased as society becomes less concerned with blaming the victim, there is still a large discrepancy between reported incidents and actual occurrences. Various writers estimate that only between 10% and 40% of rapes are reported (Amir, 1971) and the reporting rate for sexual molestation of children appears to be even lower (Finkelhor, 1979).

Indeed, Abel (1981) has provided data indicating that both rapists and child molestors are predatory, and that they average some 10 (rapists) and 70 (child molesters) victims each over their offending career. Such an extensive and dangerous problem cannot be responsibly ignored.

Society does not, of course, ignore these problems, but it does not, on the other hand, take satisfactorily responsible action. Very little money is spent on research aimed at modifying the behavior of these men or on discerning the sociocultural influences that set the stage for (one might even say incite) the commission of sexual aggression. Typically, it is far harder to secure a conviction for rape than for any other type of assaultive crime (FBI *Uniform Crime Reports*, 1980). Once a conviction is obtained, the offender is commonly sent to jail for a period of time, only to be released without treatment to once again offend. Approximately one-third of the sexual aggressors released from Canadian penitentiaries reoffend within the subsequent two years (Davidson, 1982)—or at least this proportion of them are caught. In fact, one of the many problems of using recidivism as the index of success or failure is that it reflects many things over and above reoffending (Quinsey & Marshall, 1983). In any case, it is clear that incarceration alone is not very effective with sexual aggressors (Sturup, 1972) and that the addition of the usual token treatment does not seem to help (Frisbie & Dondis, 1965).

Over the past eight or so years behavioral clinicians have become interested in this area and effective treatment and assessment procedures have been developed. This is not to say that we can now offer a completely effective program or that we now know the factors that lead to sexual assault. We certainly do have a better idea of what these might be than we did five or six years ago, but we still have a long way to go before we can confidently treat all sexual aggressors or before we can accurately diagnose these problems and predict the dangerousness of these men (Quinsey, 1981). What we appear to be in a position to do at this moment is to identify several areas of deficit or aberration that seem to be relevant to the description and treatment of sexual aggressors. This does not mean, of course, that each of these offenders suffers from defects in each and all of these areas. Just as we observe in other complex human problems, there is a significant degree of individuality in both the nature and expression of difficulties. However, these idiosyncracies usually take the form of various degrees of aberration within a limited set of areas of dysfunction; it is rare to have to look beyond these areas to describe and modify behaviors so that control over sexual aggression is achieved. These areas of dysfunction have been categorized by us as *deviant sexuality* and *social incompetence*.

DEVIANT SEXUALITY

Most behavioral researchers and clinicians working with sexual aggressors come from a background of treating and assessing other, less dangerous forms of sexual deviance. These other behaviors included fetishism, transvestism, exhibitionism, and the like, as well as alternative modes of sexual expression such as homosexuality. Early research established that men displaying these behaviors had sexual preferences that differentiated them from men who did not display such behaviors. Homosexuals, for example, showed either equivalent or greater sexual arousal to males than they did to females (Freund, 1963; McConaghy, 1967). These observations, along with the experience of working with these behaviors, led behavior therapists to assume that similar deviant sexual preferences would characterize rapists and child molestors, although it was recognized quite early that these preferences were not the only problems which characterized sexual offenders (Marshall, 1971).

Assessment

Since the early to mid 1970s, a sophisticated technology for the measurement of sexual preferences has been developed that, although highly refined, is under constant improvement. Basically, this technology involves the direct measurement of changes in the magnitude of the male's erection while he watches, listens to, or imagines sexual stimuli or acts. There is some argument about the relative value of measuring various aspects of the penis during erectile changes, but at the moment there is no easy resolution to this debate. Freund (1963) prefers to describe volume changes (i.e., changes in the size of the penis in all directions), whereas both Bancroft (Bancroft, Jones, & Pullen, 1966) and Barlow (Barlow, Becker, Leitenberg, & Agras, 1970) measure changes in the diameter (or circumference) of the penis. Recently, we (Earls & Marshall, 1982) have provided evidence for the value of measuring length changes, although there are still technical problems in doing so in a readily adaptable and economically feasible manner.

Guided as much by the research of others (e.g., Abel, Laws, and Quinsey in particular) as by our own work, we have developed a standardized procedure for assessing sexual preferences among these offenders. We use a Parks mercury-in-rubber strain gauge (see Earls and Marshall, 1982, and Rosen and Keefe, 1978, for comprehensive reviews of the erectile measurement literature), which attaches around the shaft of the penis and measures changes in circumference as the penis becomes erect.

As the penis enlarges, the sylastic rubber tubing containing the mercury stretches, thereby narrowing the column of mercury and changing its electrical resistance. These changes in electrical resistance are fed through a plethysmograph (Parks Electronics, Model 270), which converts the output of the gauge into a form that can be read by either a digital voltmeter or a polygraph. Initially the subject is asked to produce a full erection so that this measurement and that corresponding to flaccidity can be registered as anchors against which to describe responses to various stimuli. Responses to the stimuli are then described as percentages of full erection.

At the moment we use two methods of stimulus presentation: audio descriptions of various sexual acts, and slides depicting sexual materials. Slides are suitable only for discerning age preferences and they do not readily depict the dynamic features that define rape. When we want to present activities such as aggression, etc., we use audiotaped descriptions. Rapists listen to tapes that describe both mutually consenting sex and forced sex (with varying degrees of violence), while we measure their erectile responses. Child molesters view slides depicting males and females of varying ages (four years through late twenties) during one assessment procedure, while in another they listen to audio descriptions of sex with children that vary in terms of the sexual acts (fondling versus intercourse) and the amount of force used (threats, force, and beatings).

There are two basic assumptions underlying the use of this technology: 1) Measures of sexual arousal to various stimuli reflect preferences for the sexual activities depicted in the stimuli; and 2) the preferences discerned by these laboratory procedures predict actual behavior in the real world. These assumptions concern the validity of the measures and there is evidence relevant to this issue of validity.

The use of these methods for assessing sexual preferences is widespread and permits us to declare that these laboratory descriptions accurately match the expected preferences of men whose previous sexual history is unequivocal. For instance, it has been found that laboratory-assessed sexual preferences match the history of actual sexual behavior of homosexuals (Barr & Blaszczynski, 1976; Mavissakalian, Blanchard, Abel, & Barlow, 1975), fetishists and transvestites (Marks & Gelder, 1967), and exhibitionists (Langevin, Paitich, Ramsey, Anderson, Pope, Pearl & Newman, 1979)—as well child molesters (Freund, 1967; Quinsey, 1977) and rapists (Barbaree, Marshall & Lanthier, 1979). While Quinsey (1981) has found that the pretreatment sexual preferences of child molesters predict subsequent behavior, Marshall (1975) reports that relative changes induced by treatment also predict long-term behavioral changes.

Marshall found that either reduction in interest in deviant acts or an increase in arousal to appropriate sexual behaviors indicated that treatment had been successful.

Success with this approach to measurement and corresponding successes with treatment based on this approach led behavior therapists to conclude that rape and child molestation were essentially sexual acts having, on occasion perhaps, somewhat gratuitous acts of aggression present. This, we now believe, was a mistaken assumption. To illustrate this let us follow the course of our research into the deviant sexuality of rapists.

Rapists

We consider all men who sexually assault women to be rapists whether they are convicted of rape or a lesser offense (such as indecent assault, gross indecency, etc.), since our research has convinced us that almost all these men intended to have forced intercourse. Those charged with a lesser offense were interrupted in their attempts at forced penetration, couldn't get an erection, or in fact succeeded but there was not sufficient evidence for the prosecutors to secure a conviction.

Abel, Barlow, Blanchard, and Guild (1977) led the way in the assessment of rapists' sexual preferences, and indeed, Abel has led the way for the past ten years in the treatment and measurement of these men. What they found was that, while normal men showed less arousal to rape cues than they did to mutually consenting sex, rapists failed to make this discrimination. We (Barbaree, Marshall, & Lanthier, 1979) replicated these observations but interpreted the results to mean that normals were inhibited by the presence of force and violence while rapists were not. In attempting to understand this inhibition process (or rather the lack of it in rapists), we set about to disrupt it in normals in the hope that this might tell us something about the processes that eliminate it in rapists. Rapists commonly report that they are either angry or intoxicated at the time of their offense, so we took these two factors as our starting point. When we intoxicated normal males they showed erectile preferences that looked more like rapists than when they were sober. Angry normal males displayed quite marked responses to the rape cues, which were far higher than their responses before being upset.

These findings indicated that alcohol and anger interfered with the usual inhibition initiated in normal men by the presence of force or violence in sexual acts. This interference could result from a number of things, but the most obvious are: 1) alcohol or anger obscures the man's perception of the inappropriate cues (i.e., force or violence); or 2) alcohol and anger make it difficult for him to control his arousal once he has recognized that the depiction is inappropriate (supposing for the moment that this inhibition is a voluntary process); or 3) alcohol and anger make men not care about the usual social prohibitions. We (Wydra, Marshall, Barbaree, & Earls, 1981) found that both rapists and intoxicated men could identify the inappropriateness of sexual depictions just as accurately as normal men and that they were equally capable of controlling their arousal. Apparently, rapists simply do not care to control themselves, since they clearly recognize when sexual behaviors are socially aberrant and they are able to control their arousal if they wish. This suggests the possibility that factors additional to sexual arousal motivate rape.

As if to convince us of this sentiment, we (Baxter, Marshall, Barbaree, Malcolm, & Davidson, 1982) have recently completed a large-scale study including 60 rapists and 60 normals, in which we could discern no differences between the two groups. In other words, rapists did not differ from normals in terms of sexual preferences. Now these data need some comment since they appear to fly in the face of earlier studies. In addition to the findings of Abel, Barlow, Blanchard, and Guild (1977) and our own studies (Barbaree, Marshall & Lanthier, 1979), Quinsey (Quinsey, Chaplin, & Varney, 1981) has found differences between rapists and normals. It is important to note, however, that in all these studies, although these group differences were statistically significant, some of the rapists had normal profiles and some normals had rapist profiles. In any case, the rapists in our first study were those referred to us soon after we set up a treatment and assessment facility. These early referrals were made for the very good reason that they were the most dangerous sexual offenders housed in the penitentiaries where we were working at the time (Ontario Regional Federal Penitentiaries). Subjects in the later study included lower priority offenders who were judged to be less dangerous and who generally had a lower frequency of offending. From their own data, both Abel's and Quinsey's offenders seem to be more dangerous and to commit more offenses than those in our most recent study. We are inclined to believe that our latest sample is the more representative of rapists as a group.

Given these findings, then, we have begun to question the role of sexual motivation in rape. Let us make it clear right away, however, that we do not think that sexual motivation plays no part in rape. Since rape involves sexual molestation, then very clearly sexual intent is present. The question that the data we have been discussing raise concerns the importance and primacy of sexual motivation rather than whether or not it is present. Actually, these data cannot be taken as unequivocal. It may very well be that the manner in which the stimuli were presented to our recent large group of offenders and normals was not sufficiently provocative or prolonged to elicit differential arousal, despite the fact that it matches that used in our earlier study. These possibilities need further examination before we will be able to come to any firm conclusions; we are now in the process of pursuing these possibilities. However, at the same time we are also exploring alternative explanations of rape that have to do with other motivations, such as power, aggression, and the intent to humiliate or degrade the victim. Indeed, it may very well be that the particular primary motive in rape (be it sexual, power, aggression, etc.) is idiosyncratic; other authors have in fact suggested that rapists may be subclassified according to their primary motivation (e.g., Cohen, Seghorn, & Calamus, 1969).

Whatever the outcome of our studies of motivation, it remains clear that at least some rapists are sexually aberrant. A few of these men appear to be more aroused by forced sex than by mutually consenting sex, and some are equally aroused by both. It may well turn out that others are sexually excited by humiliating acts during forced sex. Just what percentage of rapists display deviant sexual preferences or an absence of the inhibitory processes normally initiated by force remains to be seen, and a careful study of a large group of these offenders tested with provocative stimuli presented for prolonged periods (5-10 minutes exposure per stimulus) is urgently needed.

Child Molesters

Contrary to our observations with rapists that the status of sexual motivation is equivocal, our research on the sexual abuse of children reveals the major focus to be sexual. While we have made quite important and somewhat novel discoveries concerning the violent proclivities of some child molestors, in those cases aggression and sex seem to be fused, whereas in rapists it appears that sex is often instrumental in achieving other goals having to do with power, aggression, and the humiliation of the victim.

Child molesters consistently show a preference for sex with children over sex with adults (Freund, 1967; Quinsey, 1977); indeed, Freund has shown specific age preferences to typify offenders who have characteristically molested only children of particular ages. While the bulk of the literature suggests that by far the majority of men who sexually abuse children are meek and mild fellows who do not attempt more than fondling, much less hurt their victim, we (Christie, Marshall, & Lanthier, 1979; Marshall, 1982b; Marshall & Christie, 1981) have found a substantial number who physically injure their victims. In a careful examination of the police reports and medical records of victims of child molestors, we (Marshall & Christie, 1981) were able to detect clear evidence in over 50% of the cases of the use of physical force over and above that necessary for the commission of the crime. In fact, only 11 of 41 offenders did not use any form of coercion or force during their sexual assaults on children. Interestingly enough, female victims were the only children to suffer beatings but penile penetration occurred across sexes. Sixty percent of female children aged 12 to 14 years were penetrated, as were 50% of boys in this age group and 38% of all children under 12 years of age (Marshall, 1982b). Clearly, child molesters are not the harmless fondlers we once thought.

Whereas erectile responses in rapists are not always pronounced when violence is portrayed, or at least they are rarely greater than responses to mutually consenting sex, in violent child molesters erectile responses appear to track the interest in physical aggression. For example, Figure 1 portrays the responses of one child molester to various levels of sex and aggression across different aged female children.

It is clear that the precise definition of erectile preferences is not a straightforward task that can be routinely administered, although we

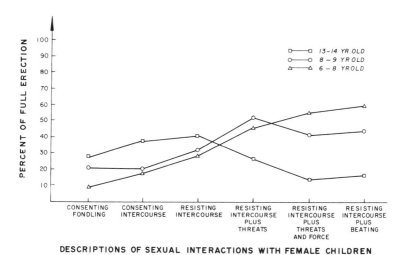

FIGURE 1. The erectile responses of a child molester to the use of force

usually detect aggressive sexual interests from our standard assessment. For some child molesters, then, aggression adds to their sexual arousal and their acts can, therefore, be reasonably construed as primarily sexual in nature.

In summary, then, our findings from the erectile assessment of sexual aggressors indicate that some rapists have deviant sexuality but most are motivated in their assaults by other needs having to do with power, aggression, and humiliation. Child molesters, on the other hand, while often acting aggressively toward their victims, are, nevertheless, primarily sexually motivated. In the treatment of child molesters, therefore, a central focus will be on changing aberrant sexuality, while with rapists the central focus will be on aggression and its related features. However, some rapists are sexually deviant and some child molesters are not. Since we cannot know this in advance in any particular case, we must routinely assess the erectile preferences of all these men, since when deviant sexuality is present it must be altered if we are to be confident that behavioral changes will endure.

Treatment

When deviant sexual interests have been established as present by testing, we need to provide treatment that will normalize these preferences. In other words, we need procedures that will reduce deviant sexual responses and others that will increase appropriate arousal where necessary.

The most popular methods for reducing deviant interests are some form of aversion therapy (Quinsey & Marshall, 1983). It was commonly assumed that classical conditioning mechanisms mediated the changes initiated by these procedures, but there is little or no evidence to support that proposal (Quinsey & Marshall, 1983). Whatever the mechanisms of change are, it is clear that these procedures work, although their effects are not always startling (Marks, 1976).

Electrical aversion therapy involves presenting a stimulus depicting the particular deviant sexual acts of relevance and following this with a mild electrical shock of an intensity selected by the patient and delivered to either the calf muscle of the leg or the lower forearm. Repeated pairings of the deviant stimulus with the unpleasant experience of shock reduce the sexual attractiveness of the deviant stimuli in most offenders. The precise manner in which this procedure is carried out appears to depend on the therapist's own preference, but we characteristically use audio depictions as the deviant stimulus (Marshall, 1973) as does Abel

(Abel, Levis, & Clancy, 1970). Quinsey has developed an interesting and, it appears, valuable variation on this theme (Quinsey, Chaplin, & Carrigan, 1980). He provides patients with feedback regarding their erectile responding to the deviant stimulus. When this responding reaches a certain criterion of erection, a red light signals aberrant arousal and an electrical shock is delivered repeatedly until responding falls below criterion. Quinsey's data suggest that this is a very powerful procedure and it is one that we intend to adopt routinely.

Covert sensitization appears to be preferred to electrical aversion in the United States, apparently because it is seen as less ethically objectionable. However, this does not seem to be a good reason to eschew electrical aversion, since the objections to this procedure are usually unfounded (Begelman, 1975) and covert sensitization does not appear to be any more ethically defensible. Covert aversion is essentially an analogue of electrical aversive therapy, where the deviant stimulus and aversive event are imagined by the subject in response to carefully prepared prompts by the therapist. Quinsey and Marshall (1983) reviewed evidence indicating limited but encouraging support for covert sensitization and suggested that the variation advocated by Maletzky (1974) may have potential. In this procedure covert aversive images are "assisted" by the simultaneous presentation of foul odors.

When aversion therapy in its various forms (electrical or covert) fails, we use "satiation therapy" (Marshall, 1979). This procedure, first described by Marshall and Lippens (1977), essentially requires the patient to masturbate continuously for one hour (whether or not he ejaculates) while verbalizing aloud every variation he can think of on his deviant fantasies. This technique seems to be particularly effective, especially for those men who masturbate quite frequently and who have a vivid fantasy life. Abel and Annon (1982) describe the use of satiation as a self-managed procedure that the patient carries out at home. In this procedure the patient records his verbalized fantasies on a tape-recorder so that the therapist can be sure the patient is actually following instructions. These therapists point out that such an approach is particularly valuable for the outpatient who is at high risk for offending, since satiation brings about a rapid loss of interest in the sexually deviant acts. Of course, this take-home variant is also clearly valuable when the patient is too shy to carry out the procedure under observation.

The most popular procedure for increasing appropriate arousal is quite similar in some respects to satiation, although it differs in strategic ways. Variously called "orgasmic reconditioning" or "masturbatory retraining," this procedure requires the patient to replace deviant fantasies

with appropriate fantasies when masturbating. There are several recommended ways to accomplish this switch (Annon, 1971; Davison, 1968;
Marquis, 1970), but the choice cannot, at the moment, be based on the
demonstrated superiority of one or another. Indeed, despite its common
use in many treatment programs, orgasmic reconditioning appears to
rest on very shaky empirical grounds (Conrad & Wincze, 1976). In our
own program we have patients carry out the procedure in the laboratory
where we provide the "appropriate" stimuli. Patients are presented with
the appropriate stimuli and instructed to masturbate to ejaculation, at
which time they are to stop, relax, and enjoy the pleasurable experiences
associated with the appropriate acts. While orgasmic reconditioning, in
one form or another, appears to be the procedure of choice for most
clinicians, much more empirical research is required before we can accept its routine application.

Other procedures for enhancing nondeviant sexual arousal have been
suggested. For instance, a classical conditioning procedure was employed
by Beech, Watts, and Poole (1971), in which the deviant stimulus served
as the unconditioned stimulus (US) and the appropriate stimulus, which
was presented immediately prior to the US, served as the conditional
stimulus. Frequent pairings of these stimuli over the course of three
months were said to have eliminated deviant sexual interests in Beech
et al.'s patient. However, it was not possible to unequivocally attribute
changes in the patient's behavior to the classical conditioning procedure,
and subsequent research has not produced encouraging results with this
approach (Herman, Barlow, & Agras, 1974; Marshall, 1974).

In summary, then, we employ electrical aversion therapy as our typical
first tactic in attempting to reduce deviant sexual arousal, using satiation
where it seems more suitable to the particular patient or where aversion
therapy has failed. Orgasmic reconditioning, conducted in the laboratory, appears to be the most promising technique for enhancing appropriate arousal, although the evidence is not at all strong. We now turn
to the broad area of social difficulties that are experienced by sexual
aggressors and that seem to maintain their aberrant behaviors.

SOCIAL INCOMPETENCE

It is generally agreed that incompetence in a broad range of social
functioning characterizes individuals who have a variety of behavioral
and emotional problems (Phillips, 1978) and that these deficits distin-

guish rapists and child molestors in particular (Abel, Blanchard, & Becker, 1977; Laws & Serber, 1975; Stermac & Quinsey, 1982). Unfortunately, however, there is no commonly agreed upon statement describing the nature or range of this incompetence, although it is understood that a lack of skills is basic to the problem (McFall, 1982).

Early work in this area took a particularly restrictive view and focused exclusively on limited aspects of interpersonal effectiveness. For example, work with neurotics emphasized the value of assertiveness (Salter, 1949; Wolpe, 1969), while rudimentary motor skills were trained in schizophrenics (Hersen & Bellack, 1976), and dating techniques were taught to heterosocially shy normals (Twentyman & McFall, 1975). Even within these restricted domains early treatment and research adopted quite limited definitions of the skill to be trained. For example, assertiveness was seen as simply being able to refuse unreasonable demands by others (McFall & Lillesand, 1971).

In recent years scientist-practitioners have identified various additional aspects of effective social functioning and have broadened their understanding of the specific elements of such behaviors. Nevertheless, within the psychological literature, social competence continues to be most commonly conceptualized in terms of conversational skills. On the other hand, from quite a different perspective, "life skills" trainers have typically considered socially ineffective individuals to be characterized by a broad range of deficiencies (Conger, 1973), although they offer little in the way of empirical support for their arguments.

Our view of the role that social incompetence plays in the misbehavior of sexual offenders is that such incompetence has two effects. First, it severely restricts access to appropriate partners and appropriate sexual behaviors. Second, being incompetent increases the level and frequency of stress in the individual's life, which in turn increases the probability that offensive behavior will occur. It is generally agreed that stress precipitates various dysfunctional states and aberrant behavior (Dohrenwend & Dohrenwend, 1974; Lazarus & Launier, 1979; Moos, 1976; Selye, 1956), and many sexual deviates claim that stress increases the likelihood that they will offend.

Our goal in identifying a range of social incompetencies is to eliminate these deficiencies in order to both increase behavioral possibilities and reduce stress, so that the probability of deviant behavior is reduced. Given this goal, we will need to look beyond a simple and restrictive range of functioning. To this end we have outlined our present conceptualization of social competence.

Elements of Social Competence

Competence in any of the areas identified below is understood to reflect an evaluation of the offender's behavior, with this judgment being a function of the adequacy of the individual's skills (McFall, 1982). It is important to note that competence is not excellence, but rather adequate execution of the skills in question. On the other hand, a normative reference for competence may not be appropriate and may even be misleading, since judgments of competence should be criterion-referenced (i.e., measured against some standard of behavior that determines adequacy). It may well be that for some skills most people are inadequate, but for individuals with specific problems (e.g., sexual aggression) this shared inadequacy may contribute to the maintenance of the deviation.

For any particular area of competence, McFall (1982) has identified three sets of skills that may be used both to evaluate competence and to define skill deficits. *Decoding skills* refer to the person's capacity to correctly perceive and interpret information from the environment (usually from other people). *Decision skills* concern the ability to identify both the behaviors necessary to perform adequately and the likely outcome of enacting these behaviors. Finally, *encoding skills* involve the coordination and effective execution of the necessary behaviors and the perception and evaluation of feedback for these behaviors.

It is important to note that anxiety may interfere with the effective execution of any skills by inhibiting or disrupting the display of behaviors that the individual has in his repertoire. Therefore, it is necessary to evaluate anxiety in the context of the behavior under analysis. If it proves to be a problem, we will then need to organize a training program to overcome anxiety. Lang (1977) has argued that the individual's capacity to deal with anxiety is itself a skill and should be trained as such. However, we have found (Gordon, Weisman, & Marshall, 1980) that simply forcing clients to endure prolonged exposure to conversational situations not only eliminates their anxiety but also permits the expression and development of adequate skilled behaviors.

Interpersonal Skills

Interpersonal ineffectiveness is perhaps the most well recognized flaw in the social functioning of sex offenders (Boozer, 1975; Cohen et al., 1969; Marshall, 1971; Murphy, Quinsey, & Marshall, 1981; Stermac & Quinsey, 1982). However, descriptions of this inadequacy have focused on conversational skills for the most part, although some therapists also point to deficiencies in sexual skills (Abel, Blanchard, & Becker, 1977; Marshall & Williams, 1975). Behaviors that serve to develop and maintain effective relationships have been neglected in both treatment and research with sex offenders.

a) *Conversational skills* include both motoric and cognitive elements combined in such a way as to effectively initiate, maintain, and terminate conversations. Low competency individuals are identified with greater consistency (Bellack, 1979; Curran, 1979) when raters employ global judgments of a particular dimension of social behavior (e.g., skill or anxiety), rather than when they are required to perform micro-analyses of discrete conversational elements (e.g., eye contact; facial expressions; rate, volume, tone and content of speech). The validation of criterion-referenced behaviors, however, is still an important goal with respect to training conversational skills; at this time, research (Conger & Farrell, 1981; Conger, Wallander, Mariotto, & Ward, 1980; Kupke, Hobbs, & Cheney, 1979) has identified a number of discrete behaviors which are functionally related to competence ratings (e.g., attention to those personal details mentioned by the conversational partner).

McFall (1982) recommends evaluating and treating the processes of conversational skills according to his model. As he points out, most of the early research in this area narrowly defined conversational skills in motoric (or verbal/motoric) terms, and it is only recently that interest has been generated in the person's ability to accurately perceive the responses of the conversational partner (Morrison & Bellack, 1981) and to time his or her own behavior to encourage and reward the other person's responses (Fischetti, Curran & Westberg, 1977). We (Marshall, & Reed, 1982) have recently shown that, indeed, rapists do have difficulty in accurately perceiving appropriate social behavior in others, although they appear to share this inadequacy with other prisoners, as well as more generally with other males from similar socioeconomic backgrounds.

In addition, conversational skills involve the capacity to consider various alternative responses, many of which may be equally appropriate and effective, when faced with a particular situation. The ability to generate these alternatives and then decide among them is an important conversational skill. So also is the capacity to assert oneself and to accurately distingush this from aggression. In our study of rapists' social perception (Marshall & Reed, 1982), we found that sexual aggressors were more likely than middle-class normal males to judge aggression to be socially appropriate and more effective than those behaviors usually defined as appropriate assertion. However, rapists did not differ in this regard from males of similarly low socioeconomic status. These observations not only indicate a difference in judgment about what is or is not acceptable behavior, but also suggest that these men feel a good deal of hostility. We (Marshall & Ruhl, 1982) have found this to be the case, although again it seems to be a socioeconomic class response rather than particular to sex offenders.

Of course, assertion is nowadays taken to mean not only standing up for one's rights and expressing negative feelings, but also the ability to declare positive feelings without overdoing it (Rimm & Masters, 1979). This latter feature is related to the vital tendency to reward or encourage one's conversational partner, although again we must guard against making this obvious. All of these abilities may be present within the person's behavioral repertoire but may be inhibited by anxiety. Anxiety management training of one sort or another should be implemented when assessment indicates that it is interfering with performance.

The assessment of conversational skills relies on a free-conversation format in which the offender is presented with a detailed scenario (e.g., approaching a woman sitting alone at a bar and trying to get to know her). He is asked to converse with the confederate as he might do in the actual situation. Interactions are videotaped and rated by independent trained observers for degree of skill and anxiety at both the global and discrete behavioral skills level. A sampling of thoughts generated by the interaction provides an estimate of the cognitive distortions or negative evaluations made by the patient (Glass & Merluzzi, 1981). Both participants (i.e., the offender and the confederate) rate each other's behavior, with the offender also being required to describe the confederate's feelings and interests. Questionnaires which describe various conversational situations call for the offender to identify the range of responses that he could emit, along with an evaluation of the possible outcome for each response. In addition to these procedures, we also measure assertiveness using a scale developed earlier with a general prison population (Keltner, Marshall, & Marshall, 1981; Marshall, Keltner, & Marshall, 1981). This scale describes a variety of situations involving either a male or female with whom the respondent is said to interact. Each situation calls for a response and the offender selects one of five alternatives, ranging from markedly unassertive to physically aggressive. Respondents are to identify both what they think they *would* do and what they think they *should* do. In this way we get not only an indication of their capacity to enact skilled behavior, but also some glimpse of their understanding of what is appropriate. We (Keltner et al., 1981) have demonstrated the validity and reliability of this scale.

These evaluations are completed before and after skills training, with new confederates being used on each occasion. We attempt to equate confederates for attractiveness, sociability, and age.

Skills training is conducted on both an individual and a group basis. Individual training involves role-playing in which the offender is: 1) given instructions on possible appropriate and less than appropriate responses, including advice on likely outcomes; 2) provided with modeled examples of these responses; 3) given the opportunity to try out these responses; and 4) provided with feedback regarding the adequacy of these responses. We emphasize the use of specific motor responses, including verbal behaviors, as well as improving overall assertiveness, increasing the precision of the timing of behavior, and directing the patients' attention to the need for reciprocity in conversations (i.e., they must reward and encourage the other person). During the course of these rehearsals, the offender is given advice concerning the accurate perception of the other person's feelings, etc., and how he might respond to these feelings. He is also encouraged to act on these perceptions. These latter procedures follow those prescribed by Greenberg and Safran (1981) and represent an attempt to intervene at the encoding stage of McFall's model. Faulty encoding is modified by perceptual retraining, which emphasizes the importance of the process of constructing one's own reality.

Within the group context, which is actually employed to train other aspects of behavior within a directed discussion-style format, offenders are encouraged to employ the skills acquired in the individual training, with the therapist correcting any errors as they occur. As an adjunct to this format, clients participate in a social skills game adapted from Quinsey and Varney (1977) by Gordon, Yates, Bellemare and Williams (1977). This provides an entertaining format that keeps offenders involved while training them in the effective use of various conversational skills.

b) *Sexual skills* are said to be deficient in sex offenders (Abel, Blanchard, & Becker, 1977; Marshall, Christie & Lanthier, 1977); these deficiencies include: lack of knowledge (Abel, Blanchard, & Becker, 1977), inappropriate attitudes toward women and children (Hegeman & Meikle, 1980), prudishness (Marshall et al., 1977; Record, 1977), and on occasion sexual dysfunctions (Abel, Blanchard, & Becker, 1977). In addition to the inappropriate attitudes toward women that have been identified by many researchers (e.g., traditional views of sex role behaviors; double standards for sexual behaviors by males and females; the belief that women who are sexually provocative, or who dress attractively, or who fail to take excessive precautions, deserve to be raped, etc.), there is evidence that sex offenders are hostile toward females (Groth, 1979) and that this is expressed in physical violence and attempts to humiliate and degrade the victims of sexual attacks (Darke, Marshall & Earls, 1982). We have recently (Darke et al., 1982) examined transcripts of interviews with convicted rapists and analyzed police reports, both of which sources reveal clear attempts to degrade and humiliate the victims. These attempts frequently have no bearing on the successful achievement of the offender's goal of raping the woman, although occasionally they seem to be incited by the offenders' failure to obtain an erection or to achieve orgasm. Whether this reflects a general tendency to sexual dysfunction or whether the dysfunction is brought on by the situation is not yet clear.

We are presently developing procedures for assessing and training these various features of behavior, but these are not yet complete. Hegeman and Meikle (1980) and Malamuth (1982) have measures of inappropriate attitudes that may be adaptable for our purposes, and Record (1977) employed a measure of prudishness that can easily be modified. As yet we have not developed satisfactory measures of the intent to do violence to the victim or to humiliate and degrade her. While erectile measures may be responsive to these features added to ongoing descriptions of forced sex, such intentions may prove to be independent of sexual motives; consequently, independent assessment will be necessary. Sexual dysfunctions should be discernible during interviews conducted before the processes outlined here are initiated. Once dysfunctions have been identified, they are assessed and treated according to existing procedures described in the literature (cf. Kaplan, 1974). An inventory of sexual knowledge is being developed. This will be based on a determination of the content of a course in sexual education that attempts to modify attitudes and prudishness as well as expanding knowledge. On this point we consider it inappropriate to focus on technical aspects of anatomy and physiology; we prefer to focus on the functional utility of behaviors and to couch explanations and information in terms suitable to the population. This group sex education also attempts to modify, by discussion and information-giving, those inappropriate attitudes noted earlier, as well as the restrictive prudish views that limit the possibility of mutual enjoyment during sex.

c) *Relationship skills* have for the most part been considered within the context of marital problems (Jacobson & Dallas, 1981). Marital satisfaction has been found to be a function of: the rewarding behaviors of each partner (Wills, Weiss, & Patterson, 1974); the perception of the significance of rewards or punishers (Jacobson & Margolin, 1979); conflict-resolution skills (Gottman, 1979); appropriate reciprocity in the relationship (Patterson & Reid, 1970); effective communication skills (Markman, 1979); and avoidance of boredom with one another (Jacobson, 1979). When these skills are absent or eroded, then marital dissatisfaction occurs, and this is often associated with an increase in arguments and the concomitant display of anger or aggression. Of course, an inability to control anger or to express it appropriately often in itself reduces marital satisfaction, and several rapists have told us that frequent arguments characterized their relationships with females. These same rapists also told us that when they were angered in this way they were far more likely to sexually assault a woman. Groth (1979) is similarly convinced that anger is a major factor in the commission of sexual assaults. Our own research has demonstrated that when normal males are angered by a female, their sexual responses to rape markedly increase (Yates, Barbaree, & Marshall, 1980). If conflict in relationships induces anger and anger increases the probability of sexual aggression, then procedures that reduce relationship conflict should be included in the treatment of sexual offenders.

We follow the procedures suggested by Jacobson, Elwood and Dallas (1981) in the assessment of the skills necessary to maintain a relationship, and these assessments focus on the behaviors outlined above. We then follow that with treatment procedures recommended by Jacobson and Dallas (1981), with adjustments made for the fact that we are working within the walls of a prison, without a partner available, and often in the absence of any ongoing relationship, These latter factors limit the scope and possibly the effectiveness of treatment, just as they do for any form of intervention we undertake. The major portion of this therapy is conducted within the context of a group, except for that aspect dealing with anger and aggression. For the latter the assessment procedures follow those recommended by Edmunds and Kendrick (1980) and include both cognitive and behavioral evaluations. Treatment of anger has been limited, but assertive training, which is included in our conversational skills program, is often sufficient to bring aggression under control (Marshall, Keltner & Marshall, 1981; Rimm, 1977). Where assertive training proves to be insufficient, either stress inoculation (Novaco, 1977) or flooding therapy (Marshall, Gauthier, & Gordon, 1979) is usually effective.

Of course, in order for a man to need effective skills in maintaining a relationship, he must first be able to secure a partner. We have already discussed some of the problems associated with initiating a relationship when considering conversational skills, but in addition a man must seek an appropriate partner. Selecting a possible partner may determine the outcome of our client's best efforts, and errors in such selection may preclude the success of even the most effective use of the skills we have taught. Unfortunately, there is no literature that addresses this issue, not even that concerned with dating skills (Curran, 1981), where one might expect this to be a key issue. It may seem unnecessary to teach clients that they are more likely to enjoy an effective long-term relationship with someone who shares similar interests and activities, but in the course of training dating skills in undergraduate clients we have found that few of them give any thought to their likely compatibility with a prospective partner. Unfortunately, there are no readily available assessment procedures for these problems, but we are working on their development. For the present, these procedures are limited to appraisals of the offenders' views on the range of features in a partner that might maximize the possibility of developing a good and relatively permanent relationship. Once we have identified the limits of their views, we use a group format and role-playing to demonstrate the consequences of choosing partners with varying degrees of compatibility.

Personal Management Skills

These skills cover: a) those necessary to seek, secure, and maintain appropriate accommodation (including budgeting and housekeeping skills) and appropriate employment; and b) the effective use of leisure, including control over intoxicated behavior and perhaps control over the actual use of alcohol or drugs. Anyone having difficulties in these areas is likely to experience stress, which, as we have already argued, will increase the probability of offensive behavior.

Little has been done within the psychological or psychiatric literature concerning any of these behaviors, except control over alcohol and drug use. Many researchers have remarked on the use of alcohol by sexual offenders and suggested that it plays a role in the commission of the crimes (Leppman, 1941; Swanson, 1968). Whether alcohol reduces social inhibitions, obscures accurate perceptions, or impairs control over sexual arousal is not clearly understood at the moment, although we have some evidence (Wydra et al., 1981) suggesting that intoxicated individuals are just as perceptive and able to exercise just as much control as are non-intoxicated subjects. In any case, control over alcohol is occasionally a relevant target for treatment with sex offenders. In this regard we follow Sobell and Sobell's (1973) procedures for both assessment and treatment. In most instances, however, we do not attempt to bring alcohol use under control; rather, we prefer to allow continued use of intoxicants, since most of our offenders will return to an environment where there is considerable pressure to continue such use. We think it is best to attempt to train individuals to behave more appropriately when intoxicated, since we have evidence that alcohol ingestion, at the least, changes quite normal individuals so that they find sexual aggression more erotically arousing (Barbaree, Marshall, Lightfoot, & Yates, 1979). Again, we are busy working on developing appropriate measurement and treatment procedures.

Similarly, we are taxing our ingenuity to develop assessment and training procedures for the other behaviors we have identified as personal management skills, although to date we have followed the well-articulated strategies of life skill coaches (Conger, 1973). It is clear that lack of attention to these factors may allow the continuation of a high level of stress in the offender's life after release. Furthermore, many offenders have told us that their urge to sexually assault a woman or child increases when they are bored. Being out of work or being unable to effectively utilize leisure time frequently leads to boredom, so that anything that improves their capacities in these areas should serve to minimize the risk of recidivism.

In closing, this section has outlined an approach to social incompetence in sex offenders which is more comprehensive than earlier models. Due to the lack of established procedures, some of our recommendations for assessment and training are necessarily speculative. We expect that as we employ these procedures under carefully controlled conditions, the data will direct us to more empirically based approaches to both treatment and assessment.

THE TREATMENT AND ASSESSMENT PROCESS

With minor variations for specific individuals, the comprehensive behavioral program that we recommend is outlined as a flow chart in Table 1.

The intake interviews focus on the patient's social and sexual history. Several sessions may be necessary to secure all this information, as well as to familiarize the patient with the setting and the approach to assess-

TABLE 1
Progression of Patients Through Behavioral Program

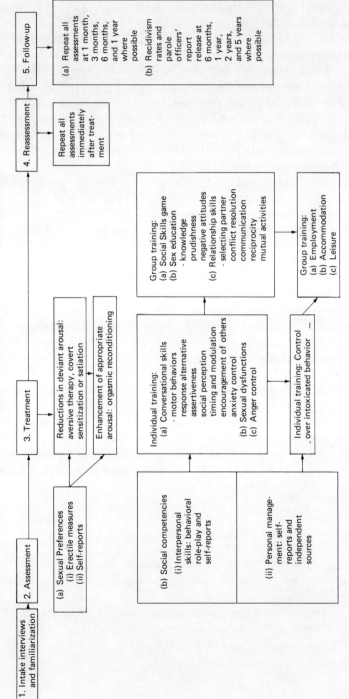

ment and treatment. Sexual deviations are conceptualized as bad habits resulting from skills deficits and the patient is advised that he can learn the skills necessary to control his behavior and enjoy a satisfactorily acceptable social and sexual adjustment. Patients are advised that a team approach is employed and, although one person is assigned as the patient's representative, at one time or another all members of the team are involved with him. All patients are required to sign a general consent form before progressing to the next step.

At the initial assessment session patients are familiarized with the procedures and given a trial run on the erectile assessment procedure so that it is clear to them what it involves. They are then required to sign an assessment consent form. Once assessments are complete, the patient is assigned to those treatment components that evaluations have shown to be necessary. Again, treatment-specific consent forms are signed before interventions commence.

Reassessments and early follow-up evaluations target the same problems, using the same measures as the pretreatment procedures. It is, of course, not always possible to secure all evaluations over extended periods, and, in fact, the outline in Table 1 is rather ideal and unlikely to be manageable in all cases. However, every attempt should be made to obtain as much data as possible.

REFERENCES

ABEL, G.G. *Treatment of sexual aggressives.* Paper presented at 3rd National Conference on the Evaluation and Treatment of Sexual Aggressives, Avila Beach, California, May, 1981.

ABEL, G.G., & ANNON, J.S. *Satiation therapy.* Paper presented at the 4th National Conference on the Evaluation and Treatment of Sexual Aggressives, Denver, April, 1982.

ABEL, G.G., BARLOW, D.H., BLANCHARD, E.B. & GUILD, D. The components of rapists' sexual arousal. *Archives of General Psychiatry,* 1977, *34,* 895-903.

ABEL, G.G., BLANCHARD, E.B., & BECKER, J.V. An integrated treatment program for rapists. In R. Rada (Ed.) *Clinical aspects of the rapist.* New York: Grune & Stratton, 1977.

ABEL, G.G., LEVIS, D., & CLANCY, J. Aversion therapy applied to taped sequences of deviant behavior in exhibitionism and other sexual deviation: A preliminary report. *Journal of Behavior Therapy and Experimental Psychiatry,* 1970, *1,* 58-66.

AMIR, M. *Patterns in forcible rape.* Chicago: University of Chicago Press, 1971.

ANNON, J.S. The extension of learning principles to the analysis and treatment of sexual problems. *Dissertation Abstracts International,* 1971, *32*(6B), 3627.

BANCROFT, J.H.J., JONES, H.G., & PULLEN, B.R. A simple transducer for measuring penile erection with comments on its use in the treatment of sexual disorder. *Behaviour Research and Therapy,* 1966, *4,* 230-241.

BARBAREE, H.E., MARSHALL, W.L., & LANTHIER, R.D. Deviant sexual arousal in rapists. *Behaviour Research and Therapy,* 1979, *16,* 215-222.

BARBAREE, H.E., MARSHALL, W.L., LIGHTFOOT, L., & YATES, E. *The effects of alcohol on sexual aggression.* Paper presented at the 2nd National Conference on the Evaluation and Treatment of Sexual Aggressives, New York, May, 1979.

BARLOW, D.H., BECKER, R., LEITENBERG, H., & AGRAS, W.S. A mechanical strain gauge for recording penile circumference change. *Journal of Applied Behavior Analysis*, 1970, *3*, 73-76.

BARR, R., & BLASZCZYNSKI, A. Autonomic responses of trans-sexual and homosexual males to erotic film sequences. *Archives of Sexual Behavior*, 1976, *5*, 211-222.

BAXTER, D., MARSHALL, W.L., BARBAREE, H., MALCOLM, B., & DAVIDSON, P. The erectile responses of rapists and normals to depictions of mutually consenting and forced sex. Unpublished manuscript. Regional Psychiatric Centre (Ontario) Canadian Correctional Services, Kingston, Ontario, 1982.

BEECH, H.R., WATTS, F., & POOLE, A.P. Classical conditioning of a sexual deviation: A preliminary note. *Behavior Therapy*, 1971, *2*, 400-402.

BEGELMAN, D.A. Ethical and legal issues of behavior modification. In M. Hersen, R.M. Eisler & P.M. Miller (Eds.) *Progress in behavior modification*, Vol. 1, New York: Academic Press, 1975.

BELLACK, A.S. Behavioral assessment of social skills. In A.. Bellack & M. Hersen (Eds.) *Research and practice in social skills*, New York: Plenum Press, 1979.

BOOZER, G. *Offender Treatment*. Presented at 7th Alabama Symposium on Justice and the Behavioral Sciences. University of Alabama, Tuscaloosa, Alabama, January, 1975.

CHRISTIE, M.M., MARSHALL, W.L., & LANTHIER, R.D. A descriptive study of incarcerated rapists and pedophiles. Report to the Solicitor General of Canada, Ottawa, 1979.

COHEN, M., SEGHORN, T., & CALAMUS, W. Sociometric study of the sex offender. *Journal of Abnormal Psychology*, 1969, *14*, 249-255.

CONGER, A.J., WALLANDER, J.L., MARIOTTO, M.J., & WARD, D. Peer judgements of heterosexual-social anxiety and skill: What do they pay attention to anyhow? *Behavioral Assessment*, 1980, *2*, 243-259.

CONGER, D.S. *Life skills coaching manual*. Prince Albert, Saskatchewan: Saskatchewan Newstart Inc., 1973.

CONGER, J.C., & FARRELL, A.D. Behavioral components of heterosocial skills. *Behavior Therapy*, 1981, *12*, 41-55.

CONRAD, S.R., & WINCZE, J.P. Orgasmic reconditioning: A controlled study of its effects upon the sexual arousal and behavior of adult male homosexuals. *Behavior Therapy*, 1976, *7*, 155-166.

CURRAN, J.P. Social skills: Methodological issues and future directions. In A.S. Bellack & M. Hersen (Eds.) *Research and practice in social skills*. New York: Plenum Press, 1979.

CURRAN, J.P. Social-skills and assertion training. In W.E. Craighead, A.E. Kazdin & M.J. Mahoney (Eds.) *Behavior modification: Principles, issues, and applications*, 2nd Edition. Boston: Houghton Mifflin, 1981.

DARKE, J., MARSHALL, W.L., & EARLS, C.M. *Intent to humiliate during sexual assaults: Cultural and treatment suggestions for the prevention of rape*. Paper presented at the 4th National Conference on the Evaluation and Treatment of Sexual Aggressives, Denver, April, 1982.

DAVIDSON, P.R. *Recidivism patterns among groups of rapists*. Paper presented at the 43rd Annual Convention of the Canadian Pychological Association, Montreal, June, 1982.

DAVISON, G. Elimination of a sadistic fantasy by a client-controlled counter-conditioning technique: A case study. *Journal of Abnormal Psychology*, 1968, *73*, 84-90.

DOHRENWEND, B.S., & DOHRENWEND, B.P. *Stressful life events: Their nature and effects*. New York: Wiley, 1974.

EARLS, C.M., & MARSHALL, W.L. The current state of technology in the laboratory assessment of sexual arousal patterns. In J.G. Greer & I.R. Stuart (Eds.) *Sexual aggression: Current perspectives on treatment*. New York: Van Nostrand Reinhold, in press, 1982.

EDMUNDS, G., & KENDRICK, D.C. *The measurement of human aggressiveness*. Chichester, England: Ellis Horwood Ltd., 1980.

FEDERAL BUREAU OF INVESTIGATION. *Uniform Crime Reports*, 1980. Washington: United States Government Printing Office, 1980.

FINKELHOR, D. *Sexually victimized children*. New York: Free Press, 1979.

FISCHETTI, M., CURRAN, J.P., & WESTBERG, H.W. Sense of timing: A skill deficit in heterosexual-socially anxious males. *Behavior Modification*, 1977, *1*, 179-194.

FREUND, K. A laboratory method for diagnosing predominance of homo- and hetero-erotic interest in the male. *Behaviour Research and Therapy*, 1963, *1*, 85-93.

FREUND, K. Diagnosing homo- and hetero-sexuality and erotic age preference by means of a psychophysiological test. *Behaviour Research and Therapy*, 1967, *5*, 209-228.

FRISBIE, L., & DONDIS, E. Recidivism among treated sex offenders. *California Mental Health Research Monographs*, 1965, *5*, 1.

GLASS, C.R., & MERLUZZI, T.V. Cognitive assessment of social-evaluation anxiety. In T.V. Merluzzi, C.R. Glass, & M. Genest (Eds.) *Cognitive assessment*. New York: Guilford Press, 1981.

GORDON, A., WEISMAN, R.G., & MARSHALL, W.L. *The effects of flooding with response freedom on social anxiety*. Paper presented at the 14th Annual Convention of the Association for the Advancement of Behavior Therapy, New York, November, 1980.

GORDON, A., YATES, E., BELLEMARE, F., & WILLIAMS, S. *A game format for training social skills*. Paper presented at the 11th Annual Meeting of the Association for the Advancement of Behavior Therapy. Atlanta, December, 1977.

GOTTMAN, J.M. *Marital interaction: Experimental investigations*. New York: Academic Press, 1979.

GREENBERG, L.S., & SAFRAN, J.D. Encoding and cognitive therapy: Changing what clients attend to. *Psychotherapy: Theory, Research and Practice*, 1981, *18*, 163-169.

GROTH, A.N. *Men who rape: The psychology of the offender*. New York: Plenum Press, 1979.

HEGEMAN, N., & MEIKLE, S. Motives and attitudes of rapists. *Canadian Journal of Behavioral Science*, 1980, *4*, 359-372.

HERMAN, S.H., BARLOW, D.H., & AGRAS, W.S. An experimental analysis of classical conditioning as a method of increasing heterosexual arousal in homosexuals. *Behavior Therapy*, 1974, *5*, 33-47.

HERSEN, M., & BELLACK, A.S. Social skills training for chronic psychiatric patients: Rationale, research findings, and future directions. *Comprehensive Psychiatry*, 1976, *17*, 559-580.

JACOBSON, N.S. Behavioral treatments for marital discord: A critical appraisal. In M. Hersen, R.M. Eisler, & P.M. Miller (Eds.) *Progress in behavior modification*, Vol. 8. New York: Academic Press, 1979.

JACOBSON, N.S., & DALLAS, M. Helping married couples improve their relationship. In W.E. Craighead, A.E. Kazdin, & M.J. Mahoney (Eds.) *Behavior modification: Principles, issues, and applications*. Boston: Houghton Mifflin, 1981.

JACOBSON, N.S., ELWOOD, R.W., & DALLAS, M. Assessment of marital dysfunction. In D.H. Barlow (Ed.) *Behavioral assessment of adult disorders*. New York: Guilford Press, 1981.

JACOBSON, N.S. & MARGOLIN, G. *Marital therapy: Strategies based on social learning and behavior exchange principles*. New York: Brunner/Mazel, 1979.

KAPLAN, H.S. *The new sex therapy*. New York: Brunner/Mazel, 1974.

KELTNER, A.A., MARSHALL, P.G., & MARSHALL, W.L. Measurements and correlation of assertiveness and social fear in a prison population. *Corrective and Social Psychiatry*, 1981, *27*, 1.

KUPKE, T.E., HOBBS, S.A., & CHENEY, T.M. Selection of heterosexual skills. 1. Criterion related validity. *Behavior Therapy*, 1979, *10*, 327-335.

LANG, P.J. Research on the specificity of feedback training: Implication for the use of biofeedback in the treatment of anxiety and fear. In J. Beatty & H. Legewie (Eds.) *Biofeedback and behavior*. New York: Plenum Press, 1977.

LANGEVIN, R., PAITICH, D., RAMSEY, G., ANDERSON, C., POPE, S., PEARL, L., & NEWMAN, S. Experimental studies of the etiology of genital exhibitionism. *Archives of Sexual Behavior*, 1979, *8*, 307-331.

LAWS, D.R., & SERBER, M. Measurements and evaluation of assertive training with sexual offenders. In R.E. Hosford & C.S. Moss (Eds.) *The crumbling walls: Treatment and counseling of prisoners.* Champaign, Ill.: University of Illinois Press, 1975.

LAZARUS, R.D., & LAUNIER, R. Stress-related transactions between person and environment. In L.A. Pervin & M. Lewis (Eds.) *Internal and external determinants of behavior.* New York: Plenum, 1979.

LEPPMAN, F. Essential differences between sex offenders. *Journal of Criminal Law and Criminology,* 1941, *32,* 366.

MALAMUTH, N. *Factors related to aggression against women.* Paper presented at the 43rd Annual Convention of the Canadian Psychological Association, Montreal, June, 1982.

MALETZKY, B.M. "Assisted" covert sensitization in the treatment of exhibitionism. *Journal of Consulting and Clinical Psychology,* 1974, *42,* 34-40.

MARKMAN, H.J. Application of a behavioral model of marriage in predicting relationship satisfaction of couples planning marriage. *Journal of Consulting and Clinical Psychology,* 1979, *47,* 743-749.

MARKS, I.M. Management of sexual disorders. In H. Leitenberg (Ed.) *Handbook of behavior modification and behavior therapy.* Englewood Cliffs, N.J.: Prentice-Hall, 1976.

MARKS, I.M., & GELDER, M. Transvestism and fetishism: Clinical and psychological changes during faradic aversion. *British Journal of Psychiatry,* 1967, *113,* 711-729.

MARQUIS, J.N. Orgasmic reconditioning: Changing sexual choice through controlling masturbatory fantasies. *Journal of Behaviour Therapy and Experimental Psychiatry,* 1970, *1,* 263-271.

MARSHALL, P.J., KELTNER, A.A., & MARSHALL, W.L. Anxiety reduction, assertive training and enactment of consequences: A comparative treatment study in the modification of nonassertion and social fear. *Behavior Modification,* 1981, *5,* 85-102.

MARSHALL, W.L. A combined treatment method for certain sexual deviations. *Behaviour Research and Therapy,* 1971, *9,* 292-294.

MARSHALL, W.L. The modification of sexual fantasies: A combined treatment approach to the reduction of deviant sexual behavior. *Behaviour Research and Therapy,* 1973, *11,* 557-564.

MARSHALL, W.L. The classical conditioning of sexual attractiveness: A report of four therapeutic failures. *Behavior Therapy,* 1974, *5,* 298-299.

MARSHALL, W.L. The prediction of treatment outcome with sexual deviants based on changes in erectile responses to deviant and nondeviant stimuli. Unpublished report, Queen's University, Kingston, Ontario, 1975.

MARSHALL, W.L. Satiation therapy: A procedure for reducing deviant sexual arousal. *Journal of Applied Behavior Analysis,* 1979, *12,* 10-22.

MARSHALL, W.L. The classification of sexual aggresors. In S. Verdun-Jones & A. Keltner (Eds.) *Sexual aggression and the law.* Simon-Fraser University Press: Burnaby, B.C., 1982a.

MARSHALL, W.L. *Aggression in child molestors.* Paper presented at the 8th International Congress on Law and Psychiatry, Quebec City, June, 1982b.

MARSHALL, W.L., & CHRISTIE, M.M., & LANTHIER, R.D. *Social competence, sexual experience, and attitudes to sex in incarcerated rapists and pedophiles.* Report to Solicitor General of Canada, Ottawa, 1977.

MARSHALL, W.L., GAUTHIER, J., & GORDON, A. The current status of flooding therapy. In M. Hersen, R.M. Eisler, & P.M. Miller (Eds.) *Progress in behavior modification,* Vol. 7. New York: Academic Press, 1979.

MARSHALL, W.L., & LIPPENS, K. The clinical value of boredom: A procedure for reducing inappropriate sexual interests. *Journal of Nervous and Mental Diseases,* 1977, 165, 283-287.

MARSHALL, W.L., & REED, M. The accuracy of social perception in rapists. Unpublished manuscript, Queen's University, Kingston, Ontario, Canada, 1982.

MARSHALL, W.L., & RUHL, M. Hostility and assertiveness in sex offenders. Unpublished manuscript, Queen's University, Kingston, Ontario, Canada, 1982.

MARSHALL, W.L., & WILLIAMS, S.M. *A behavioral treatment program for incarcerated sex offenders: Some tentative results.* Paper presented at the Annual Convention of the Association for the Advancement of Behavior Therapy, San Francisco, December, 1975.

MAVISSAKALIAN, M., BLANCHARD, E.B., ABEL, G.G., & BARLOW, D.H. Responses to complex erotic stimuli in homosexual and heterosexual males. *British Journal of Psychiatry,* 1975, *126,* 252-257.

McCONAGHY, N. Penile volume changes to moving pictures of male and female nudes in heterosexual and homosexual males. *Behaviour Research and Therapy,* 1967, *5,* 43-48.

McFall, R.M. A review and reformulation of the concept of social skills. *Behavioral Assessment,* 1982, *4,* 1-33.

McFALL, R.M., & LILLESAND, D.B. Behavior rehearsal with modeling and coaching in assertion training. *Journal of Abnormal Psychology,* 1971, *77,* 313-323.

MOOS, R.H. *Human adaptation: Coping with life crises.* Lexington, Mass.: D.C. Heath, 1976.

MORRISON, R.L., & BELLACK, A.S. The role of social perception in social skill. *Behavior Therapy,* 1981, *12,* 69-79.

MURPHY, W.D., QUINSEY, V.L., & MARSHALL, W.L. *Social skills of sexual aggressives.* Paper presented at the 3rd National Conference on the Evaluation and Treatment of Sexual Aggressives, Avila Beach, California, March, 1981.

NOVACO, R.W. Stress inoculation: A cognitive therapy for anger and its application to a case of depression. *Journal of Consulting and Clinical Psychology,* 1977, *45,* 600-608.

PATTERSON, G.R., & REID, J.B. Reciprocity and coercion: Two facets of social systems. In C. Neuringer & J.L. Michael (Eds.) *Behavior modification in clinical psychology.* New York: Appleton-Century-Crofts, 1970.

PHILLIPS, E.L. *The social skills basis of psychotherapy.* New York: Grune & Stratton, 1978.

QUINSEY, V. The assessment and treatment of child molestors: A review. *Canadian Psychological Review,* 1977, *18,* 204-220.

QUINSEY, V.L. *Prediction of recidivism and the evaluation of treatment programs for sex offenders.* Paper presented at Sexual Aggressives and the Law: A Symposium. Vancouver, October, 1981.

QUINSEY, V.L., CHAPLIN, T.C., & CARRIGAN, W.F. Biofeedback and signalled punishment in the modification of inappropriate sexual age preferences. *Behavior Therapy,* 1980, *11,* 567-576.

QUINSEY, V.L., CHAPLIN, T.C., & VARNEY, G. A comparison of rapists' and non-sex offenders' sexual preferences for mutually consenting sex, rape, and physical abuse of women. *Behavioral Assessment,* 1981, *3,* 127-135.

QUINSEY, V. & MARSHALL, W.L. Procedures for reducing deviant arousal: A comparative evaluation. In J.G. Greer & I.R. Stuart (Eds.) *Sexual aggression: Current perspectives on treatment.* New York: Van Nostrand, 1983.

QUINSEY, V.L., & VARNEY, G.W. Social skills game: A general method for the modelling and practice of adaptive behaviors. *Behavior Therapy,* 1977, *8,* 279-281.

RECORD, S.A. Personality, sexual attitudes and behavior of sex offenders. Unpublished doctoral thesis, Queen's University, Kingston, Ontario, 1977.

RIMM, D.C. Assertive training and the expression of anger. In R.E. Alberti (Ed.) *Assertiveness: Innovations, applications, issues.* San Luis Obispo, Calif.: Impact Publishers, 1977.

RIMM, D.C., & MASTERS, J.C. *Behavior therapy: Techniques and empirical findings* 2nd Edition. New York: Academic Press, 1979.

ROSEN, R.C., & KEEFE, F.J. The measurement of human penile tumescence. *Psychophysiology,* 1978, *15,* 366-376.

SALTER, A. *Conditioned reflex therapy.* New York: Capricorn, 1949.

SELYE, H. *The stress of life.* New York: McGraw-Hill, 1956.

SOBELL, M.B., & SOBELL, L.C. Individualized behavior therapy for alcoholics. *Behavior Therapy,* 1973, *4,* 49-72.

STERMAC, L.E., & QUINSEY, V.L. Social competence in rapists. Unpublished manuscript. Mental Health Centre, Penetanguishene, 1982.

STURUP, G.K. Castration: The total treatment. In H.L.P. Resnick & M.F. Wolfgang, (Eds.) *Sexual Behavior.* Boston: Little, Brown, 1972.

SWANSON, D.W. Adult sexual abuse of children. *Diseases of the Nervous System,* 1968, *29,* 677-683.

TWENTYMAN, C.T., & McFALL, R.M. Behavioral training of social skills in shy males. *Journal of Consulting and Clinical Psychology,* 1975, *43,* 384-395.

WILLS, T.A., WEISS, R.L., & PATTERSON, G.R. A behavioral analysis of the determinants of marital satisfaction. *Journal of Consulting and Clinical Psychology,* 1974, *42,* 802-811.

WOLPE, J. *The practice of behavior therapy.* New York: Pergamon Press, 1969.

WYDRA, A., MARSHALL, W.L., BARBAREE, H.E., & EARLS, C.M. *Control of sexual arousal by rapists and nonrapists.* Paper presented at the 42nd Annual Convention of the Canadian Psychological Association, Toronto, June, 1981.

YATES, E., BARBAREE, H.E., & MARSHALL, W.L. *The effects of "anger" on sexual arousal to rape cues.* Paper presented at the 14th Annual Convention of the Association for the Advancement of Behavior Therapy, New York, November, 1980.

8

Behavioral Research and Therapy: Its Impact on the Alcohol Field

LINDA C. SOBELL and MARK B. SOBELL

INTRODUCTION: PHENOMENOLOGICAL AND EMPIRICAL CONCEPTUALIZATIONS OF ALCOHOL PROBLEMS

Over the past two decades, the conceptual framework of the alcohol field has been unprecedentedly challenged. This challenge has emanated from many factors, including: 1) public health and economic concerns regarding the consequences of alcohol use and abuse; 2) the relative ineffectiveness of traditional alcohol treatment approaches; 3) increased funding for alcohol research; and, in particular, 4) the early success of behavioral research and treatment in the alcohol field.

The alcohol field's protracted failure to make significant clinical and research advances prior to the mid 1960s relates to the fact that the field has been guided by a model of alcoholism that has a phenomenological rather than an empirical basis (Pattison, Sobell, & Sobell, 1977). In large part, the traditional model of alcoholism is a collection of unvalidated premises which have guided and directed most alcohol research and treatment (see Pattison et al., 1977). Basically, the model is a set of *beliefs*, rather than a set of working hypotheses. Consequently, the traditional model has made it difficult to conduct research which might produce results incongruent with the prevailing tenets.

While traditionalists in the alcohol field have been guided by a model of alcoholism, behaviorists have used a model of behavior to study alcohol problems. The behavioral model relies on scientific method to test and validate theoretical propositions. Interestingly, while the greatest and most consistent strength of behavioral research has been its reliance on scientific method, this reliance has also resulted in behavioral research findings being inconsistent with many elements of the traditional model of alcoholism. In this regard, by way of caveat, Rankin and his colleagues (Rankin, Hodgson, & Stockwell, 1979), noting the traditional model's phenomenological origins, have cogently pointed out that the "experimental results were not, as it is sometimes assumed, at variance with the clinical facts, merely at variance with the overgeneralization of the clinical anecdote" (p. 389).

Behavioral and other empirical research in the alcohol field has now produced an impressive body of data that conflict with the traditional model. The synthesis of these findings will be referred to as the empirically-based model of alcohol problems. It would be beyond the scope of this chapter to review in detail old and new conceptualizations in the alcohol field. However, it will be helpful to briefly compare and contrast conclusions about the nature of alcohol problems that derive from the empirically-based model with those that derive from the traditional model. When one compares the two models, it is readily apparent that one model relies heavily on empirical data, while the other primarily uses phenomenological evidence. These two different ways of approaching the study of alcohol problems have led to radically different conceptualizations of alcohol problems and of persons with alcohol problems.

For the purposes of this chapter, only a tabular presentation of the major conceptual differences between the two models is necessary. The differences, listed in Table 1, have been discussed in greater detail by Pattison et al. (1977) and Sobell (1981).

These two highly discordant models also define treatment objectives and relapse quite differently. For traditionalists there is only one treatment objective—abstinence. Of course, from this perspective any drinking is considered problematic. The empirical model, however, stresses avoiding drinking that is likely to result in negative consequences. Not surprisingly, each model's definition of relapse is tied to its definition of treatment objectives. From the traditional perspective, *any* drinking constitutes a relapse, whereas in the empirically-based model relapse refers only to drinking that incurs or is likely to incur adverse consequences.

TABLE 1
The Traditional (Phenomenologically-Based)
and Empirically-Based Models of Alcohol Problems

Topic	Traditional Model	Empirically-Based Model
The Nature of Alcohol Problems	A uniform phenomenon (basically the same for all).	A variable phenomenon (defined by physical, psychological, and/or social consequences of alcohol consumption; individuals differ in types and severity of consequences of drinking).
Who Can Develop Alcohol Problems?	Certain people are biologically pre-disposed to alcoholism.	Anyone who drinks (however, there are differential risks based on physical, psychological, and environmental factors).
Control Over Drinking	Alcoholics cannot reliably stop drinking once they start drinking.	Even chronic alcoholics demonstrate excellent control of their drinking, if environmental contingencies are appropriately arranged.
Addiction and Alcohol Consumption	For the once-addicted person, even a small amount of drinking (one or a few drinks) will initiate physical dependence.	Even for chronically addicted persons, physical dependence is only initiated by very heavy, continuous drinking over a two- to five-day period.
The Natural History of Alcohol Problems	Progressive deterioration, whenever the person drinks (characterized by the development of a reliable sequence of symptoms).	Variable over time (the majority of persons move into and out of periods of alcohol problems of varying severity, separated by periods of abstinence or nonproblem drinking; a minority, about 30%, show progressive deterioration).
Reversibility of Alcohol Problems	A permanent disorder (alcoholics can never drink again without eventually experiencing adverse consequences).	A reversible disorder for some (those with less severe histories are more likely to achieve nonproblem drinking).
Treatment Approaches	A standardized, optimal treatment for all.	Treatment is tailored to individual case needs.
Drinking Behavior and Life Health in Treatment Outcome	Abstinence = Improvement in all areas of life health. Drinking = Impairment in multiple areas of life health.	Variable over cases; drinking (or nondrinking) behavior may be positively or negatively, or entirely unrelated to other areas of life health.

PURPOSE OF THIS CHAPTER

In recent years it has become clear that behavioral research and treatment have had a marked impact on many aspects of the alcohol field. The purpose of this chapter is twofold: 1) to identify and discuss major behavioral contributions to the alcohol field and their resultant impact; and 2) to show how behavioral studies have, over time, played a significant role in altering the scientific community's conceptualization of alcohol problems. The intent of this chapter is not to exhaustively review all of the important behavioral studies that have been conducted, but, rather, to highlight and review the major and seminal behavioral contributions to the field of alcohol studies. Therefore, failure to reference a particular study should not be interpreted as suggesting that the study lacks merit.

At the outset, we would like to emphasize that the work of many behavioral scientists has contributed to conceptual changes in the alcohol field. While these contributions can be viewed individually, they have also had a collective influence. In fact, in some cases two different sets of investigators have independently developed and published similar behavioral innovations. For example, both Lovibond and Caddy (1970) and Sobell and Sobell (1973, 1978) developed controlled drinking trials in the early 1970s, but each on a different continent. The taste-rating task was also independently conceived by Marlatt, Demming, and Reid (1973) and by Miller and Hersen (1972).

Finally, as will be apparent from the following review, behavioral research has had a surprisingly diverse impact on the alcohol field, an impact that goes well beyond the simple development of treatment techniques. For organizational purposes, the contributions will be presented and discussed within the context of three major topical areas: basic research, applied research, and assessment and treatment outcome evaluation methodology.

BASIC RESEARCH

The pioneering research of Mendelson and Mello in the early 1960s formed the foundation of basic behavioral research in the alcohol field (e.g., Mello, 1972; Mendelson, 1964). In the ensuing decade, the research of these investigators, as well as the research of three other major groups of behavioral scientists (*Baltimore group*—Bigelow and his colleagues; *Rutgers group*—Nathan and his colleagues; *Patton group*—Schaefer, M.

Sobell, and Mills), individually and collectively provided some very enlightening evidence about the relationships between alcohol problems and drinking behavior. Incredible as it now seems, drinking behavior had not been systematically studied prior to the 1960s. While space does not permit addressing these early advances in detail, they have been reviewed in a number of articles and chapters (Adesso, 1980; Caddy & Gottheil, 1983; Mello, 1972; Nathan & Briddell, 1977). The major contributions of these early basic research studies are outlined in Table 2.

Collectively, these early basic research advances had a sizable impact on the conceptualization of alcohol problems. Most of the early advances derived from controlled studies of experimental intoxication of clinical subjects (subjects were studied while they consumed alcohol under controlled conditions). It should also be noted that these studies exemplify the most fundamental application of scientific method to the study of alcohol problems, i.e., systematic observations of the phenomena under study. While experimental intoxication studies were not the exclusive domain of behavioral researchers, their laboratories accounted for much of this research.

One of the early basic research advances in the alcohol field revealed major differences in the topography of drinking behaviors between chronic alcoholics and normal drinkers. Several studies, including a cross-cultural replication, have now shown that alcoholics and normal drinkers differ on measures of total ethanol consumed, sip size, and rate of drinking (reviewed in Sobell & Sobell, 1978). The other two basic

TABLE 2

Major Contributions of Early Basic Behavioral Research Studies—
Experimental Intoxication Procedures

---

* Laboratory Studies of *Ad Lib* Drinking
    Acute studies (single drinking session): described the topography of drinking behaviors of alcoholics and normal drinkers
    Chronic studies (drinking over extended periods of time): demonstrated that chronic alcoholics, even when addicted, typically modulate their drinking over time

* Studies of the Relationship Between Alcohol Consumption and Physical Dependence (Addiction)
    Established that physical dependence only develops after very large amounts of alcohol are consumed daily for two to five days (minimum necessary condition)

* Studies Demonstrating that the Drinking Behavior, Even of Chronic Alcoholics, Can Be Readily Modified by Environmental Contingencies

---

research advances listed in Table 2, in particular, set the stage for explicit evaluations of nonabstinent treatment goals. First, some of these early studies established that, contrary to traditional notions, physical dependence on alcohol, as indicated by clinical withdrawal symptoms upon cessation of drinking, was not initiated in chronic alcoholics by ingestion of one or a few drinks; rather, it was found that very heavy prolonged drinking was necessary for the development of physical dependence (Ballenger & Post, 1978; Gross, Lewis, & Hastey, 1974; Mello & Mendelson, 1976; Turner, 1980). Typically, an individual has to consume at least the equivalent of a fifth of spirits daily over the course of two to five days. Second, several clinical research studies were published showing that even chronic alcoholics could manifest excellent control over their drinking when environmental contingencies related to their drinking were appropriately arranged (reviewed in Caddy & Gottheil, 1983; Nathan & Briddell, 1977; Pattison et al., 1977; Sobell & Sobell, 1975).

Beyond these early advances, several other basic research advances have contributed notably to the study of alcohol problems. Again, these will only be briefly summarized, since they, too, have been extensively reviewed in the literature (Adesso, 1980; Collins & Marlatt, 1981; Marlatt & Rohsenow, 1980; Nathan & Briddell, 1977; Wilson, 1978). The major contributions of these more recent studies are summarized in Table 3.

TABLE 3

Major Contributions of Recent Basic Behavioral Research Studies

---

Studies Using Primarily Normal Drinker Subjects

* Investigations of Determinants of Drinking, and of the Effects of Drinking of Other Behaviors:
  Use of the balanced-placebo design to separate cognitive (instructional) and pharmacological effects of alcohol—demonstrated that simply being instructed that one is consuming, or has consumed, alcohol can have a significant effect on behavior
  Use of the "taste test" as an unobtrusive behavioral measure of drinking
  Demonstration of a highly robust social influence (co-action) effect on drinking behavior

Studies Using Primarily Clinical Subjects

* The Development of Behavioral Measures of Dependence
* Investigations Further Demonstrating Contingency Control Over Drinking
* Investigations of Conditioning Processes as Related to Drinking Behavior:
  Studies of taste-mediated learning (taste aversion)
  Studies of the conditioning basis (or lack of a basis) for specific treatments (e.g., electrical aversive conditioning, cue exposure)
  Studies of conditioning processes involved in the development of tolerance to alcohol

---

In contrast to early basic research, recent basic behavioral research investigations have focused more on the drinking behavior of normal subjects than on that of clinical subjects. Most of the studies using normal drinker subjects have used one of two major research strategies to examine the relationships between drinking behavior and several other variables. In the first design, alcohol administration is controlled (an independent variable) and the effects of alcohol are measured (e.g., on aggression, anxiety, sexual arousal). In the second, the effect of an experimental manipulation (e.g., social modeling of drinking, arousal of interpersonal anxiety) on alcohol consumption (a dependent variable) is assessed.

Two notable innovations have greatly facilitated the more recent basic research advances. The first involves the use of a balanced placebo research design (see Marlatt & Rohsenow, 1980; Wilson, 1981). This design consists of four experimental conditions achieved by crossing beverage administration (consume alcohol, consume placebo) with instructions (told beverage contains alcohol, told beverage does not contain alcohol). Two of the four experimental conditions are particularly noteworthy in that the instructions and beverage administration are discrepant. In perhaps the most interesting condition, subjects are instructed that they are drinking an alcoholic beverage, when in fact the beverage does not contain alcohol. This manipulation evaluates the effects of cognitive influences on behavior, since no alcohol is actually consumed. In the other condition, subjects are instructed that their beverage contains no alcohol, when in fact it does. This condition evaluates the pharmacological effects of alcohol. The most important contribution derived from research using the balanced placebo design has been the finding that, regardless of the beverage actually consumed, instructions (a cognitive variable) can exert a significant influence on a variety of behaviors, including aggression, reported sexual arousal, mood, and to a lesser extent, psychomotor behaviors (reviewed in Marlatt & Rohsenow, 1980). A good example of this research can be found in the work of Wilson and his colleagues. In one study Wilson and Lawson (1976) found that males who believed they had consumed alcohol, although they had in fact consumed a placebo beverage, reported greater sexual arousal to erotic stimuli. Physiological measurement, however, showed the subjects' sexual arousal to be unchanged.

The second important innovation, the taste test, derived from procedures originally developed by Schachter (see Marlatt, 1978a). The taste test provides an unobtrusive measure of drinking behavior. In this task, subjects are instructed to rate several beverages for their taste characteristics. However, rather than the taste ratings, the actual dependent variable of interest is the total quantity of alcohol consumed by subjects while participating in the test. The taste test has been used extensively in research with normal drinker subjects and has also been found to reliably differentiate alcoholic from nonalcoholic subjects (Marlatt et al., 1973).

As mentioned earlier, in recent years only a handful of basic research studies have examined the drinking behavior of clinical subjects. The major contributions of these studies, shown in Table 3, include the findings that speed of drinking is correlated with severity of dependence (Rankin, Hodgson, & Stockwell, 1980) and that conditioning processes, both Pavlovian and operant, may play a role in the development of tolerance to alcohol (Poulos, Hinson, & Siegel, 1981). The most important implication of the latter research is that stimuli associated with alcohol consumption may come to elicit a preparatory response (preparing the organism to counteract the effects of the depressant drug, alcohol) that is opposite in direction to the acute affects of alcohol, i.e., aversive. This conditioned response may then heighten the likelihood of drinking. If this is the case, then extinction of the conditioned response should facilitate treatment success.

Surprisingly, little speculation exists for why recent research studies have primarily used normal drinkers rather than alcohol abusers as subjects. In this vein, both Wilson (1981) and Agras and Berkowitz (1980) have recently suggested that the paucity of clinical research is related to the academic research setting, where resource limitations, as well as time and publication pressures, make it easier and more sensible to implement analogue studies using normal subjects than applied studies using clinical populations.

APPLIED RESEARCH

As will be seen, the basic research studies of the 1960s and early 1970s quite strongly influenced the course of applied behavioral research. Behavioral treatment research is probably the most noteworthy and easily identified of the three major research areas which have had an impact on the alcohol field. There are two reasons for this. First, behavioral methods have gained acceptance and recognition because they have been used in some of the few well designed and well controlled studies which have demonstrated positive treatment effects with alcohol abusers. Second, behavioral clinical research studies have been at the vanguard of empirical studies validating the use of nonabstinent treatment goals.

One general indication of how behavioral approaches have influenced the alcohol field is reflected in the series of Special Reports on Alcohol and Health prepared by the National Institute on Alcohol Abuse and Alcoholism (1971, 1975, 1978, 1981). In reviewing these reports, it can be noted that the first report, in 1971, stated that behavioral methods had "only begun to be developed experimentally" (p. 25). In contrast, the most recent report, a mere ten years later, states that "There appears to be an acceptance of behavioral therapy techniques, if not theory" (p. 152).

Further support for the impressive findings of behavioral treatment approaches is contained in Emrick's 1979 review of all randomized controlled alcohol treatment studies reported in the English language literature from 1952 to 1978. After evaluating the 90 studies meeting these criteria, one of Emrick's two positive conclusions was that "some behavioral approaches have been found to be relatively effective in reducing problem drinking" (p. 82).

Several studies have contributed to these advances, but once again space limits the number that can be mentioned. As before, failure to cite a particular study is not a reflection of the value of that study. The major contributions of behavioral treatment research to the alcohol field are summarized in Table 4.

Among the advances listed in Table 4, the best known and most controversial is the demonstrated efficacy of nonproblem drinking treatment goals—the controlled drinking studies. Before discussing this research, it is important to recognize that over three dozen studies published prior to 1970 had reported nonproblem drinking outcomes for alcohol abusers, but in nearly every case the treatment goal had been abstinence (see Pattison et al., 1977). In contrast to these studies, behavioral researchers have specifically investigated the efficacy of non-

TABLE 4

Major Contributions of Behavioral Treatment Research

---

* Demonstrated Efficacy of Nonproblem Drinking Treatment Goals

* Development of Specific Treatments for Problem Drinkers

* Demonstrations of the Efficacy of Skill Training Treatments (alternatives to drinking)

* Demonstrations of the Efficacy of Contingency Management Treatments (however, implementation problems have made their use difficult)

* Development of Relapse Prevention and Early Intervention Treatments

---

abstinent treatment goals and, thus, they can be considered as pioneering treatment research specifically designed to achieve nonproblem drinking goals. The two earliest behavioral studies to use an experimental design to evaluate a controlled drinking treatment goal were those of Lovibond and Caddy (1970) and Sobell and Sobell (1973, 1978). As already suggested, in some ways these and similar studies were a natural outgrowth of the basic behavioral research conducted in the 1960s.

Another important and often overlooked contribution of behavioral treatment research studies is that several studies concerned the development and evaluation of treatments specifically designed for problem drinkers (i.e., persons who have serious alcohol problems but do not drink in a pattern conducive to the development of physical addiction, and whose overall impairment is usually less severe than that of chronic or addicted alcoholics). The development of treatments for problem drinkers is a good example of how behavioral research interfaced with other advances in the alcohol field to further our understanding and treatment of individuals with alcohol problems. At least four major factors contributed to the development of treatments for problem drinkers. First, epidemiological research published in the early 1970s (e.g., Cahalan & Room, 1974) clearly established that there was a large population of individuals who could be defined as problem drinkers. Second, such persons were, and still are, greatly underrepresented in treatment programs and in Alcoholics Anonymous. Third, for a long time traditionalists in the alcohol field failed to recognize the treatment needs of this population, presumably because the traditional ideology focuses almost exclusively on addicted drinkers. Fourth, and very important, behavioral researchers accepted these epidemiological findings and recognized their implications. This, of course, led quite naturally to the development and evaluation of treatments for problem drinkers.

The focus on problem drinkers was further strengthened when treatment research findings indicated that successful nonproblem drinking outcomes were positively correlated with a less severe history of drinking problems (reviewed in Sobell, 1978). Some of the earliest and best known studies using problem drinkers were those of William Miller and his colleagues (Miller, 1978; Miller & Taylor, 1980), Pomerleau and his colleagues (Pomerleau, Pertschuk, Adkins, & Brady, 1978) and Sanchez-Craig (1980).

A third major contribution of behavioral treatment research has been the development and evaluation of skills training treatments for alcohol abusers. The innovations here were, of course, quite similar to those in other areas of behavior therapy, but tailored to the treatment of individuals with alcohol problems. In general, the majority of treatments have been oriented toward providing individuals with specific skills to enhance their ability to respond differently in what would otherwise be drinking situations (reviewed in P.M. Miller, 1976). The best known social skills training study with alcohol abusers was conducted by Chaney, O'Leary, and Marlatt (1978). Other skills training studies have examined more generic coping or problem-solving skills training (Sanchez-Craig, 1980; Sobell & Sobell, 1973, 1978).

Contingency management treatments have also been shown to be efficacious. Specifically, two well designed studies, one by Azrin (1976) and the other by Peter Miller (1975), have demonstrated that contingency management treatments implemented in the subjects' natural environment can be quite effective. However, in general, the implementation and continuation of contingency management procedures have been hampered by serious practical problems, such as the need for an extensive and continuing investment of resources, and the unwillingness of contingency managers (e.g., community agencies) to continue the contingencies beyond the research phase despite demonstrated effectiveness. Consequently, the clinical value of contingency management as an *enduring* treatment approach remains questionable.

The final major contribution of behavioral treatment research, as noted in Table 4, is Marlatt's theoretical conceptualization of the relapse process (Cummings, Gordon, & Marlatt, 1980; Marlatt, 1978b; Marlatt & Gordon, 1980). While the traditional model of alcoholism suggests that recovery from alcohol problems is an all-or-none phenomenon, the treatment outcome literature convincingly demonstrates that alcohol problems tend to be recurrent, even when clients show considerable improvement over time (Polich, Armor, & Braiker, 1981). In this regard, Marlatt's theorizing has led to research on the precipitants of relapse and to the development of methods of relapse prevention and early intervention.

Marlatt's work is an excellent example of the development of programmatic, empirically-based research. First, he studied alcohol abusers' self-reported precipitants of relapse. Second, based on those data he developed techniques to assist individuals to avoid drinking in situations that have a high risk of relapse. Third, procedures were developed to encourage early intervention when problem drinking occurs. Although long-term treatment outcome data for these procedures are not yet available, this line of research is important because it exemplifies an empirically-derived treatment approach. Finally, given the recurrent nature of alcohol problems, it must be considered unfortunate that it was not until the late 1970s that treatment strategies were specifically developed to deal with the relapse process.

ASSESSMENT AND TREATMENT OUTCOME EVALUATION METHODOLOGY

As stated earlier, we have categorized behavioral research contributions to the alcohol field into three major areas of impact. Besides the basic and applied research contributions, the third area which has had a marked impact on the alcohol field is that of assessment and treatment outcome evaluation methodology. The major contributions of behavioral research to this area are listed in Table 5.

The specific methodological advances listed in Table 5 have significantly altered the assessment and evaluation of alcohol treatments (reviewed in Sobell & Sobell, 1982). While these contributions have stemmed from behavioral research, we should stress that many simply reflect the application of sound scientific method to fundamental research questions. One of the advances noted in Table 5—the quantification and measurement of drinking behavior—nicely illustrates this point. As discussed earlier, traditionalists essentially consider any posttreatment drinking as synonymous with failure. Quite naturally, from this perspective it is somewhat superfluous to evaluate the extent of any drinking by alcoholics either before or after treatment; in the end, it is simply the presence or absence of drinking that defines outcome. From

TABLE 5

Major Contributions to Alcohol Assessment
and Treatment Outcome Evaluation Methodology

---

* Precise Quantification of Daily Drinking Behavior

* Frequent Follow-up Assessments
    Minimizes attrition (subjects lost to follow-up)
    Possible therapeutic benefit

* Research on the Veridicality of Data
    Alcohol abusers' self-reports of drinking and drinking-related events are generally valid, if subjects are alcohol-free when interviewed
    No single data source, even "official records," is error free; thus, data should be obtained from multiple sources and conclusions based on a convergence of evidence

* Methodologies for Use in Other Areas of Alcohol Research
    (e.g., epidemiology, clinical pharmacology)

---

a behavioral perspective, the obvious way to evaluate changes in drinking behavior is simply to measure that behavior over time. However, prior to 1970, no major empirical study had ever measured the actual amount of daily drinking by alcohol abusers. Interestingly, the measurement of daily drinking behavior, which had its roots in one of the first behavioral controlled treatment trials in the alcohol field, derived from a rather straightforward need to evaluate the actual extent, rather than mere occurrence, of drinking. The first study to measure daily drinking behavior (Sobell & Sobell, 1973, 1978) did so because of a need to assess the effectiveness of a nonproblem drinking goal. In this regard, the existing traditional dichotomization of alcohol abusers' drinking behavior as either abstinent or drunk was simply not suitable for reflecting nonproblem drinking outcomes.

Interestingly, over the last decade, there has been a growing recognition of the need to precisely quantify drinking behavior for treatment research purposes, irrespective of treatment goal. This recognition, in fact, is reflected in a recent state-of-the-art review which found that close to one-third of the recent alcohol treatment outcome studies surveyed used quantified drinking as an outcome variable (Sobell & Sobell, 1982).

The quantification and measurement of daily drinking behavior also represents a good example of how one methodological advance precipitated other advances. Prior to the development of a daily drinking behavior measure, follow-up data had typically been gathered through a single follow-up interview conducted months or years after treatment termination. The use of a single follow-up interview, however, is obviously not adequate for gathering daily drinking data over long time intervals. Also, it was speculated in the literature that a long time lapse between treatment termination and the gathering of follow-up data might result in a high percentage of subjects lost to follow-up. Most assuredly, in relation to evaluating a nonproblem drinking goal, a high attrition rate would have seriously weakened any conclusions that could have been made about the efficacy of such a controversial treatment goal. Thus, to specifically deal with this problem, an alternative follow-up strategy was developed. In order to gather daily drinking behavior data, it was necessary to conduct multiple follow-up assessments at frequent intervals.

The use of frequent, multiple follow-up contacts also resulted in additional contributions to the alcohol field. First, those studies that have used frequent contacts have reported a remarkably high percentage of subjects found for follow-up. The importance of this finding is that several studies now suggest that failure to present outcome data for a high percentage of subjects in a study may result in positively biased outcome conclusions (reviewed in Sobell & Sobell, 1982). The second contribution of frequent, multiple follow-up contacts was the suggestion that the very nature and intensity of the contacts may have therapeutic benefits for the research subjects (Sobell & Sobell, 1981). Finally, collecting outcome data at multiple intervals provides an opportunity to analyze individual temporal patterns of outcome.

Another major contribution of behavioral reasearch to assessment and treatment outcome evaluation methodology derives from research on the reliability and validity of pretreatment and treatment outcome measures. Until the mid 1970s, the prevailing belief of traditionalists, as well as that of the general public, was that alcohol abusers' do not validly self-report their drinking behavior. It was strongly asserted that alcohol abusers lie, deny, and distort accounts of their drinking and related behavior. Despite this claim, it is paradoxical that in almost all traditional alcohol treatment programs, self-reports have constituted the major or sole source of data upon which clinical assessments and treatment outcome conclusions have been based. Indeed, whatever the claim, it is difficult to imagine how one might realistically measure pre- and post-treatment drinking behavior without relying to some extent on self-reports.

As could have been expected, reports of successful nonproblem drinking outcomes gave rise to further claims that alcohol abusers' self-reports cannot be trusted. Since most of the nonproblem drinking research studies were behavioral in nature, it quite naturally followed that behavioral scientists would approach the question of the validity of alcohol abusers' self-reports in the same way that they approached other issues in the alcohol field. Basically, recognizing that questions about the validity of alcoholics' self-reports lacked an empirical basis, they decided to put these questions to scientific test.

In general, an extensive amount of research has now determined that, in contradiction to popular beliefs, alcohol abusers' self-reports of drinking and drinking-related events are quite reliable and valid, when gathered in a clinical or research setting and when subjects are alcohol-free when interviewed (reviewed in Sobell & Sobell, 1982). This line of research is yet another example of how behavioral scientists pioneered research that should have been conducted by others in the alcohol field long before the advent of behavior therapy.

One final comment about research on self-reports is in order. In most of these studies some small proportion of alcohol abusers' self-reports have been found to be invalid. Acknowledging this, investigators have conducted additional research to determine how best to gather valid data. The results of this research have clearly demonstrated that no data source is error free; even "official records" are sometimes inaccurate. The importance of this extended line of research on self-reports is that it has led to the development of a data-gathering strategy that stresses obtaining assessment and outcome data from multiple sources, and then basing assessment and treatment outcome conclusions on a convergence of mutually corroborative evidence (Sobell & Sobell, 1980).

One contribution of behavioral treatment evaluation research not included in Table 5 concerns the conduct of long-term treatment evaluations. A major criticism of behavioral treatment research in general has been the failure of investigators to conduct extended outcome evaluations (i.e., beyond six months; reviewed in Agras & Berkowitz, 1980). Interestingly the conduct of long-term follow-up has been a distinct strength of behavioral alcohol treatment research studies; most of the major behavioral alcohol treatment studies have used a minimum 12-month evaluation interval (see Sobell & Sobell, 1982).

A final point about the impact of behavioral research on the alcohol field is that some of the technological advances in the area of assessment and treatment outcome evaluation have provided improved procedures for use in other areas of alcohol research. The following example is but one illustration of how behavioral methods can be broadly applied to the study of alcohol problems. A well-known major objective of public health research has been to identify health impairment related to ethanol consumption. In public health epidemiological research, drinking behavior has typically been assessed by estimation formulae. The most frequently used formula has been the quantity-frequency (QF) method. Since this method can only derive a measure of *average or typical* daily drinking, questions have arisen about whether it can accurately portray actual drinking behavior (e.g., Room, 1977). This concern is further heightened when one considers that many people, especially young males, show great variability in their drinking patterns (e.g., Cahalan, Cisin, & Crossley, 1969). In addressing this concern, a recent study (Sobell, Celluci, Nirenberg, & Sobell, 1982) compared drinking behavior data gathered by a quantity-frequency method with data gathered by a time-line daily drinking method (Sobell, Maisto, Sobell, & Cooper, 1979), and found that the quantity-frequency method obscured alcohol abusers' actual drinking patterns. Specifically, the quantity-frequency method failed to identify certain types of ethanol consumption days, especially those associated with health risks. Thus, as can be seen, a methodological advance from behavioral research has provided epidemiological researchers with some provocative data.

CONCLUSIONS

From the preceding review and discussion, it can be concluded that both basic and applied behavioral research has had a profound and pervasive influence on the field of alcohol studies and on the treatment of alcohol problems. This impact has resulted from behavioral researchers applying sound scientific methods to the investigation of fundamental research questions. In slightly over a decade, behavioral research has influenced the alcohol field in two very important ways. First, it has clearly broadened our understanding of the nature of alcohol problems. Second, behavioral approaches have been recognized as some of the most effective treatments for alcohol problems.

REFERENCES

ADESSO, V.J. Experimental studies of human drinking behavior. In H. Rigter & J. Crabbe, Jr. (Eds.), *Alcohol tolerance and dependence.* New York: North-Holland Biomedical Press, 1980.

AGRAS, W.S., & BERKOWITZ, R. Clinical research in behavior therapy: Halfway there. *Behavior Therapy,* 1980, *11,* 472-487.

AZRIN, N.H. Improvements in the community-reinforcement approach to alcoholism. *Behaviour Research and Therapy,* 1976, *14,* 339-348.

BALLENGER, J.C., & POST, R.M. Kindling as a model for alcohol withdrawal syndromes. *British Journal of Psychiatry,* 1978, *133,* 1-14.

CADDY, G.R., & GOTTHEIL, E. Contributions to behavioral treatment from studies on programmed access to alcohol. In M. Galanter (Ed.), *Recent developments in alcoholism, Volume 3.* New York: Plenum Press, 1983.

CAHALAN, D., CISIN, I.H., & CROSSLEY, H.M. *American drinking practices: A national study of drinking behavior and attitudes.* Monograph No. 6. New Brunswick, NJ: Rutgers Center of Alcohol Studies, 1969.

CAHALAN, D., & ROOM, R. *Problem drinking among American men.* New Brunswick, NJ: Rutgers Center of Alcohol Studies, 1974.

CHANEY, E.F., O'LEARY, M.R., & MARLATT, G.A. Skill training with alcoholics. *Journal of Consulting and Clinical Psychology,* 1978, *46,* 1092-1104.

COLLINS, R.L., & MARLATT, G.A. Social modeling as a determinant of drinking behavior: Implications for prevention and treatment. *Addictive Behaviors,* 1981, *6,* 233-240.

CUMMINGS, C., GORDON, J.R., & MARLATT, G.A. Relapse: Prevention and prediction. In W.R. Miller (Ed.), *Addictive behaviors: Treatment of alcoholism, drug abuse, smoking, and obesity.* New York: Pergamon Press, 1980.

EMRICK, C.D. Perspectives in clinical research: Relative effectiveness of alcohol abuse treatment. *Family and Community Health,* 1979, *2,* 71-88.

GROSS, M.M., LEWIS, E., & HASTEY, J. Acute alcohol withdrawal syndrome. In B. Kissin & H. Begleiter (Eds.), *The biology of alcoholism, volume 3: Clinical pathology.* New York: Plenum Press, 1974.

LOVIBOND, S.H., & CADDY, G.R. Discriminated aversive control in the moderation of alcoholics' drinking behavior. *Behavior Therapy,* 1970, *1,* 437-444.

MARLATT, G.A. Behavioral assessment of social drinking and alcoholism. In G.A. Marlatt & P.E. Nathan (Eds.), *Behavioral approaches to alcoholism.* New Brunswick, NJ: Rutgers Center of Alcohol Studies, 1978(a).

MARLATT, G.A. Craving for alcohol, loss of control, and relapse: A cognitive-behavioral analysis. In P.E. Nathan, G.A. Marlatt, & T. Løberg (Eds.), *Alcoholim: New directions in behavioral research and treatment.* New York: Plenum Press, 1978(b).

MARLATT, G.A., DEMMING, B., & REID, J.B. Loss of control drinking in alcoholics: An experimental analogue. *Journal of Abnormal Psychology,* 1973, *81,* 233-241.

MARLATT, G.A., & GORDON, J.R. Determinants of relapse: Implications for the maintenance of behavior change. In P. Davidson & S. Davidson (Eds.), *Behavioral medicine: Changing health lifestyles.* New York: Brunner/Mazel, 1980.

MARLATT, G.A., & ROHSENOW, D.J. Cognitive process in alcohol use: Expectancy and the balanced placebo design. In N.K. Mello (Ed.), *Advances in substance abuse: Behavioral and biological research.* Greenwich, CT: JAI Press, 1980.

MELLO, N. Behavioral studies of alcoholism. In B. Kissin & H. Begleiter (Eds.), *The biology of alcoholism, volume 2: Physiology and behavior.* New York: Plenum Press, 1972.

MELLO, N.K., & MENDELSON, J.H. The development of alcohol dependence: A clinical study. *McLean Hospital Journal,* 1976, *1,* 64-84.

MENDELSON, J.H. (Ed.), Experimentally induced chronic intoxication and withdrawal in alcoholics. *Quarterly Journal of Studies on Alcohol,* 1964, *25,* Supplement 2.

MILLER, P.M. A behavioral intervention program for chronic public drunkenness offenders. *Archives of General Psychiatry,* 1975, *32,* 915-918.

MILLER, P.M. *Behavioral treatment of alcoholism.* New York: Pergamon Press, 1976.

MILLER, P.M. & HERSEN, M. Quantitative changes in alcohol consumption as a function of electric aversive conditioning. *Journal of Clinical Psychology,* 1972, *28,* 590-593.

MILLER, W.R. Behavioral treatment of problem drinkers? A comparative outcome study of three controlled drinking therapies. *Journal of Consulting and Clinical Psychology,* 1978, *46,* 74-86.

MILLER, W.R., & TAYLOR, C.A. Relative effectiveness of bibliotherapy, individual and group self-control training in the treatment of problem drinkers. *Addictive Behaviors,* 1980, *5,* 13-24.

NATHAN, P.E., & BRIDDELL, D.W. Behavioral assessment and treatment of alcoholism. In B. Kissin & H. Begleiter (Eds.), *The biology of alcoholism, volume 5: Treatment and rehabilitation of the chronic alcoholic.* New York: Plenum, 1977.

NATIONAL INSTITUTE ON ALCOHOL ABUSE AND ALCOHOLISM. Alcohol and Health, M. Keller & S.S. Rosenberg (Eds.). First Special Report to the U.S. Congress on Alcohol and Health from the Secretary of Health, Education, and Welfare, December, 1971. DHEW Pub. No. (HSM)72-9099. Washington, D.C., Supt. of Docs.: Govt. Print. Off., 1971.

NATIONAL INSTITUTE ON ALCOHOL ABUSE AND ALCOHOLISM. Alcohol and Health, New Knowledge, M. Keller (Ed.). Second Special Report to the U.S. Congress on Alcohol and Health from the Secretary of Health, Education and Welfare, June, 1974. DHEW Pub. No. (ADM)75-212. Washington, D.C., Supt. of Docs.: Govt. Print. Off., 1975.

NATIONAL INSTITUTE ON ALCOHOL ABUSE AND ALCOHOLISM. Alcohol and Health, E.P. Noble (Ed.). Third Special Report to the U.S. Congress on Alcohol and Health from the Secretary of Health, Education, and Welfare, June, 1978. DHEW Pub. No. (ADM)79-832. Washington, D.C., Supt. of Docs.: U.S. Govt. Print. Off., 1978.

NATIONAL INSTITUTE ON ALCOHOL ABUSE AND ALCOHOLISM. Alcohol and Health, J.R.

DeLuca & J. Wallace (Eds.). Fourth Special Report to the U.S. Congress on Alcohol and Health from the Secretary of Health, Education, and Welfare, January, 1981. DHEW Pub. No. (ADM)81-1080. Washington, D.C., Supt. of Docs.: U.S. Govt. Print. Off., 1981.

PATTISON, E.M., SOBELL, M.B., & SOBELL, L.C. *Emerging concepts of alcohol dependence.* New York: Springer, 1977.

POLICH, J.M., ARMOR, D.J., & BRAIKER, H.B. *The course of alcoholism: Four years after treatment.* New York: John Wiley, 1981.

POMERLEAU, O.F., PERTSCHUK, M., ADKINS, D., & BRADY, J.P. A comparison of behavioral and traditional treatment for middle-income problem drinkers. *Journal of Behavioral Medicine,* 1978, *1,* 187-200.

POULOS, C.X., HINSON, R.E., & SIEGEL, S. The role of Pavlovian processes in drug tolerance and dependence: Implications for treatment. *Addictive Behaviors,* 1981, *6,* 205-212.

RANKIN, H., HODGSON, R., & STOCKWELL, T. The concept of craving and its measurement. *Behaviour Research and Therapy,* 1979, *17,* 389-396.

RANKIN, H., HODGSON, R., & STOCKWELL, T. The behavioral measurement of dependence. *British Journal of Addiction,* 1980, *75,* 43-47.

ROOM, R. Measurement and distribution of drinking patterns and problems in general populations. In G. Edwards, M.M. Gross, M. Keller, J. Moser, & R. Room (Eds.), *Alcohol-related disabilities.* Geneva: World Health Organization, 1977.

SANCHEZ-CRAIG, M. Random assignment to abstinence or controlled drinking in a cognitive-behavioral program: Short-term effects on drinking behavior. *Addictive Behaviors,* 1980, *5,* 35-40.

SOBELL, L.C., MAISTO, S.A., SOBELL, M.B., & COOPER, A.M. Reliability of alcohol abusers' self-reports of drinking behavior. *Behaviour Research and Therapy,* 1979, *17,* 157-160.

SOBELL, L.C., CELLUCCI, T., NIRENBERG, T., & SOBELL, M.B. Do quantity-frequency data underestimate drinking-related health risks? *American Journal of Public Health,* 1982, *72,* 823-828.

SOBELL, L.C., & SOBELL, M.B. Convergent validity: An approach to increasing confidence in treatment outcome conclusions with alcohol and drug abusers. In L.C. Sobell, M.B. Sobell, & E. Ward (Eds.), *Evaluating alcohol and drug abuse treatment effectiveness: Recent advances.* New York: Pergamon Press, 1980.

SOBELL, L.C., & SOBELL, M.B. Frequent follow-up with alcohol abusers as data gathering and continued care with alcoholics. *International Journal of Addictions,* 1981, *16,* 1077-1086.

SOBELL, L.C., & SOBELL, M.B. Alcoholism treatment outcome evaluation methodology. In National Institute on Alcohol Abuse and Alcoholism Alcohol and Health Monograph No. 3 *Prevention, intervention, and treatment: Concerns and models.* Washington, D.C.: National Institute on Alcohol Abuse and Alcoholism, 1982.

SOBELL, M.B. Alternatives to abstinence: Evidence, issues and some proposals. In P.E. Nathan, G.A. Marlatt, & T. Løberg (Eds.), *Alcoholism: New directions in behavioral research and treatment.* New York: Plenum Press, 1978.

SOBELL, M.B. The nature of alcohol problems: Old concepts and new. *Progress in Neuropsychopharmacology,* 1981, *5,* 475-481.

SOBELL, M.B., & SOBELL, L.C. Individualized behavior therapy for alcoholics. *Behavior Therapy,* 1973, *4,* 49-72.

SOBELL, M.B., & SOBELL, L.C. The need for realism, relevance and operational assumptions in the study of substance dependence. In H.D. Cappell & A.E. LeBlanc (Eds.), *Biological and behavioral approaches to drug dependence.* Toronto: Addiction Research Foundation, 1975.

SOBELL, M.B., & SOBELL, L.C. *Behavioral treatment of alcohol problems: Individualized therapy and controlled drinking.* New York: Plenum Press, 1978.

TURNER, T.B. Clinical aspects of ethanol tolerance and dependence. In H. Rigter & J. Crabbe, Jr. (Eds.), *Alcohol tolerance and dependence.* New York: North-Holland Biomedical Press, 1980.

WILSON, G.T. Booze, beliefs, and behavior: Cognitive processes in alcohol use and abuse. In P.E. Nathan, G.A. Marlatt, & T. Løberg (Eds.), *Alcoholism: New directions in behavioral research and treatment.* New York: Plenum Press, 1978.

WILSON, G.T. Expectations and substance abuse: Does basic research benefit clinical assessment and therapy? *Addictive Behaviors,* 1981, *6,* 221-232.

WILSON, G.T., & LAWSON, D.M. Expectancies, alcohol and sexual arousal in male social drinkers. *Journal of Abnormal Psychology,* 1976, *85,* 587-594.

9

Cue Exposure for Relapse Prevention in Alcohol Treatment

NED L. COONEY, LAURENCE H. BAKER,
and OVIDE F. POMERLEAU

While many treatment programs can help alcohol abusers achieve initial remission of their problems, a review of the treatment literature (Emrick, 1974) indicated that 35-65% of treated alcohol abusers relapsed within a year. Similar rates of relapse were found in other substance use disorders (Hunt, Barnett, & Branch, 1971). At the Behavioral Medicine Unit of Newington, Connecticut, Administration Medical Center, we have been exploring methods for preventing relapse in alcohol abuse patients, starting with a skill training approach described by Chaney, O'Leary, and Marlatt (1978). This approach emphasizes group training of social skills and cognitive problem-solving techniques for coping with potential relapse situations. Situations such as being offered a drink by a friend, feeling frustrated or angry with another person, or being turned down for a job are examples of situations in which alcohol abusers are likely to relapse (Marlatt & Gordon, 1980). Effective skills for coping with these situations may decrease a patient's relapse risk.

The authors are grateful to Joanne Fertig for assistance in data collection. The research was partially supported by NIAAA Alcoholism Center Grant 1-P50-AA 03510-04 and NIAAA Training Grant 5-T32-AA 07290-02.

In one of our early groups utilizing role-playing procedures, a patient remarked, "All this play-acting doesn't mean much here in the hospital. What counts is when you have to do it out there with the real thing!" Taking this advice to heart, we purchased some cold beer prior to the next group. When it came time to role play refusing a drink offered by a friend, we asked the patients to use beer as props. The patients were initially startled to see alcoholic beverages in the hospital, and their behavior in the group indicated to us that some very significant processes were occurring.

When questioned about their reactions to the sight of the cold beer, several mentioned that their mouths watered and others noted that they became tremulous and slightly nauseous. One patient remarked how sitting there with a cold beer in his hand "felt comfortable, like being with an old friend." Some volunteered that they immediately began thinking about the pleasant feelings they had when drinking, including the pleasant taste and smell of the beer. Other patients admitted to wrestling with the thought of actually drinking the beer in the treatment group. One patient even refused to touch the drinks, saying "If I touch it, I'll drink it." Patients also reported feeling guilty; they apparently observed themselves desiring a drink and became angry with themselves. It was as if simply desiring a drink constituted a relapse. Without even taking a sip they appeared to experience a decrease in confidence about their abilities to resist drinking. These unpleasant feelings persisted in some patients up to a day after the first alcohol cue exposure. Certainly, not all patients reacted strongly. Some said that the beer didn't seem real, that the smell was bitter and unpleasant; they denied any desire to drink. However, as we began to incorporate real alcoholic beverages in our skill training groups, the groups became more lively, and patients appeared to apply themselves in earnest to the role-playing.

In order to understand the responses which we were generating in the clinic, we began to explore the literature on cue exposure in addictive behaviors and began a research program on the physiological and cognitive effects of cue exposure. We have also taken our laboratory findings back to the clinic in an attempt to develop new assessment and treatment approaches.

BEHAVIORAL THEORIES OF RELAPSE

Behavioral models of relapse all share the view that addictive problems in general and alcohol abuse in particular are in part learned behavior disorders (as opposed to innate physical or psychological dispositions or traits), and can be understood through the principles of classical and operant conditioning and social learning theory.

Conditioning Models of Relapse

Wikler (1965) proposed a model for opiate relapse based on respondent conditioning principles. In Pavlov's conditioning paradigm, a neutral stimulus is repeatedly paired with an unconditioned stimulus that naturally elicits an unconditioned response. With repeated trials the neutral stimulus becomes a conditioned stimulus and elicits a conditioned response. Wikler's model uses classical conditioning to explain "craving" for a drug in the absence of physical dependence. Certain environmental stimuli are repeatedly paired with pharmacological withdrawal symptoms arising due to episodes of acute abstinence during periods of physical dependence. These previously neutral stimuli become capable of producing conditioned withdrawal reactions long after physical dependence has been abolished. These reactions may be labeled "craving" by the ex-addict (Ludwig & Wikler, 1974) and may motivate the individual to seek relief through substance use. Siegel (1979) proposes a different mode of acquisition of conditioned craving. In his model, the environmental stimuli that reliably predict drug effects (e.g., the sight and smell of beverage alcohol) enable the addict to make adaptive drug compensatory physiological responses in anticipation of these effects. These conditioned responses are opposite to the acute drug effects and thus maintain homeostatic balance. However, when they are not followed by drug consumption these conditioned physiological reactions may be experienced as withdrawal symptoms or craving.

Thus, Wikler suggests that conditioned responses are acquired during withdrawal while Siegel suggests that conditioned responses are acquired during drug administration. This distinction may be academic, however, since an addicted individual is frequently experiencing a cyclical peak in pharmacological withdrawal immediately before the next drug administration. Both models suggest that stimuli closely associated with drug effects come to elicit conditioned craving/withdrawal reactions.

Pomerleau (1981) has proposed a two-factor model in which the above-mentioned respondent conditioning paradigm is combined with an operant paradigm. In the two-factor model, conditioned craving/withdrawal responses serve as discriminative stimuli for avoidance and/or escape from withdrawal through drug self-administration.

Cognitive Models of Relapse

Some theorists (Marlatt & Gordon, 1980; Wilson, 1978) have argued for the importance of cognitive variables in the relapse process. Expectations play a prominent role in these cognitive models of relapse. Bandura (1977) classifies expectations into efficacy and outcome expectations. An *outcome expectation* is defined as the belief that a given behavior (e.g., drinking alcoholic beverages) will produce a given outcome (e.g., relaxation, increased coping ability). An *efficacy expectation* is defined as the conviction that one is capable of successfully performing a given coping behavior. These expectations are said to determine whether or not an individual initiates coping behavior, what form it takes, and how long it is maintained in the face of obstacles and aversive experiences.

Bandura postulates that these expectations are acquired through a variety of processes. He suggests that the most powerful means for modifying efficacy expectations is through performance-based procedures and *in vivo* mastery experience. Verbal persuasion, modeling, and modification of emotional arousal are also means for changing efficacy expectations.

Marlatt and Gordon (1980) have integrated efficacy and outcome expectations into a model of relapse. According to this model, relapse occurs when an individual is exposed to a challenge to his/her coping ability, a high-risk situation, and lacks an effective coping response. This failure to cope produces a decreased sense of self-efficacy. At the same time, the individual may experience a shift in his/her outcome expectancies regarding substance use, anticipating positive effects of the substance, such as decreased anxiety, increased coping ability, etc. Decreased efficacy expectations, positive substance use outcome expectations, and cues signaling substance availability may then precipitate a relapse.

The conditioning and cognitive models of relapse are not mutually exclusive and may describe parallel or interactive processes. Figure 1 shows a simplified schematic of the two models. Several interactions could be hypothesized. For example, substance use outcome expectations may mediate conditioned responding to cue exposure. Eaglen and Mackenzie (1982) have demonstrated that knowledge of the absence of the unconditioned stimulus can lead to rapid cessation of conditioned responding in humans. Another possibility is that self-observed conditioned withdrawal reactions during exposure lead to decreased but more accurate estimates of self-efficacy. For example, a patient in an abstinence oriented hospital program who experiences an increase in craving

MARLATT COGNITIVE MODEL

WIKLER/SIEGEL CONDITIONING MODEL

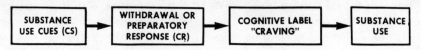

FIGURE 1. Models of relapse

when exposed to alcohol during a weekend pass may return to the hospital with his rose-colored glasses removed. At this point these and other interactive hypotheses are purely speculative, but they could be subjected to empirical tests.

What are the implications of these relapse models for relapse prevention? If, as the conditioning model suggests, conditioned craving is a determinant of relapse, then extinction procedures (exposure to eliciting stimuli in the absence of drug effects) should reduce conditioned craving and decrease the likelihood of relapse. On the other hand, if, as the cognitive model suggests, expectations are important determinants of relapse, then performance-based skill training procedures and *in vivo* mastery experiences should enhance efficacy expectations about coping with temptation and reduce the likelihood of relapse. Although it is possible to design treatments which pit these models against each other, it is easy to envision treatment procedures combining these two elements—extinction and skill training.

Both models imply that exposure to eliciting stimuli (high-risk situations) is important in treatment. What, then, are these stimuli? The models suggest that they will be idiosyncratic to some degree, and careful assessment may be required to identify them (e.g., Marlatt, 1976). However, there is one final common pathway in all relapse—substance administration cues. The sight and smell of beverage alcohol, an available pack of cigarettes, or a slice of cheesecake may elicit strong reactions in persons with histories of abusing these substances.

BASIC RESEARCH EVIDENCE

Several laboratories have independently studied the effects of substance use cues on opiate addicts, obese persons, and alcohol abusers. These studies will be discussed with reference to the behavioral models of relapse. The obesity and drug abuse literature will be examined first.

Responsivity to Drug Cues

O'Brien (1976) reports anecdotally that abstinent opiate addicts relate withdrawal "sickness" and craving to specific environmental stimuli, including: "being offered a taste by an old copping buddy"; "seeing a few bags of heroin"; and "seeing a friend shooting up." O'Brien further provides a demonstration of conditioned withdrawal responses. Subjects receiving daily methadone were given injections of naloxone, a short-acting narcotic antagonist, as the unconditioned stimulus in order to precipitate a pharmacological withdrawal reaction. The conditioned stimuli consisted of a tone and an odor. After six to 11 conditioning trials (pairings of UCS and CS), five out of eight subjects showed evidence of conditioned withdrawal responses, which included yawning, tearing, rhinorrhea, and a subjective feeling of "sickness."

To demonstrate the effects of drug administration cues, Sideroff and Jarvik (1980) presented a videotape showing heroin-related stimuli to heroin addicts finishing a 14-day detoxification program. Cue exposure resulted in changes, including increased anxiety, depression, and craving ratings, as well as an increase in GSR and heart rate. Non-blind experimenter observations indicated increased yawning, sniffing, and half-closed eyelids in experimental subjects after exposure. These are usually the signs of a heroin withdrawal syndrome.

Teasdale (1973) also explored the effects of cue exposure. Opiate addicts responded more to slides of drug-related material than to neutral material. Responses included self-reported tension, confusion, and withdrawal distress.

Responsivity to Food Cues

Conditioned salivary responding to food cues was first studied by Pavlov (1927). More recently, Rodin (1978) has demonstrated an endocrine response to food cues, with human subjects showing enhanced secretion of insulin following presentation of the stimulus.

Wooley, Wooley, and Woods (1975) found that responsivity to food cues is a function of degree of obesity and of prior food consumption. A salivary response to food cues was observed among all subjects after a low calorie preload, but after a high calorie preload only obese subjects responded to the cues. Further research (Wooley, Wooley, & Williams, 1978) indicated that chronic dieting ("restrained" eating patterns), even among the non-obese, was associated with greater reactivity to food cues after a high calorie preload.

Rodin (1981) suggests another variable influencing responsivity to food cue exposure—generalized external responsivity. Externality is defined as greater responsiveness to salient cues. Rodin and Slochower (1976) found that when normal weight persons were placed in a food-abundant summer camp, those who were initially more responsive to external cues subsequently gained the most weight.

In summary, the variables influencing responsivity to food cue exposure include prior food consumption, degree of obesity, history of chronic dieting, and generalized external responsivity.

Cognition During Food Exposure

Several studies investigated the influence of cognitions in responsivity to food cue exposure. Wooley and Wooley (1973) manipulated instructional sets accompanying exposure. Subjects who were told they could eat the food after exposure had a significantly greater salivary response than subjects told they could not eat. Furthermore, Wooley and Wooley observed a salivary response in the absence of food cues in subjects instructed to think about food.

Walter Mischel (1974) conducted a series of studies on delay of gratification in children. In this paradigm, subjects were given a choice between a small immediate food reward and a delayed, larger reward. Mischel demonstrated that cognitions about a food cue, not what was physically present, determined the length of delay behavior in children.

> Regardless of the stimulus in their visual field, if (subjects) imagine real objects as present they cannot wait very long for them. But if they imagine pictures (abstract representations) of the objects they can wait for long time periods (and even longer than when they are distracting themselves with abstract representations of objects that are comparable but not relevant to the rewards for which they are waiting). By means of instructions (given before the child begins to wait) about what to imagine during the delay period, it is possible

to completely alter (in fact, to reverse) the effects of the physically present reward stimuli in the situation, and to cognitively control delay behavior with substantial precision. While arousal-generating cognitions about the real objects in the contingency significantly impede delay, cognitions about their nonconsummatory (nonmotivational) qualities and associations, or about their abstract representations enhance delay (pp. 285-286).

Taken together, the findings of the Wooleys and Mischel suggest cognitive mediation of responsivity to food cues.

Responsivity to Alcohol Cues

There are several laboratory demonstrations of the ability of alcohol-associated cues to elicit craving and withdrawal symptoms in former addicts. A cue common to all users of orally ingested drugs such as alcohol is the flavor of the drug-containing substance. The so-called "loss of control" exhibited by alcohol abusers who taste beverage alcohol is well known in clinical lore. Ludwig, Wikler, and Stark (1974) tested abstinent alcohol abusers for craving after consuming a placebo dose, a low dose, or a high dose of alcohol. Only half of the subjects were exposed to alcohol cues and had reason to believe they were actually drinking alcohol. The main finding of this experiment was a significant increase in craving several hours after both low and high doses, but only for the group led to believe it had consumed alcohol. Physiological, behavioral, and self-report measures of craving all showed a similar pattern of results.

Hodgson, Rankin, and Stockwell (1979) also tested the hypothesis that a dose of alcohol can elicit craving. Abstinent alcohol abusers were given no alcohol, a low dose, or a high dose, and craving was assessed three hours later. Pulse rate was higher at that assessment after consuming the high dose than after either the low dose or no dose. An interaction was found between severity of alcohol dependence (Edwards & Gross, 1976) and a behavioral measure of craving (speed of drinking), with the more dependent subjects having greater craving after a high dose. These effects were not matched by a significant change in subjective desire.

Also working with abstinent alcohol abusers, Kaplan, Meyer, and Stroebel (in press) found predictors of a laboratory analogue of relapse. Increased subjective craving and heart rate in response to alcohol cues and higher scores on a questionnaire assessing withdrawal symptoms in the past 30 days of drinkings (alcohol dependence) predicted choice of a beer over a lottery ticket in the lab. These laboratory studies demonstrate that formerly dependent, abstinent alcohol abusers respond with increased craving after consuming a dose of alcohol and that these responses predict drinking in the laboratory.

While of great theoretical interest, these assessment procedures have limited practical value since they require alcohol consumption, which is proscribed in most clinical settings. Pomerleau, Fertig, Baker, and Cooney (in press) have addressed this issue by assessing reactivity to alcohol cues in the absence of alcohol consumption. Eight alcohol abusers in treatment were compared with ten non-abusing controls. Five-minute "sniff trials" were provided in which subjects smelled either cedar chips or their favorite alcoholic beverage, in a labeled container. Swallowing rate (as measured by Digastricus EMG spikes) and self-rated desire to drink alcohol were significantly elevated in alcohol sniffing trials for alcohol abusers in treatment compared with non-abusers; cardiac rate and galvanic skin response duration were also elevated in alcohol abusers, though not significantly.

As part of the Pomerleau et al. (in press) study, a validation experiment was done to compare two different measures of salivary response in alcohol abusers. The Digastricus EMG measure was compared with a simpler measurement technique using cotton dental rolls (Wooley & Wooley, 1973). Three 1½-inch dental rolls were placed in the mouth (one sublingually, two bucally bilaterally) and left in place for a five-minute collection period. Within-subject comparisons of response during alcohol and cedar sniffing trials showed that swallowing (as measured by Digastricus EMG) was highly correlated with saliva collections (as measured by dental roll weight change). Taken together, these findings suggest that salivary responses which appear to be conditioned responses can be observed in alcohol abusers.

Observed "conditioned" salivary responses might serve as a quantitative physiological index of desire to drink. A laboratory study was done to examine the relationship between salivary responses in alcohol abusers and cognitive variables measured in the presence of alcohol cues (Cooney, Baker, Pomerleau, & Josephy, in press). High positive correlations were found between salivary response and ratings of desire to drink alcohol and of expected palatability of the drink. Ratings of the expected positive effects of drinking on Southwick, Steele, Marlatt, and Lindell's (1981) Alcohol-Related Expectancies scale showed strong correlations between salivary response and expectations of greater "stimulation/perceived dominance," greater "pleasurable disinhibition," and less "be-

havioral impairment" from drinking. Thus, there is evidence that a physiological response to alcohol cues (salivation) is associated with concurrent
positive drinking outcome expectation in alcohol abusers.

In summary, basic laboratory studies show that cue exposure can elicit
reactions which look like withdrawal reactions in opiate addicts. The
obesity literature suggests that responsivity to food cues is a function of
level of deprivation, degree of obesity, history of dieting, generalized
external responsivity, and instructionally induced cognitive set. The cognitive control of responsivity is especially interesting because it provides
a potential means for intervention. The alcohol literature suggests that
abstinent alcohol abusers respond with increased craving after consuming a dose of alcohol. Cue exposure in the absence of consumption elicits
increased desire to drink, salivary responding, and positive drinking
outcome expectations. Drawing from a diverse literature on cue exposure, it is evident that exposure to substance use cues generates a reaction
in subjects with both cognitive and physiological components. Behavioral
theory suggests that these reactions are important determinants of relapse. The relationship between these reactions and actual relapse is a
fertile area for future clinical research. The usefulness of behavioral
methods such as cue exposure for the prevention of relapse is ripe for
exploration.

CUE EXPOSURE IN ALCOHOL TREATMENT SETTINGS

The findings in the previous section imply that physiological and cognitive reactions to alcohol consumptions cues should be taken into account in the clinical assessment and treatment of problem drinkers.
Traditional alcohol treatment settings are often intentionally devoid of
alcohol consumption cues. While many "controlled drinking" treatments
have provided cue exposure experience, patients engaged in abstinence
oriented treatment may also benefit from exposure to alcohol related
stimuli.

Implications for Assessment

"I'll never drink again" is an inaccurate prediction too often made by
alcohol abusers who have recently achieved a period of abstinence. Many
clinicians have learned to distrust such verbal assessments and have
sought more reliable measures of relapse risk. The ability to predict

accurately a given patient's risk for relapse after treatment would benefit clinicians and program evaluators. With such an assessment tool practitioners would be better able to match length of treatment and discharge plans to individual patient needs. Evaluators would be able to determine the immediate effects of treatment procedures, thus accelerating the development of innovative treatments.

Miller, Hersen, Eisler, and Elkin (1974) validated a "taste test" technique in which alcohol abusers are asked to taste and rate several alcoholic beverages. Subjects who had poorest outcome one year after treatments consumed a greater quantity of beverage during a taste-rating task given at the end of treatment.

Taste tests have limited applicability in settings or cases in which the consumption of even the smallest amounts of alcohol is contraindicated. Kennedy (1971) exposed patients to beverage alcohol at the beginning and end of a ten-week inpatient treatment regimen. Patients who showed a decrease in pupillary dilation in response to alcohol cues were most likely to show maintenance of treatment gains at a three-month follow-up. In a previously described analogue relapse prediction study, Kaplan et al. (in press) found that, among other factors, increased heart rate to the presentation of a beer was predictive of subsequent choice of beer rather than a lottery ticket among abstinent alcohol abusers. A minimally invasive (i.e., no alcohol consumption) procedure for the assessment of physiological reactivity to alcohol cues may be possible using measures of salivary response to the sight and smell of beverage alcohol. In our treatment unit at the Newington, Connecticut, Veterans Administration Medical Center, we have been using dental rolls (cf. Wooley & Wooley, 1973) to assess salivary responding to a neutral substance (i.e., cedar chips) and to patients' preferred alcoholic beverages in the manufacturer's bottle (Pomerleau et al., in press). The sight and smell of a preferred alcoholic beverage is a cue common in all relapse situations. Collected during five-minute "sniffing trials" with a five-minute intertrial interval, the difference in weight of the saliva on the two trials conveys the degree of salivary responding. This measure, along with self-reported desire to drink during exposure, could be used in treatment and discharge planning. For example, a patient who shows a decrease in response after starting to take disulfiram (Antabuse ®) would be encouraged to use that drug as a relapse prevention strategy. A patient who showed high responsiveness to alcohol cues just prior to discharge would be encouraged to seek an environment which minimizes drinking cues, such as a halfway house. Further research is needed to investigate the predictive validity of cue exposure assessment.

Treatment Implications

Exposure to the relevant cues has been a widely used procedure in the treatment of a variety of problem behaviors, such as phobic avoidance (Marks, 1978) and obsessions and compulsions (Rachman & Hodgson, 1980). Several case reports of cue exposure treatment have been reported in the alcohol literature. Hodgson and Rankin (1976) report the application of alcohol cue exposure procedures in the case of a 43-year-old man with a 23-year history of alcohol abuse. The patient reported that after having one drink he was unable to cease drinking. Over six daily sessions the patient was administered a priming dose of vodka (40 or 160 ml) and then asked to resist the subsequent desire to drink. By the sixth day the patient's self-reported desire to drink several hours after the priming dose fell to nearly zero. During six months of follow-up this patient reported six lapses from abstinence, but in all cases abstinence was quickly regained.

Blakey and Baker (1980) describe six cases in which patients were gradually exposed to a variety of individualized cues, including trips to their favorite pubs where they observed others drinking while they consumed soft drinks. At the end of treatment (up to 40 exposure trials) patients reported no desire to drink, and five of six patients reported continued abstinence at follow-up periods varying from two to nine months.

Several psychological processes may underlie the effects of cue exposure procedures for alcohol abuse. Extinction of conditioned withdrawal responses would occur provided the unconditioned stimulus (i.e., ethanol) is not consumed. Thus, repeated presentations of the sight and smell of an alcoholic beverage without consumption should eventually result in a decrease in conditioned withdrawal symptoms.

Operant processes may also play a role in exposure treatments. Repeated exposure while blocking consummatory responses may decrease the discriminative stimulus characteristics of alcohol cues. Thus, the sight and smell of an alcoholic beverage would no longer signal the availability of reinforcement (i.e., avoidance of withdrawal symptoms). Cue exposure also provides an opportunity for acquiring and practicing coping skills, such as refusing a drink. With repeated trials and appropriate reinforcement, alcohol cues may become a discriminative stimulus for performance of these new skills. Relaxation may be another coping skill, as Strickler, Bigelow, and Wells (1976) demonstrated. They taught seven abstinent alcoholics to use relaxation procedures while listening to an audiotape of a problem drinker in a bar. As compared to seven abstinent alcoholics who did not learn relaxation procedures, the relaxation group showed greater reduction of muscle tension in response to alcohol-related cues.

Finally, exposure procedures may produce their effects through a process of altered cognitions. With repeated guided exposure to alcohol cues, patients observe themselves coping with high-risk drinking situations without consuming alcohol. Their sense of self-efficacy should, theoretically, increase, enhancing the likelihood they will persist at coping without drinking in other high-risk situations. Patients may also rehearse alternative cognitions in the presence of alcohol cues. For example, patients may practice imagining the aversive consequences of drinking. With repeated exposure and cognitive restructuring, patients' outcome expectations may come to focus on the negative rather than positive consequences of drinking.

In summary, with repeated practice and exposure, a variety of behavioral and cognitive coping skills may come to be performed in the presence of cues which previously elicited a desire to drink. As noted above, these respondent, operant, and cognitive processes are not mutually exclusive and may be occurring simultaneously and, perhaps, in interaction.

At this time it seems prudent to employ procedures which combine extinction and skill training processes. Initial attempts to design treatments based on extinction processes alone have not met with success. Meyer, Randall, Barrington, Mirin, and Greenberg (1976) used naltrexone, a narcotic antagonist, in an extinction-based treatment for heroin addicts. Patients receiving naltrexone were encouraged to repeatedly go through the ritual of heroin self-administration. Each administration supposedly constituted an extinction trial with exposure to powerful drug administration cues in the absence of drug effects. Patients receiving naltrexone quickly stopped self-administering heroin on the ward. However, upon return to the community, patients who received naltrexone had a relapse rate similar to those who had self-administered heroin without the narcotic blockade. Meyer and his colleagues suggest that extinction did not occur in their protocol because the consumption of the narcotic antagonist signaled the unavailability of heroin effects. Another interpretation of the results is that the extinction-based procedure did not involve acquisition or practice in coping skills. For this to occur, cue exposure must occur in a context where drug effects are potentially available. It remains for future research to unravel the mechanism of such extinction-based treatment procedures.

Current Applications

An example of a clinical application of cue exposure procedures comes from our development of a skill training group as part of an inpatient program for the treatment of male dependent drinkers. The treatment emphasizes learning new skills for coping with high-risk situations (Chaney et al., 1978; Marlatt & Gordon, 1980) and extends this approach by conducting skill training in the presence of salient drinking cues (i.e., alcoholic beverages). A portable bar with glassware, ice bucket, napkins, etc., as well as a wide variety of beers, wines, and distilled spirits, is stored in the pharmacy and brought to the treatment room for the group sessions. Patients are told that they will be asked to hold, look at, and smell their favorite alcoholic beverage *without* consuming it. The therapists acknowledge that this may make some patients uncomfortable and they provide a therapeutic rationale for enduring this discomfort.

Initially, skill training focuses on practicing skills for turning down a drink offered by another group member. Each patient takes turns practicing drink refusal in the face of his preferred alcoholic beverage. This is based on Bandura's (1977) participant modeling procedure, which has been demonstrated to enhance self-efficacy. As we mentioned initially, patients report that role-plays which use genuine alcoholic beverages seem more "real" and they see their newly acquired skills as more relevant responses. Another behavioral rehearsal includes finding a hidden bottle of a favorite beverage and pouring it down the sink. These are but two examples of a variety of behavioral rehearsals which involve cue exposure.

A second group of exercises focuses on learning cognitive skills for coping with the desire to drink. Patients are instructed to sit with a glass or bottle of their favorite beverage in a quantity sufficient to elicit the desire to drink. After several minutes a group discussion is initiated in which patients describe their current craving experience. Unpleasant sensations similar to withdrawal symptoms are frequently mentioned. A shift toward more positive outcome expectations is also often described by patients.

Many patients become aware of an acute decrease in self-efficacy. Prior to exposure, recently detoxified patients note a strong sense of optimism and report absolutely no desire to drink. One traditional approach has been to label this as "denial" and to confront it. Based on our exposure treatment experience, naiveté may be operating for many patients. After cue exposure many patients reevaluate their ability to remain abstinent and apply themselves more assiduously to treatment.

Cognitive coping strategies are also practiced while patients are exposed to alcohol cues and are experiencing an increased desire to drink. We ask patients to practice imagining the negative consequences of their drinking while they are exposed to drinking cues. In this manner, we hope to overcome the shift towards positive outcome expectations. Patients may practice relaxation procedures to cope with the desire to drink. We also invite patients to rehearse calling a close friend or AA sponsor while experiencing the desire to drink.

Finally, after a desire to drink is elicited, patients are asked to self-monitor and record their desire for the next several days. This procedure allows patients to become more aware of the desire to drink, and they notice how their desire to drink changes over time and across situations.

Our use of exposure as part of relapse prevention training involves teaching new coping skills in the presence of alcohol cues. It is unlikely that a respondent extinction process occurs during the limited exposure (10 hours) that patients typically receive. However, patients may acquire useful skills for coping with their reactions to alcohol cues. While our procedures have yet to be subjected to rigorous empirical study, they are derived from basic behavioral theory and research and are testable. What is striking in our work has been the reliability with which cue exposure can elicit the desire to drink. Clinicians can now initiate the onset of a phenomenon to which previously there was only limited access. Patients can practice coping skills in a guided fashion prior to discharge into an environment brimming over with drinking cues.

REFERENCES

BANDURA, A. Self-efficacy: Toward a unifying theory of behavioral change. *Psychological Review,* 1977, *84,* 191-215.

BLAKEY, R., & BAKER, R. An exposure approach to alcohol abuse. *Behaviour Research and Therapy,* 1980, *84,* 319-325.

CHANEY, E.F., O'LEARY, M.R., & MARLATT, G.A. Skill training with alcoholics. *Journal of Consulting and Clinical Psychology,* 1978, *46,* 1092-1104.

COONEY, N.L., BAKER, L., & JOSEPHY, B. Cognitive and physiological factors associated with craving in abstinent alcoholics. Unpublished manuscript, University of Connecticut Medical School, 1982.

COONEY, N.L., BAKER, L.H., POMERLEAU, O.F., & JOSEPHY, B. Salivation to drinking cues in alcohol abusers: Toward the validation of a physiological measure of craving. *Addictive Behaviors,* in press.

EAGLEN, A., & MACKENZIE, B. Overlearning and instructional control of extinction of vasomotor responding. *Behaviour Research and Therapy,* 1982, *20,* 41-48.

EDWARDS, G., & GROSS, M.M. Alcohol dependence: Provisional description of a clinical syndrome. *British Medical Journal,* 1976, *1,* 1058-1061.

EMRICK, C.D. A review of psychologically oriented treatment of alcoholism. I. The use and interrelationship of outcome criteria and drinking behavior following treatment. *Quarterly Journal of Studies on Alcohol*, 1974, *35*, 523-529.

HODGSON, R.J., & RANKIN, H.J. Modification of excessive drinking by cue exposure. *Behaviour Research and Therapy*, 1976, *14*, 305-307.

HODGSON, R., RANKIN, H., & STOCKWELL, T. Alcohol dependence and the priming effect. *Behaviour Research and Therapy*, 1979, *17*, 379-387.

HUNT, W.A., BARNETT, L.W., & BRANCH, L.G. Relapse rates in addiction programs. *Journal of Clinical Psychology*, 1971, *27*, 455-456.

KAPLAN, R.F., MEYER, R.E., & STROEBEL, C.F. Alcohol dependence and responsivity to an ethanol stimulus as predictors of alcohol consumption. *British Journal of Addiction*, in press.

KENNEDY, D.A. *Pupilometrics as an aid in the assessment of motivation, impact of treatment, and prognosis of chronic alcoholics.* Unpublished dissertation, University of Utah, 1971.

LUDWIG, A.M., & WIKLER, A. "Craving" and relapse to drink. *Quarterly Journal of Studies on Alcohol*, 1974, *35*, 108-130.

LUDGWIG, A.M., WIKLER, A., & STARK, L.H. The first drink: Psychobiological aspects of craving. *Archives of General Psychiatry*, 1974, *30*, 539-547.

MARKS, I.M. Exposure treatments: Clinical application. In W.S. Agras (Ed.), *Behavior modification: Principles and clinical applications*, (2nd ed.). Boston: Little Brown, 1978.

MARLATT, G.A. The drinking profile: A questionnaire for the behavioral assessment of alcoholism. In E.J. Mash & L.G. Terdal (Eds.), *Behavior therapy assessment: Diagnosis, design, and evaluation*. New York: Springer, 1976.

MARLATT, G.A., & GORDON, J.R. Determinants of relapse: Implications for maintenance of behavior change. In P. Davidson & S. Davidson (Eds.), *Behavioral medicine: Changing health lifestyles*. New York: Brunner/Mazel, 1980.

MEYER, R., RANDALL, M., BARRINGTON, C., MIRIN, S., & GREENBERG, I. Limitations of an extinction approach to narcotic antagonist treatment. In O. Julius, & P. Renault (Eds.), *Narcotic antagonists: Naltrexone progress reports*. Research Monograph, Rockville, MD: NIDA, 1976.

MILLER, P.M., HERSEN, M., EISLER, R.M., & ELKIN, T.E. A retrospective analysis of alcohol consumption on laboratory tasks related to therapeutic outcome. *Behaviour Research and Therapy*, 1974, *12*, 73-76.

MISCHEL, W. Processes in delay of gratification. In L. Berkowitz (Ed.), *Advances in experimental social psychology*, Vol. 7. New York: Academic Press, 1974, p. 249-292.

O'BRIEN, C.P. Experimental analysis of conditioning factors in human narcotic addiction. *Pharmacological Review*, 1976, *27*, 533-543.

PAVLOV, I.P. *Conditioned reflexes* (G.V. Anrep trans.) London: Oxford, 1927.

POMERLEAU, O.F. Underlying mechanisms in substance abuse: Examples from research on smoking. *Addictive Behaviors*, 1981, *6*, 187-196.

POMERLEAU, O.F., FERTIG, J., BAKER, L., & COONEY, N. Reactivity to alcohol cues in alcoholics and non-alcoholics: Implications for a stimulus control analysis of drinking. *Addictive Behaviors*, in press.

RACHMAN, S., & HODGSON, R. *Obsessions and compulsions*. Englewood Cliffs, NJ: Prentice-Hall, 1980.

RODIN, J. Has the distinction between internal versus external control of feeding outlived its usefulness? In G. Bray (Ed.), *Recent advances in obesity research: II*. London: Newman, 1978.

RODIN, J. Current status of the internal-external hypothesis for obesity. What went wrong? *American Psychologist*, 1981, *36*, 361-372.

RODIN, J., & SLOCHOWER, J. Externality in the nonobese: Effects of environmental responsiveness on weight. *Journal of Personality and Social Psychology*, 1976, *33*, 338-344.

SIDEROFF, S.I., & JARVIK, M.W. Conditioned responses to a videotape showing heroin related stimuli. *International Journal of Addictions*, 1980, *15*, 529-536.

SIEGEL, S. The role of conditioning in drug tolerance and addiction. In J.D. Keehn (Ed.), *Psychopathology in animals: Research and clinical applications*. New York: Academic Press, 1979.

SOUTHWICK, L., STEELE, C., MARLATT, A., & LINDELL, M. Alcohol-related expectancies: Defined by phase of intoxication and drinking experience. *Journal of Consulting and Clinical Psychology*, 1981, *49*, 713-721.

STRICKLER, D., BIGELOW, G., & WELLS, D. *Electromyograph responses of abstinent alcoholics to drinking related stimuli: Effects of relaxation instructions.* Paper presented at the meeting of the Association for Advancement of Behavior Therapy. New York, 1976.

TEASDALE, J.D. Conditioned abstinence in narcotic addicts. *International Journal of Addictions*, 1973, *8*, 273-292.

WIKLER, A. Conditioning factors in opiate addiction and relapse. In D. Wilner & G. Kassenbaum (Eds.), *Narcotics*. New York: McGraw-Hill, 1965.

WILSON, G.T. Booze, beliefs, and behavior: Cognitive processes in alcohol use and abuse. In P.E. Nathan, G.A. Marlatt, & T. Løberg, (Eds.), *Alcoholism: New directions in behavioral research and treatment*. New York: Plenum, 1978.

WOOLEY, S.C., & WOOLEY, O.W. Salivation to the sight and thought of food: A new measure of appetite. *Psychosomatic Medicine*, 1973, *35*, 136-142.

WOOLEY, O.W., WOOLEY, S.C., & WILLIAMS, B.S. Restraint of appetite and sensitivity to calories. *International Journal of Obesity*, 1978.

WOOLEY, O.W., WOOLEY, S.C., & WOODS, W.A. Effect of calories on appetite for palatable food in obese and nonobese humans. *Journal of Comparative and Physiological Psychology*, 1975, *89*, 619-625.

10
The Nature and Treatment of Chronic Tension Headache

CLARE PHILIPS

Over the past decade, an intriguing puzzle has been developing about the nature and the treatment of headache. Psychologists, interested in applying their expertise within medicine, have focused a great deal of attention upon tension headache—one of the most pervasive chronic pain problems. As the nature of the disorder appeared to be well-established (Diamond & Dalessio, 1978; Ostfeld, 1962; Wolff, 1963), it seemed possible to derive therapeutic approaches directly from an accepted model. In many ways, this has proved fruitful, and useful therapeutic results have been reported. However, these studies, as well as the psychophysiological investigations they inspired, also produced some entirely unexpected results, unpredicted by the prevailing view of tension headache. These results have undermined the prevailing view of the disorder and the justification for current psychological treatment approaches. We find ourselves, therefore, in the position of having moderately effective procedures without understanding the process by which they achieve these effects—a not uncommon state of affairs in both psychology and medicine.

This chapter considers the background to the current preoccupation with EMG activity both in the assessment and treatment of tension headache. A different view of the nature of the pain problem, based on a

211

tripartite approach to its assessment, is proposed. The assessment would include the qualities of the pain experience, the pain-motivated behavior, and the psychophysiological correlates. The implications of such a shift in our view of tension headache are considered, with special reference to current treatment methods.

Happily, these new developments in our understanding of tension headache are clearing the way for a more rational basis for treatment and, as we shall see, one of the most promising methods is an old friend.

The Nature of Tension Headache

Prevalence

Tension headache is the most common of the chronic pain problems, entailing periodic and, for some individuals, continuous experience of head discomfort and pain. The experience is reversible and does not lead to any permanent deficits. However, although the headaches are not serious in this respect, when suffered severely and frequently they may profoundly affect the person's ability to lead a normal life.

Virtually everyone in the population experiences this type of headache periodically—a fact brought home to anyone trying to collect a headache-free control group. It has been estimated (Ostfeld, 1962) that approximately 10% of headache sufferers will be found to have an organic basis for their problems (i.e., inflammatory, traction, etc.), 10% will have migraine, and 80% will have tension headache or a mixed problem with tension and migraine features. Thus, most headaches are of the tension variety, though only 10 in every 100 sufferers experience severe episodes of pain (Philips, 1977b). Women are considerably more prone both to suffer and to report headaches of this type (Philips, 1977b; Philips & Hunter, 1982a). It has been held that headache is more common in individuals with psychiatric illness, but it turns out that the prevalence of tension headache is very similar when general practice and psychiatric populations are compared. However, the intensity of pain report in the psychiatric population is considerably higher (Philips & Hunter, 1982b).

Characterization

In 1962 a classification system for headache was formalized by an ad hoc committee of neurologists and physicians, representing the prevailing view on each of 15 distinguishable types of headache (Friedman,

1962). Tension or muscular contraction headaches were defined as follows:

> Ache or sensation of tightness, pressure, or constriction widely varied in intensity, frequency and duration sometimes long-lasting and commonly sub-occipital. It is associated with sustained contraction of the skeletal muscles in the absence of permanent structural change, usually as part of the individual's reaction during life stress.

Migraine, in contrast, is distinguished by a set of symptoms—unilateral onset, sensory prodromata, and accompanied nausea/vomiting—which are held to be due to excessive cranial and cerebral vasoconstriction and vasodilatory activity.

Despite the ambiguities inherent in the definition of tension headaches (i.e., with respect to essential qualities and locus of pain), the necessary and differentiating feature of these headaches is clear. The putative basis of these headaches lies in the "sustained contraction" of the muscles in the region of the head and neck.

Clinically, the diagnosis of tension headache is not made on the basis of EMG assessments—as might have been expected. This diagnosis is made largely by a process of exclusion. If no organic evidence can be found to explain the head pain and a quorum of migrainous features is not present, it is concluded that the problem is due to muscle tension.

The model of the disorder upon which the diagnosis is being made is, in fact, a straightforward muscular illness model. The symptoms of discomfort and pain in the head are due to an underlying dysfunction in the muscles, the underlying pathogenic factor. It implies a clearly univariate approach to the headache pain problem, in that a 1:1 link is firmly drawn between the pathogenic factor (the muscle contraction) and the pain phenomenon. The implications for treatment and management are straightforward. If the underlying pathology or dysfunction can be reduced or removed, pain will cease. This may be done by direct or indirect pharmacological action (muscular relaxants, tranquilizers) or by the more lengthy psychotherapeutic avenue of modifying the individual's muscular reactions to stress.

This view of the nature of tension headache persisted for some time and remains the accepted view today. This is perhaps a testament to the stability (or inertia!) of thinking, if one considers two important changes that have occurred over the 20 years since the ad hoc committee report. Let us consider these changes in turn.

Conception of Pain

The first—the shift in our views concerning pain—is the more remarkable, as it represents a change in thinking which has far-reaching
consequences (Melzack, 1973, 1975; Rachman & Philips, 1975; Weisen-
burg, 1977), highlighting the influence of cognitive-emotional, motivational, and behavioral factors on pain experience. The change came
about largely because of the collaboration of Ronald Melzack and Patrick
Wall (1965) in their now well-known gate control theory of pain. In
brief, the theory focused upon the potency of central influences in determining and modifying pain. The theory postulates the physiological
mechanism by which messages coming from the periphery along the
spinal cord can be changed or halted ("gated") by messages moving
downward from the brain. The downward influences include cognitive,
attentional, emotional, and anticipatory factors. The influence of such
psychological variables is held to occur before (and after) the peripheral
messages reach the brain. Using this framework, it became possible to
account for a number of clinical findings that had been inexplicable (i.e.,
hypnotic analgesia, football injuries, Beecher's soldiers, placebos, chronic
pains, etc.).

There is, needless to say, a good deal of debate about the neurological
underpinnings of the gating mechanism, but the theory certainly has
had a profound effect on thinking about pain, both in drawing attention
to the central determinants of pain and in emphasizing the importance
of a multivariate approach to understanding the nature of a pain problem.

Psychophysiological Studies

The second change, which concerns the way we view the nature of
tension headache itself, has occurred as a consequence of psychophysiological investigations of people suffering from tension headaches. The
original studies that laid the basis for the prevailing muscular model
came from the work of Wolff and his colleagues in the 1950s (Wolff,
1963). By current standards, the research lacks the necessary controls
and is a crude analogue study. Subjects (non-headache) were fitted with
a metal band around the head that went over the forehead and tem-
ples—like a metallic tennis sweatband. A screw device allowed the band
to be made progressively tighter. Not surprisingly, this led to increased
EMG activity and synchronous reports of increasing discomfort and
pain. As this pain was similar in locus and quality to a tension headache,

it was concluded that muscle tension was the likely basis for naturally occurring tension headache.

No comparable studies were undertaken until psychological interest was awakened by the growth of interest in headaches in the 1970s, encouraged by the biofeedback enthusiasts and the lure of behavioral medicine.

a) In these studies the resting EMG levels of the key muscles of the head, neck, and shoulders of groups of tension headache sufferers were compared to those of headache-free people and of migraine sufferers. It was predicted from the medical model that only the tension headache cases would show a sustained and elevated level of muscle activity.

Although some studies reported a significant difference between the tension headache cases and the non-headache controls (i.e., frontalis elevation: Boxtel & Van der Ven, 1978; Philips, 1977a; Vaughn, Pall, & Haynes, 1977; neck: Bakal & Kaganov, 1977; Pozniak-Patewicz, 1976; temporalis: Philips & Hunter, 1982a; Pozniak-Patewicz, 1976) a substantial number of studies have found no EMG abnormality (frontalis: Bakal & Kaganov, 1977; Martin & Mathews, 1977; Philips & Hunter, 1982a; neck: Boxtel & Van der Ven, 1978; Martin & Mathews, 1977; Philips, 1977a). In a recent study (Philips & Hunter, 1982a) that assessed frontalis and temporalis levels, 30% of the tension headache cases (psychiatric sample) showed no detectable muscular abnormality when compared to appropriate controls. These subjects were indistinguishable from the 70% with muscular abnormality with respect to their headache characteristics (intensity, frequency, duration, chronicity, etc.). In a previous study in a general practice, 8.3% of tension cases had normal muscular levels (Philips, 1977a). It is clear from the size of standard deviations in both this work and in the studies already quoted that there is a wide range of tension levels. This implies that there were some people in each study with tension headache but no resting muscular abnormality. Such variations may explain the equivocal results reported above.

Contrary to expectation, when tension and migraine cases were compared, significantly *higher* EMG resting levels were found in migraine (Bakal & Kaganov, 1977; Philips, 1977a; Pozniak-Patewicz, 1976). Thus, it appears that EMG levels cannot be used to differentiate tension headache from migraine headaches.

b) Assessments of all the key muscles—frontalis, temporalis, neck and trapezius—have revealed that there is not a generalized overactivity in the muscles of the head, neck, and shoulders. Rather, it appears that the frontalis or temporalis muscles are abnormal and that this abnormality may be evident at rest, in response to stress, or at both times. The correlation between these muscles at rest has been found to be .03 (Philips & Hunter, 1982a), thus confirming the specificity of any muscular reaction involved.

c) More detailed assessments of the relationship between pain intensity and EMG levels (Epstein, Abel, Collins, Parker, & Cinciripini, 1978) have revealed an inconsistent relationship. For example, in one person the correlation was strong (i.e., $r = .47$), while in another it was small and negative ($r = -.14$). In an earlier study, correlations were insignificant for all five cases (Epstein & Abel, 1977). Haynes, Giffin, Mooney, and Parise (1975) observed that several subjects did not demonstrate the expected relation between headache occurrence and EMG increments. In a comparison of subjects with and without headache (Philips, 1977a), I have found *no* significant increments on any of the four muscles. If one examines this issue by looking at the degree of association between general headache characteristics (intensity, frequency, and duration) and average EMG level at rest, similar dissociations are found (Philips, 1977a; Philips & Hunter, 1982a) with no significant correlations between muscle tension levels and any of the three characteristics. There appears to be a remarkable lack of concordance between the pain experienced and the supposed putative basis—muscle tension.

d) Finally, a remarkable degree of desynchrony has been found between EMG levels and headache during biofeedback trials. Cases without EMG abnormality show improvement in headache (Martin & Mathews, 1977). Significant EMG decrements may be associated with stability of the headache problem (Philips & Hunter, 1981b), while EMG increases may lead to no worsening of headaches or even therapeutic improvement (Andrasik & Holroyd, 1980).

Although there are a number of methodological limitations in these studies (such as failure to ensure assessement of the most abnormal muscle and the failure to separate longstanding and recent onset cases), it is clear that the results undermine the muscular model of tension headache. In chronic sufferers, tonic muscle tension is neither a necessary nor a differentiating criterion. It seems possible that the muscular activity may in fact be part of an associated reaction to pain, rather than its cause. This view is now under consideration by some neurologists (e.g., Raskin & Appenzeller, 1980).

Alternative Approach

The upshot of these developments (both in headache studies and more general research on pain mechanisms) is to suggest that a preoccupation with the activity of a set of mucles is an inadequate basis for explaining the nature of tension headache.

Over the last few years, I have been exploring an alternative assessment approach which investigates the problem without concern for establishing the original predisposing factor(s) or original etiology. Instead, it explores the nature of chronic headache in terms of its measurable aspects—psychophysiological, cognitive and behavioral—and their relationship to one another. The medical model of headache—as with other painful disorders—has assumed the existence of a close, if not 1:1:1 link, between these three aspects of the pain. That is to say, it has been thought that the amount of distress and pain and the extent of behavioral disruption motivated by pain are predictable from the extent of physiological dysfunction in the muscles. By setting aside this assumption we can gain a better understanding of the nature of the problem by exploring each of the three aspects of headache.

SUBJECTIVE EXPERIENCE

To the sufferer from headache, it is his or her own experience of pain which is paramount. Paradoxically, this aspect of headache has received little attention. The intensity of an episode usually is evaluated on analogue or adjectival scales and its duration estimated. But the experienced qualities of the pain—sensory and emotional—have been ignored. This is particularly odd when one remembers that tension headache is defined in terms of "ache or sensation of tightness and pressure," etc. (Friedman, 1962).

Using a group of severe chronic headache sufferers, we have looked in detail at the qualities of the pain experience and how they relate to the frequency, rated intensity, and duration that are obtained using a daily diary (Hunter & Philips, 1981). This work was facilitated by the McGill Pain Questionnaire (MPQ) developed by Ronald Melzack (1975)

FIGURE 1
The McGill Pain Questionnaire Scale Names and Pain Quality
Descriptors

Scale No.	Scale Name	Pain descriptors
Sensory scales		
1	Temporal	Flickering, quivering, pulsing, throbbing, beating, pounding
2	Spatial	Jumping, flashing, shooting
3	Punctate pressure	Pricking, boring, drilling, stabbing, lancinating
4	Incisive pressure	Sharp, cutting, lacerating
5	Constrictive pressure	Pinching, pressing, gnawing, cramping, crushing
6	Traction pressure	Tugging, pulling, wrenching
7	Thermal	Hot, burning, scalding, searing
8	Brightness	Tingling, itchy, smarting, stinging
9	Dullness	Dull, sore, hurting, aching, heavy
10	Sensory miscell.	Tender, taut, rasping, splitting
Affective scales		
11	Tension	Tiring, exhausting
12	Autonomic	Sickening, suffocating
13	Fear	Fearful, frightening, terrifying
14	Punishment	Punishing, gruelling, cruel, vicious, killing
15	Affective/miscell.	Wretched, blinding
Evaluative		
16	Evaluative	Annoying, troublesome, miserable, intense, unbearable
Miscellaneous scales		
17		Spreading, radiating, penetrating, piercing
18		Tight, numb, drawing, squeezing, tearing
19		Cool, cold, freezing
20		Nagging, nauseating, agonizing, dreadful, torturing

to allow a fine grained assessment of the sensory, affective, and evaluative qualities of a pain experience. It consists of a set of intensity-graded scales (see Figure 1) of pain descriptors categorized into three major factors: sensory, affective, and evaluative. Research with this scale has

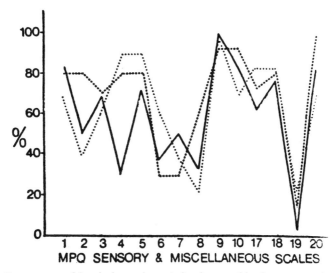

FIGURE 2. Percentages of headache patients (migraine psychiatric – – –, tension psychiatric———, tension general practice . . .) choosing sensory and miscellaneous scales of the McGill Pain Questionnaire.

revealed stable profiles that are qualitatively different in varied pain groups (Melzack, 1975).

Although headaches are considered a minor disorder, our results have revealed that the level of distress should not be underestimated (Hunter & Philips, 1981). The MPQ enables an objective comparison to be made between the pain experience of different patient groups. Severe chronic headache in general population subjects and psychiatric subjects showed a level of pain experience approximating that of cancer pain, phantom limb, and post-herpatic pain cases (Melzack, 1975).

The sensory pain descriptors most frequently used are those of dullness (i.e., sore, hurting, aching), temporal quality (i.e., pulsing, throbbing), incisive pressure (i.e., sharp, cutting), and constrictive pressure (i.e., pressing, gnawing). No difference was evident between migraine and tension pain on these qualities (Figure 2).

Tension headache sufferers were, however, more frequent users of the affective scales. The affective pain experience was more intense in the tension headache cases (from the psychiatric population) than in any other pain group reported by Melzack (1975).

BEHAVIOR

A sufferer from chronic headache finds himself with less and less scope for his normal life. He restricts his activities (social, work, personal) either to minimize pain or to prevent its occurrence. In acute pain, withdrawal and inactivity are common, and it has been argued that withdrawal serves an important function in allowing tissue rejuvenation and general recuperation (Wall, 1979). In chronic pain conditions without organic dysfunction, as in headache and low back pain, a comparable behavioral pattern is elaborated. In these cases, however, it appears to have no recuperative function and, in time, becomes non-adaptive. The reason for this may be that it actively inhibits the sufferers from distraction and the positive activities which would raise their tolerance of headache. Fordyce (1976) has argued that the pain behavior is reinforced by immediate environmental consequences and consequently persists or increases in strength. Certainly this has been shown to be a factor in exercise/work avoidance and complaint behavior. However, there are many kinds of behavior in chronic headache cases that are not easily explained by the operant thesis. They result in considerable punishment and yet are strongly endorsed.

Headache studies have on the whole been content to monitor behavior disability simply by collating medication rate. The problems of compliance, variations in attitudes to pill-taking, as well as past efficacy of such drugs, have been found in our work to make this measure blunt and far from adequate. As a consequence we have been developing an instrument to assess a sufferer's characteristic pain-motivated behavior (Philips & Hunter, 1981a). This takes the form of a checklist inventory which covers a variety of behavior: verbal and nonverbal complaining, avoidance of and escape from a variety of stimuli and activities (noise, bright lights, social events, sexual encounters, etc.), self-help coping strategies, and self-medication. The results reveal a wide range of behavior both in anticipation of pain provocation and as a direct consequence of the pain experienced. The most frequently reported are: 1) avoidance or minimizing of noise (82%), physical activity and social activity (approximately 70% for both), and bright lights (approximately 60%), 2) verbal complaining about pain (80%), and 3) nonverbal complaining (pressing/massaging pain locus) (80%).

Confirming the inadequacy of pill-taking as a single measure of the level of behavioral disruption, we have found less than 50% of the cases use drugs despite the high level of pain reported. The correlation between medication rate (assessed from a daily diary) and avoidance or complaint behavior was also found to be insignificant. Complaining and avoidance behavior were significantly correlated, but the size of the correlation was low (.38), suggesting that separable aspects of the behavior are being sampled.

The overall quality of the pain behavior has a lot in common with the withdrawal behavior commonly seen in anxiety states and depression. The latter has often been associated with chronic pain conditions and, as we have seen, the pain experience of tension headache entails strong affective qualities. In fact, significant correlations were evident in the group studied between both complaint and avoidance behaviors, and neuroticism (Eysenck Personality Questionnaire, Eysenck & Eysenck, 1976), while avoidance behavior was highly correlated with Wakefield Depression scores (Snaith, Ahmed, Melita, & Hamilton, 1971).

PSYCHOPHYSIOLOGY

Having described a number of the findings from the psychophysiological investigations, let me emphasize two conclusions that can be drawn from our own work. First, there is no objective support for the division of headaches into vascular and muscular types (migraine/tension headache). Tension headache (or muscular contraction as it is called) is characterized by less muscle tension—on average—than migraine. People with either type of headache show significantly higher elevations of tension (in certain muscles) than do headache-free subjects. EMG tension is a correlate of headache and not a distinguishing characteristic of one particular type of headache. These data have contributed to the conclusion drawn by Bakal and Kaganov (1977) and others that we may be dealing with a continuum of headache intensity rather than two discrete types. As the dysfunction increases in intensity, increasing vascular characteristics will be evident, as well as increasing muscle tension. Second, tension headache sufferers form a heterogeneous group with respect to the presence, form, locus, and extent of the muscular involvement. As noted above, a sizeable number of cases—especially in psychiatric practice—have no EMG abnormality. However, with respect to their headache experience, these individuals are indistinguishable from those with EMG abnormality. In chronic tension headache, pain reports are not always predicated upon sustained elevations of muscle tension and we must consider other psychological determinants of, or influences on, the pain experience.

INTERRELATION OF THE THREE ASPECTS

Having delineated the nature of chronic headache in terms of three measurable aspects—physiological, behavioral, and subjective—it is possible to consider the relationships among them.

In a correlational analysis of data from a group of severe tension headache sufferers, Philips and Hunter (1982c) found:

1) *No significant* associations between any physiological measure (EMG frontalis and temporalis at rest, in response to stress, temporal artery pulse abnormality at rest, in response to stress) and any of the behavioral or subjective indices discussed above.
2) In contrast to this demonstration of discordance, we found two strong links between the behavioral and subjective measures. The first is between the sensory pain qualities and the medication rate, such that more intense sensory experiences are associated with increasing pilltaking. The second link is between the *affective* pain experience and pain behavior, such that fearful and punishing pain experiences are associated with increased complaint and avoidance behavior.

It appears from a study on back pain (Zarkowska, 1981) that the degree of association between the behavior and subjective indices may be a function of the chronicity of the disorder. As the problem persists, a closer and closer association builds up between these two aspects of the problem. It seems possible that a similar process may occur as any pain becomes a chronic problem. It is, of course, true that a correlational approach to the interrelationship between the three aspects of headache is only the first step in clarifying their nature. It gives information about the relative independence of the physiological parameters, but the associations require further research and are the subject of a study in progress.

At this stage it is possible to state that chronic tension headache is associated with a severe sensory and affective experience which is closely correlated to extensive maladaptive behaviors (in the sense that no amelioration of the pain problem ensues). Psychophysiological activity, though often evident in the form of muscular tension in frontalis or temporalis muscles, is not directly associated with the pain experience or the behavior motivated by it. It is possible that psychophysiological activity plays a significant role in the development of the pain problem. However, in its chronic form, muscle tension appears to be of secondary importance—probably part of the person's physiological response to repeated and noxious pain experiences.

TREATMENT

Theoretical Basis

Turning to the question of psychological treatment, the predominant approaches, adopted over the last decade, are firmly based upon the muscular model of chronic tension headache. As muscular overactivity is the putative basis of the pain, any method which results in the systematic and permanent reduction of this muscle tension will, ipso facto, reduce and eliminate the problem. The close link of muscular abnormality and the pain symptom has made tension headache an ideal candidate for biofeedback enthusiasts keen to demonstrate the practical value of their costly expertise. It is against this background that both biofeedback and progressive relaxation have flourished and become almost mandatory treatments in pain clinics. This occurred despite the results discussed above, which have made evident the inadequacy of the muscular model in explaining chronic pain.

Interpretation of Results

There has been what can only be termed a flood of studies reporting on the efficacy of biofeedback. Only more recently has the potency of general relaxation been reconsidered. I will not systematically review these studies, as it has been done adequately in a number of recent surveys (Martin, 1981; Neuchterlein & Holroyd, 1980; Williamson, 1981; Young & Blanchard, 1980). On the whole, the outcome data have indicated that a sizeable proportion of tension headache sufferers improve when given these treatments. Young and Blanchard (1980) have summarized the improvement rates of biofeedback studies up to 1980 at 65-95% improvement. This implies a procedure that may be indistinguishable from a placebo condition at the lower rate (65%), but which may attain undisputed potency at the higher rates. The American Biofeedback Society reflected this optimism in asserting that tension headache is one of five disorders treatable by biofeedback, and pain clinics are now under pressure from patients to provide this service.

Although some equivocal results remain to be explained, progressive relaxation techniques appear to produce improvement rates remarkably similar to biofeedback. The interpretation of these results has been as follows. Specific EMG self-control or general EMG relaxation results in the attenuation of the pathogenic cause of the headaches. The EMG decrements, when monitored (and this has not always been done), are regarded as the cause of the symptom improvement. The fall in EMG levels is said to be a function of the development of muscular control—either specific self-control (biofeedback) or more general bodily relaxation (progressive relaxation). Finally, the therapeutic effects are taken as further support for the muscular thesis.

The position is not this simple, and there is growing evidence which leads one to doubt these interpretations.

a) *Subject selection.* Subjects have been selected for frontalis biofeedback treatment on the basis of the diagnosis of tension headache, even in the absence of physiological data on the presence, locus, and form of any muscular abnormalities. Given the results reviewed earlier, a proportion of these cases will be inappropriate candidates for biofeedback training. Where resting EMG levels are reported, it is clear that a proportion of the cases are without abnormality of the frontalis (e.g., Martin & Mathews, 1977; Philips, 1977a) but may nevertheless improve. In these individuals it is unclear why their headaches should improve as a function of treatment. Subjective behavioral improvements take place without EMG changes.

b) *Evidence of desynchronies.* Although parallel drops in EMG levels and pain report have often been found, symptomatic improvement has been reported when EMG levels have been stabilized or even increased during treatment. In a study by Andrasik and Holroyd (1980) all subjects believed they were lowering their frontalis tension levels. In fact, only one of the groups was doing so. The other groups were working to maintain or to increase their frontalis activity. The results reveal comparable improvement irrespective of the EMG levels produced. The opposite direction of effect has also been produced in a study of our own (Philips & Hunter, 1981b). In this case successful large decrements in frontalis or temporalis EMG levels were produced by biofeedback training. In fact, the levels reached towards the end of treatment were indistinguishable from that found in age-matched nonheadache controls (see Figure 3). However, both behavioral and subjective measures of the headache pain were remarkably stable. The significant reduction in EMG was not associated wth any substantial change in the headache problems.

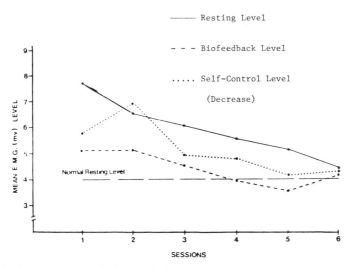

FIGURE 3. Mean E.M.G. levels during the 6 sessions of treatment at rest (———), during biofeedback trials (– – – –) and when instructed to "decrease" tension level, i.e. self-control level (. . . .).

c) *The assessment of self-control.* The belief in the rationale of biofeedback has been so strong that the (presumed) specific training of muscle control has not been assessed and the validity of the procedure was assumed. It is thus argued that successful decrements in resting muscle tension are due to increasing self-control of the muscle involved. In a recent trial, we have looked to see how justified this conclusion may be (Philips & Hunter, 1981b). Subjects were asked to demonstrate their growing capacity to reduce the tension in the abnormal muscle (frontalis or temporalis) before each session (Figure 3). They demonsrated some modest skill in doing this prior to treatment and the levels attained continued to drop during treatment, to lower and lower levels. However, when the falling resting level was controlled (in a covariance analysis), there was no further improvement on their initial capacity to control the muscle (Figure 4). Consequently, no improvement in *specific* self-control was demonstrated. It would be incorrect to explain the significant fall in the level of EMG as due to the development of self-control of the muscle involved. No specific effect of training was evident.

Therefore, it appears that the clinical success of biofeedback has encouraged too rosy an interpretation of the results. The evidence reviewed on discordance of EMG levels and pain, as well as that showing desynchronous adjustments during treatment, makes the muscular model un-

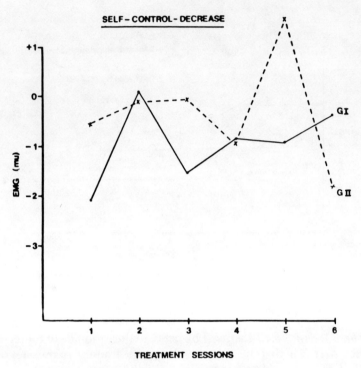

FIGURE 4. Mean EMG levels of self-control independent of resting level, at each of the six treatment sessions for Group I (———) and Group II (– – – –) respectively.

tenable and casts doubt on the justification for biofeedback. Retaining this point of view is likely to hold back progress in understanding and treating these problems. In recent onset cases, the role of muscle tension may be more important, but in this discussion I have limited myself to the consideration of *chronic* sufferers and to the maintenance of the problem, rather than etiology.

This review may be disappointing for those hoping to validate their use of (or specialization in) biofeedback. However, it may mark the beginning of a new period in psychological work on chronic headache. The fact is that, despite the failure to confirm the muscular view of headache, a treatment is available that undoubtedly improves headaches in a large proportion of cases. If this is not a function of physiological mediators (EMG changes), we must find the potent nonphysiological mediators—or "nonspecific factors" as they have been called—that can explain the results. We are faced with a multivariate pain phenomenon and not a simple muscular disorder. The tripartite approach that considers the subjective, behavioral and physiological components of headache may prove useful in the attempt to explain biofeedback successes.

The questions to be answered now are: Why do so many cases improve? What are the influential factors at play? If therapeutic success is not a function of EMG changes, what are the powerful "nonspecific" elements that are mobilized by biofeedback and progressive relaxation which are giving relief to individuals with severe persistent headache, sometimes with 10- to 20-year histories of headache?

Perhaps the answer may be found by looking more carefully at the behavioral and subjective aspects of the pain problems. It has been possible to demonstrate significant links between these two—linkage that may strengthen with the persistence of the problem. In light of this, it is worth considering whether the therapeutic results can be explained in terms of changes in either the behavior or in the subjective experience.

It has been suggested (i.e., Andrasik & Holroyd, 1980) that biofeedback may result in changes in the sufferer's behavior and this leads to the improvement in the headaches. The implication is that there is an important functional relationship between pain behavior and the pain problem.

This suggestion has been developed in the operant pain treatments of Fordyce (1976), in which structured behavioral programs have been found to result in remarkable rehabilitation of chronic cases. Unfortunately, there is no assessment of the extent to which behavioral intervention actually modifies pain experiences—sensory and affective. There is some suggestion that treatment may be motivating courageous *performance*, rather than attenuating pain experience. However, the approach has been to increase activity rates, rather than to reduce the specific avoidance behavior we have found to occur so commonly in headache sufferers. This avoidance behavior may, in fact, have a more important role in maintaining or even aggravating pain experience. In fear research it has been clearly demonstrated that avoidance of a phobic object, though bringing temporary relief, results in strengthening subsequent fear reactions. Exposure, on the other hand, leads to progressive and marked decrements in fear (subjective and physiological expressions thereof). It is feasible that the pronounced avoidance behavior found in chronic pain may be maladaptive in a comparable manner. Avoidance may increase oversensitivity and reduce tolerance of stress stimuli, even though it is likely to bring temporary relief. Treatments which effectively result in reduced avoidance of stress stimuli may do considerably more than rehabilitate the sufferer behaviorally. They may also systematically reduce sensory and/or affective pain experience in response to potent stimuli. We are currently engaged in examining this issue in more detail.

The more recent cognitive treatments of tension headache (Holroyd & Andrasik, 1978; Holroyd, Andrasik, & Westbrook, 1977) may be seen as providing cognitive encouragement for reducing and minimizing avoidance of stress and increasing tolerance/exposure to these stimuli. The cognitions may act as diverting stimuli—an interpretation suggested by the authors themselves.

Alternatively, the nonspecific factor of importance may be the effect biofeedback procedures have upon the subjective component itself. The biofeedback treatment is impressive and the subject is made to believe that he is gaining control over his muscles and, therefore, his pain. The adjustments in feelings of helplessness and anxiety/general arousal are probably significant. It is quite feasible that treatment results in a growing mental calm which reduces the affective, if not the sensory, pain qualities. This implies a shift in the subjective component as the key process occurring in biofeedback, with consequent effects upon pain behavior. Behavior change would then be a result of the reductions in subjective experience and not vice versa, as was speculated above. Future research which assesses changes in behavior and experience during treatment will help tease out the underlying factors mediating improvement.

Current practice: Guidelines

In the meantime, what can the clinician do for headache sufferers? For the majority of chronic cases, the most useful and cost-effective approach is simple and familiar—progressive relaxation. This will be particularly effective for individuals with pronounced emotional reactions associated (directly or indirectly) with their pain problem (Philips & Hunter, 1981c). However, there is likely to be a small subgroup of cases with recent onset, in whom a close association can be established between pain report and EMG levels of activity. In such individuals, a biofeedback approach is justified and may prove a more useful initial step.

Although it has become clear that the value of biofeedback has been overestimated, it would be unwise to react by entirely dismissing it. Criteria other than specific cost-effectiveness are often important in clinical decisions. Biofeedback is a potent mediator of nonspecific effects and may be of particular importance in individuals with classical medical conceptions of their pain problem (a not unusual occurrence in pain sufferers). More generally, biofeedback tends to break the passive recipient attitude that develops in these patients. The training requires that the individual actively participate in his own muscular retraining, developing a strong sense of self-control. The attitude shift that results is likely to ameliorate the depressive mood so often a correlate of chronic pain and to help motivate behavioral adjustments. Thus, although progressive relaxation is the best single option for headache pain, we may find biofeedback techniques of use for certain individuals as part of an integrated approach.

However, irrespective of treatment choice, it is important to reduce (if not eliminate) complaint and active avoidance behaviors, with particular concern for those that occur in anticipation of pain ("I'd better not go shopping, in case it brings on my pain, etc."). These behavioral changes can be achieved by graded retraining, to increase the frequency and length of distracting and rewarding activities. Monitoring his own pain variation in face of his behavior allows the patient to recognize the potent factors and derive and practice coping strategies (i.e., relaxation, alternative activities). Finally, it is often necessary to rectify a drug abuse problem, as many chronic sufferers have developed psychological and sometimes physiological dependence on large amounts of unprescribed and prescribed drugs. Some of the migraine drugs have now been found to produce headache in certain cases—a headache which is indistinguishable from the original migraine. Gradual wthdrawal over a six-week period during treatment is a relatively simple and essential step.

Here, as in other forms of therapy, there is a need to evaluate the effects of our methods both in the individual case and generally. Useful measures of assessment are now available to evaluate pain experience and pain behavior, using adjectival and behavioral checklists (Hunter & Philips, 1981; Melzack, 1975; Philips & Hunter, 1981a). Psychophysiological assessment of the extent and relevance of temporalis and frontalis muscles with respect to appropriate stressors and during periods of pain is easily achieved. What remains to be done is for clinicians to take seriously the heterogeneity of this group and to assess each case with respect to the extent of the problem—physiologically, behaviorally, and subjectively. From such an assessment they can more rationally select their treatment approach and monitor the efficacy of the intervention.

CONCLUSION

From the review of the results of both investigations and treatments of tension headache, it is becoming evident that, after a period of preliminary and necessary clarification, we now are in a better position to work on the problem of headache pain. The time for preoccupying ourselves with EMG potentials is over, and the importance of clarifying the psychological influences on a chronic pain problem is paramount. It seems likely that progress will be aided by two important considerations: 1) the evident heterogeneity of the group of tension headache sufferers with respect to physiological, subjective, and behavioral components of the phenomenon; and 2) the relevance of clarifying the functional relationship between these components in the chronic sufferer. The tripartite assessment approach utilized in this paper may prove a useful framework for future work.

REFERENCES

ANDRASIK, F., & HOLROYD, K.A. A test of specific and non specific effects in biofeedback treatment of tension headache. *Journal of Consulting and Clinical Psychology,* 1980, *48*(5), 575-586.

BAKAL, D.A., & KAGANOV, J.A. Muscle contraction and migraine headache: A psychophysiological comparison. *Headache,* 1977, *5,* 208-216.

BLANCHARD, E.B., ANDRASIK, F., AHLES, T.A., TEDERS, S.J., & O'KEEFE, D. Migraine and tension headache: A meta-analytic review. *Behavior Therapy,* 1980, *11,* 613-631.

BOXTEL, V. A., & VAN DER VEN, J.R. Different EMG activity in subjects with muscle contraction headaches related to mental effort. *Headache,* 1978, *17,* 233-237.

DIAMOND, S., & DALESSIO, D.J. *The practicing physician's approach in headache.* Baltimore: Williams & Wilkins, 1978.

EPSTEIN, L.H., & ABEL, G.G. An analysis of biofeedback training effects for tension headache patients. *Behavior Therapy,* 1977, *8,* 37-47.

EPSTEIN, L.H., ABEL, G.G., COLLINS, F., PARKER, L., & CINCIRIPINI, P.M. The relationship between frontalis muscle activity and self-report of headache pain. *Behaviour Research and Therapy,* 1978, *16,* 3 153-160.

EYSENCK, H.J., & EYSENCK, S.B.G. *Manual of Eysenck Personality Questionnaire.* London: Hodder & Stoughton, 1976.

FORDYCE, W.E. *Behavioral methods for chronic pain and illness.* St. Louis: Mosby, 1976.

FORDYCE, W.E. Learning processes in pain. In R.A. Sternbach (Ed.), *The psychology of pain.* New York: Raven Press, 1978.

FRIEDMAN, A.P. "Ad Hoc" Committee on Classification of Headache: Classification of headache. *Journal of the American Medical Association,* 1962, *179,* 717-718.

GANNON, L.R., HAYNES, S.N., SAFRANEK, R., & HAMILTON, J. A psychophysiological investigation of muscular contraction and migraine headache. *Journal of Psychosomatic Research,* 1981, *25*(4), 271-280.

HAYNES, S.N., GIFFIN, P., MOONEY, D., & PARISE, M. EMG, biofeedback and relaxation instruction in the treatment of muscular contraction headache. *Behavior Therapy,* 1975, *6,* 672-678.

HOLROYD K.A., & ANDRASIK, F. Coping and self-control of chronic tension headache. *Journal of Consulting and Clinical Psychology,* 1978, *46*(5), 1036-1045.

HOLROYD, K.A., ANDRASIK, F. & WESTBROOK, T. Cognitive control of tension headache. *Cognitive Therapy and Research,* 1977, *1,* 121-133.

HUNTER, M., & PHILIPS, C. The experience of headache—Assessment of the qualities of tension headache pain. *Pain,* 1981, *10,* 209-219.

MARTIN, P.R. Behavioral management of headaches: A review of evidence. *International Journal of Mental Health*, 1981, *9*(1 & 2), 88-110.

MARTIN, P.R., & MATHEW, A.M. Tension headaches: A psychophysiological investigation. *Journal of Psychosomatic Research*, 1977, *22*, 389-399.

MELZACK, R. *The puzzle of pain*. Harmondsworth, England: Penguin Educational Series, 1973.

MELZACK, R. The McGill Pain Questionnaire: Major properties and scaling methods. *Pain*, 1975, *1*, 277-299.

MELZACK, R., & WALL, P. Pain mechanisms: A new theory. *Science*, 1965, *150*, 971-979.

NEUCHTERLEIN, K.H., & HOLROYD, J.C. Biofeedback in treatment in tension headache. *Archives of General Psychiatry*, 1980, *37*, 866-873.

OSTFELD, A.M. *The common headache syndrome: Biochemistry, pathophysiology, therapy*. Springfield, Ill.: Charles C. Thomas, 1962.

PHILIPS, C. A psychological analysis of tension headache. In S. Rachman (Ed.) *Contributions to medical psychology*, Vol. I. Oxford: Pergamon Press, 1977a.

PHILIPS, C. Headache in general practice. *Headache*, 1977b, *16*(6), 322-329.

PHILIPS, C., & HUNTER, M. Pain behaviour in headache sufferers. *Behaviour Analysis and Modification*, 1981a, *4*, 257-266.

PHILIPS, C., & HUNTER, M. The treatment of tension headache: I. Muscular abnormality and biofeedback. *Behaviour Research and Therapy*, 1981b, *19*, 485-498.

PHILIPS, C., & HUNTER, M. The treatment of tension headache: II. EMG 'normality' and relaxation. *Behaviour Research and Therapy*, 1981c, *19*, 499-507.

PHILIPS, C., & HUNTER, M. The psychophysiology of tension headache. *Headache*, 1982a, *22*, 173.

PHILIPS, C., & HUNTER, M. Headache in a psychiatric population. *Journal of Nervous and Mental Disorders*, 1982b, *170*, 1.

PHILIPS, C., & HUNTER, M. Unpublished manuscript, 1982c.

POZNIAK-PATEWICZ, E. Cephalic spasm of head and neck muscles. *Headache*, 1976, *15*, 261-266.

RACHMAN, S.J., & PHILIPS, C. *Psychology and medicine*. London: Temple Smith, 1975.

RASKIN, N.M., & APPENZELLER, O. *Headache*. Philadelphia: W.B. Saunders & Co., 1980, pp. 172-185.

SNAITH, R.P., AHMED, S.N., MELITA, M.C., & HAMILTON, M. Assessment of severity of primary depressive illness. *Psychological Medicine*, 1971, *1*, 143-149.

VAUGHN, R., PALL, M.L., & HAYNES, S.N. Frontalis EMG response to stress in subjects with frequent muscular contraction headaches. *Headache*, 1977, *16*, 313-317.

WALL, P.D. On the relation of injury to pain. *Pain*, 1979, *6*, 253-264.

WEISENBERG, M. Pain and pain control. *Psychological Bulletin*, 1977, *84*(5), 1008-1044.

WILLIAMSON, D.A. Behavioral treatment of migraine and muscular contraction headaches: Outcomes and theoretical explanations. In M. Hersen, R.M. Eisler, & P.M. Miller (Eds.), *Progress in behavior modification*, Vol. II. New York: Academic Press, 1981.

WOLFF, H.G. *Headache and other head pain*. New York: Oxford University Press, 1963.

YOUNG, L.D., & BLANCHARD, E.B. Medical applications of biofeedback training—A selective review. In S. Rachman (Ed.), *Contributions to medical psychology*, Vol. II. Oxford: Pergamon Press, 1980.

ZARKOWSKA, E.A. The relationship between subjective and behavioural aspects of pain in people suffering from low back pain. University of London: M. Phil. dissertation, 1981.

11
Advances in Social Skills Training for Chronic Mental Patients

DAVID W. FOY, CHARLES J. WALLACE, and ROBERT P. LIBERMAN

Social skills can be broadly defined as those interpersonal behaviors necessary 1) to accomplish instrumental goals and 2) to establish and maintain social relationships. Disruptions in one or more of the affective, cognitive, verbal, and behavioral domains seriously affects an individual's potential for enjoying and sustaining interpersonal relationships which, for most of us, are the essence of "quality of life." Chronic mental disorder, intended to mean recurring psychotic conditions such as schizophrenia and major affective disorders, poses enduring social disruptions for affected individuals. These disorders involve such impairment that not only is the individual's social quality of life adversely affected by his/her symptoms, but capability for learning or relearning adaptive social behaviors is also hampered.

The advent of neuroleptic drugs in the treatment of schizophrenia was a major advance for controlling acute symptoms in the short and intermediate term. Widespread use of neuroleptics paved the way for de-institutionalization of chronic mental patients by the thousands in the past two decades. However, the anticipated improvement in social quality of life, as patients were released to be reintegrated into community social networks, was not forthcoming. Not only does a long-term neuroleptic drug regimen present problems with medication side effects, but there is no evidence to show that these drugs per se promote acquisition of essential instrumental and social behaviors necessary for community survival. For many chronic mental patients, a drug control regimen for psychotic symptoms means living in a "revolving door," with a psychiatric ghetto on one side and hospitalization on the other. Frequently, on neither side of the door does the possibility of specific treatment aimed at social rehabilitation exist (Falloon, Flanagan, Foy, Liberman, Lukoff, Marder, & Wittlin, in press).

As will be shown in this chapter, there is a budding clinical technology for teaching essential social behaviors to chronic mental patients. In its present form it is expensive in terms of staff and patient time and effort, does not work with some patients, and, worst of all, is presently available in only a few experimental settings. However, in the span of only 10 years social skills training for chronic mental patients has undergone rapid evolution in its comprehensiveness. Until unlikely quantum leap advancements are made in other forms of treatment for schizophrenia, the task of developing focused social rehabilitation techniques remains a critical one.

The purpose of this chapter is to describe a comprehensive social skills training approach for chronic mental patients as it is currently conducted in our clinical research center in Los Angeles. A working definition and a comprehensive model of social skills will be presented. Selected studies demonstrating the development of social skills training for chronic mental patients will be reviewed, and consideration will be given to what constitutes the "state of the art" in this form of social rehabilitation oriented treatment. Social skills training will be presented in the context of a broader stress-diathesis model of schizophrenia.

STRESS-DIATHESIS MODEL OF SCHIZOPHRENIA

Improving our understanding of schizophrenia and our ability to treat it is an important challenge for mental health professionals. Schizophrenia occurs universally at a rate of approximately 1% of the population. Its direct and indirect costs are staggering for the affected individual and his/her family, as well as for the society to which the individual belongs. A stress-diathesis model (Zubin & Spring, 1977) presents schizophrenia as a complex disorder involving biological, environmental, and behavioral factors which interact in its onset and remission.

In this model the diathesis or biological vulnerability for schizophrenia may be exacerbated, producing psychotic symptoms by:

1) occurrence of stressful life events for which the individual has ineffective coping skills;
2) adverse changes in the individual's social support network;
3) adverse changes in or insufficient interpersonal problem-solving skills.

For the individual at risk (biological diathesis) for schizophrenia, balance between 1) the amount of *stress* experienced from life events and social relationships and 2) the individual's problem-solving *skills* and social support may be critical. The stress-diathesis model predicts that psychotic symptoms arise or reappear when stressors overwhelm the individual's coping capacites and available social support. It is important to note that this model is bidirectional, i.e., an imbalance (producing symptoms) is created in situations when too *many* environmental stressors occur or the individual uses too *few* coping skills. The active role of the individual's problem-solving skills and social network in reducing vulnerability for schizophrenic symptoms is underscored in this model (Liberman, Wallace, Vaughn, Snyder, & Rust, 1980).

Treatment implications of the stress-diathesis model are broad in nature. Clearly, for many patients a neuroleptic drug regimen is indicated for reduction of the biological diathesis. Additionally, different environmental stressors need to be identified, the social network carefully evaluated for sources of stress and support, and the individual's cognitive and interpersonal problem-solving skills assessed. Family therapy and social skills training in a problem-solving context may become vital components of broad spectrum treatment when such a comprehensive assessment is undertaken.

There is substantial empirical support for the stress-diathesis model's emphasis on coping skills. The consistent positive relationship between premorbid social adjustment and posthospitalization outcome is well-documented (cf. Hersen & Bellack, 1976; Phillips & Zigler, 1961; Strauss & Carpenter, 1974). To the extent that social adjustment involves interpersonal problem-solving skills, this general finding of better outcome for individuals with higher social skills appears to support the model. Additionally, there is evidence that deficiences in *cognitive* problem-solving skills in schizophrenic patients are associated with higher indices of psychotic psychopathology and poorer premorbid competence (Platt & Siegal, 1976). Finally, studies comparing schizophrenic patients with normal controls indicate that chronic mental patients show deficiencies in important components of social skills (e.g., less eye contact, more speech dysfluencies) and perception of relevant situational cues necessary for effective problem-solving (cf. Hersen & Bellack, 1976; Liberman et al., 1979).

Social Skills Defined

While the general concept of social skills is often limited to interpersonal *behaviors*, the working definition of social skills used in current training approaches is more comprehensive in nature. It includes affective, cognitive, and motor behavioral domains, as well as verbal and nonverbal channels of communication. One of the best definitions is offered by Hersen and Bellack (1977), who describe social skills as the ability to

> express both positive and negative feelings in the interpersonal context without suffering consequent loss of social reinforcement. Such skill is demonstrated in a large variety of interpersonal contexts and involves the coordinated delivery of appropriate verbal and nonverbal responses. In addition, the socally skilled individual is attuned to the realities of the situation and is aware when he is likely to be reinforced for his efforts. The overriding factor is effectiveness of behavior in social interactions. However, determination of effectiveness depends on the context of the interaction . . . and, given any context, the parameters of the specific situation (p. 512).

This working definition avoids limitations inherent in trait or molecular behavioral descriptive approaches to social skills (McFall, 1982). Wallace, Nelson, Liberman, Aitchison, Lukoff, Elder, and Ferris (1980) identified four major elements of social skills necessary in a comprehensive definition:

1) the individual's *internal state*—his/her feelings, attitudes, perceptions of the interpersonal context;
2) the topography of the individual's behaviors—the rate of behaviors such as eye contact, hand gestures, body posture, speech dysfluencies, voice volume, and latency of verbal response;
3) the outcome of the interaction as reflected in the achievement of the individual's goals;

4) the outcome of the interaction as reflected in the attitudes, feelings,
behaviors, and goals of the other participant(s) (p. 43).

Interestingly, three groups of clinical researchers have independently
developed remarkably similar models of social skills. Trower, Bryant
and Argyle (1978) emphasize 1) *perception* of relevant characteristics in
interpersonal situations, 2) *translation* of perceptions into alternative
courses of action and deciding upon the best alternative, and 3) *implementing* the chosen alternative through interpersonal behaviors. This
clinical research group trains chronic mental patients in observation
skills, listening skills, and speaking skills.

Wallace et al. (1980) distinguish between instrumental and social af-
filiation types of social situations. Instrumental situations involve obtaining a specific outcome from the environment, while establishing or
maintaining social relationships is the objective in social/affiliative situations. While training methods are specific to the kind of situation, the
model of social skills includes *receiving* skills, *processing* skills, and *sending*
skills. Receiving involves cognition necessary for accurate comprehension of relevant situational parameters. Processing is cognitive problem-
solving which includes evaluating response options and selecting an appropriate one. Sending skills are verbal and nonverbal behavioral responses necessary to present the selected option in the interpersonal
context.

Similarly, McFall (1982) recently proposed a social skills model composed of *decoding* skills, *decision* skills, and *encoding* skills. Included in the
decoding process are reception, perception, and interpretation of the
stimulus situation. Decision skills involve response searching, response
testing, response selection, repertoire searching, and utility evaluation.
Encoding skills include execution and self-monitoring. Regardless of
which current model of social skills one chooses, three major cognitive
and behavioral processes are incorporated so that cognitive problem-
solving skills and interpersonal communication skills are emphasized.

SOCIAL SKILLS TRAINING FOR CHRONIC MENTAL PATIENTS

Social skills training is a behavior treatment approach aimed at increasing the individual's performance competence in critical life situations. It is assumed that each individual tries to do the best he/she can,
given the person's biological endowment, cognitive limitations, and previous social learning experiences. When an individual's "best effort" fails

to meet interpersonal needs and goals, it is an indication of a functional deficit in the individual's repertoire. This deficit might arise from a diathesis for schizophrenia, from lack of experience, or from extreme amounts of social stressors (e.g., criticism and/or overinvolvement of a close family member). Therefore, the objective of training is to improve the individual's ability to cope with a wide variety of interpersonal situations, regardless of the source of the skill deficits. Implementation of training is based upon the situationally specific aspects of instrumental and social-emotional encounters between people. Thus, the training can be done in vivo with the people actually involved with the patient's real-life problems, or it can take place through simulated encounters commonly referred to as "role-playing."

Since it is often not possible to consistently involve patients' significant others in a series of training sessions, role-playing with surrogate participants (other patients or co-trainers) is the most frequently used training vehicle. Focused instructions, goal-setting, modeling, feedback, and social reinforcement are the behavioral techniques, taken from social learning principles, used by the trainer. Videotaping is frequently used to present modeling performances and provide feedback. Target behaviors identified for change usually include both response topography (e.g., eye contact, voice volume or intonation, response latency, smiles, or other affective expressions) and content behaviors (e.g., requests for change, compliance, hostile comments, asking questions for more information).

At the end of each role-played scene the trainer reviews the patient's performance, provides positive and corrective feedback, and gives instructions to use other behaviors presumed to improve performance on the next trial. Each training scene is role-played until performance meets a criterion agreed upon by the trainer and the patient. Training sessions may vary in length from 15 to 90 minutes and training may be offered in individual or group formats. Individual training allows more extensive focus on a single patient's behavior and more opportunity for practice within sessions, while the group format provides vicarious learning opportunities from observation of other patients' training trials. Other advantages and disadvantages of the two formats have been outlined in detail (cf. Liberman, King, DeRisi, et al., 1975; Trower et al., 1978).

In social skills training the content is as important as the teaching methods used. It seems of little use to train individuals in situations which they are unlikely to encounter in their natural environments. Systematic history-taking, behavioral probes on high probability difficult situations, consultation with the individual's significant others, and self-report assessment instruments are methods which may be used to iden-tify individualized training situations. Comprehensive discussion of the relative merits and limitations in the various social skills assessment meth-ods is available (Hersen, 1979; McFall, 1982), and thorough review of these issues is recommended before systematic social skills training is attempted.

While the general procedures for social skills training have been shown to be useful with normals and a wide range of psychiatric diagnostic groups, there are several important differences in their use with chronic patients with more severe disorders. First and perhaps foremost, pa-tients' psychotic symptoms (hallucinations, delusions, other thought dis-turbances) mut be under control so that attentional or other cognitive aberrations do not obstruct the extensive learning and retention required (Hersen & Bellack, 1976). This most often means that chronic patients' symptoms must be relatively well-controlled by a neuroleptic regimen in order for training to be effective. Secondly, procedures for chronic patients are intensified, as compared to training for less impaired psy-chiatric patients or normals. More problem situations are trained, more trials per scene are used, and more focused instructions, feedback, and prompting are required of the trainer. In this connection it is particularly important to note that *modeling* is a critical training component for chronic patients, while instructions alone may be sufficient for less im-paired individuals (Eisler, Blanchard, Fitts, & Williams, 1978).

Since 1971 when Serber and Nelson published one of the earliest applications of social skills training with schizophrenic patients, an ad-ditional 35 published studies reflecting development of increasingly com-prehensive technology have appeared. Thorough critical reviews of these studies are already available (e.g., Hersen, 1979; Wallace et al., 1980). However, the improvements in training methodology can be demon-strated by examining three training protocols from an eight-year period of development.

Early social skills training for chronic psychiatric patients was directed by a molecular behavioral model of social skills which emphasized train-ing situation-specific "sending" skills. Foy, Eisler, and Pinkston (1975) used seven training scenes depicting a 56-year-old male patient's actual work-related interpersonal conflicts. Evaluation of the patient's re-sponses during pretreatment baseline led to sequential training on the target behaviors depicted in Figure 1. As shown, 15 training sessions were held in which modeling and then modeling plus instructions were used to effect changes in targeted behaviors. In this early work only *content* behaviors were trained in a few situations in one functional area.

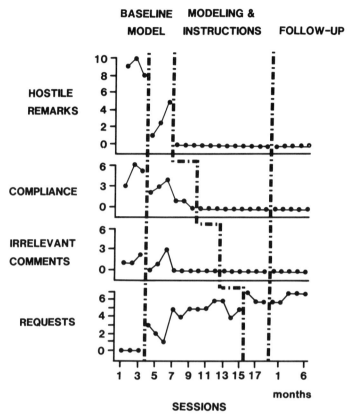

FIGURE 1. Social skills training (Foy, Eisler, & Pinkston, 1975)

Perhaps most importantly, the use of a multiple baseline design across target behaviors to evaluate ongoing training effects was also demonstrated in this early single case design study.

In 1977, Finch and Wallace reported results from a group design study with schizophrenic patients which extended training methodology to include "receiving" skills as well as sending skills. Figure 2 shows the targeted sending behaviors which were systematically trained over 12 group sessions. Compared to the matched, untreated control group, the social skills treatment group performed significantly better at posttreatment on each of the targeted behaviors. In this study both topographical and *content* "sending" behaviors were included for training. Additionally, several procedures were included which focused upon "receiving" skills. The primary receiving area which the study addressed was inattentive-

TARGET SKILL AREAS	MEAN RATINGS (0-5)	

1. **Sending Skills**

		Tx Group	Control
A.	LOUDNESS	4.3	2.3
B.	FLUENCY	4.3	1.9
C.	AFFECT	3.8	1.9
D.	CONTENT	4.4	1.8
E.	EYE CONTACT	3.8	1.8
F.	OVERALL	4.1	1.9

2. **Receiving Skills**

"INCREASING ATTENTIVENESS"

A. Maintaining good eye contact

B. Patients' input solicited for practice

C. Simple instructions

D. Patients provide performance feedback to role-players

E. Therapist prompting for inattention

FIGURE 2. Social skills training (Finch & Wallace, 1977)

ness. Figure 2 displays the specific procedures used to establish and maintain subjects' attentiveness to the group social skills training procedures during the training sessions. Unfortunately, no data were provided regarding the effectiveness of the receiving skills training.

The Foy et al. (1975) and the Finch and Wallace (1977) studies exemplify early, limited attempts to improve social skills in chronic mental patients. However, the relatively few hours spent in training on a small sample of problem situations in both these studies could hardly be expected to produce sufficient change in patients' daily social functioning to positively impact on overall quality of life. In fact, there is convergence across studies with chronic psychiatric patients that generalization of training to situations outside the training setting remains an unsolved problem (Wallace et al., 1980). Practically, what this means is that patients could be trained to perfection in the treatment setting and still be unable to get their interpersonal needs met in the natural environment.

Not only is generalization of training a remaining problem, but there is also the matter of the magnitude of social and personal rehabilitation needs which many chronic psychiatric patients present. A recent study by Sylph, Ross, and Kelward (1978) examined the extent of social disability found in two samples (n = 147) of chronic psychiatric patients. Major deficits were found in over 50% of the patients in many social and personal functional areas, such as: personal hygiene and grooming; dressing, clothes selection and maintenance; money management; use of public transportation; domestic chores; competitive or sheltered employment; reading; and vocabulary and sentence construction. Social skills training techniques following a molecular behavioral model aimed only at interpersonal situations can hardly be expected to change chronic mental patients' quality of life in the face of such profound functional deficiencies.

The social skills training protocol in use and undergoing further development in our Los Angeles clinical research center represents an extension of the methods described in the Foy et al. (1975) and Finch and Wallace (1977) studies. However, the training program is designed to more adequately deal with the range and severity of social rehabilitation needs presented by many chronic mental patients. In fact, the training approach might be more appropriately labeled "social and independent living skills" training.

In the training program, full use is made of the comprehensive receiving, processing, and sending skills model of social skills developed by Wallace et al. (1980). Cognitive goal-setting and problem-solving skills are trained with intensity equal to that given interpersonal skills training. The structural and functional unit of the training program is labeled a "module." A module is composed of a category of skills falling within a major life domain area. Modules are constructed so that problem-solving skills and interpersonal skills needed in major functional areas are taught simultaneously. When the program is fully operational, modules will be available in each of the following areas:

1) conversational skills
2) vocational rehabilitation (job-seeking, interviewing, maintenance skills)
3) home finding and home maintenance
4) medication management (drug effects, side effects, self-monitoring)
5) leisure and recreation management
6) self-care and personal hygiene
7) use of public transportation
8) food preparation
9) money management
10) use of community agencies

Design of the Modules

As shown in Figure 3, each module consists of a set of sequential exercises designed to teach patients the skills that constitute the module, train them to solve the problems they might encounter in the use of

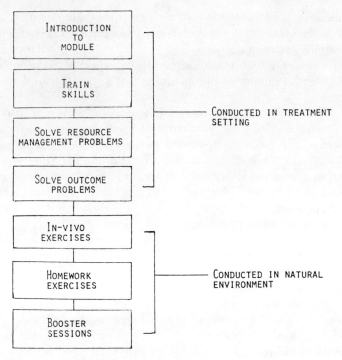

FIGURE 3. Overview of Training Components in a Module

these skills, and have them practice the skills in both the training sessions and the "real world."

Introduction to module. The objective of this exercise is to have patients actively identify the goals of a module, the consequences that will occur if the goal is achieved, and the steps necessary to achieve the goal. (Each of the steps is one of the skills that will be taught in the next exercise.) After a module is briefly described, patients are asked the following set of questions:

a) What is the goal of this module?
b) What is the problem?
c) If you get (*goal*), what will happen?
d) Do you have time, money, skills, people to help?
e) What are the steps to get (*goal*)?

Questions and corresponding correct answers are available to the therapist on a "data sheet"; therapists compare patients' answers to those on the data sheet and institute a correction procedure if any answer is incorrect. The number of correct answers is recorded.

Train skills. The skills are taught in the same order as that necessary to achieve the goal of the module. Each one is taught using a combination of videotaped modeling and role-played practices. After reviewing the "place" of the skill in the sequence of steps necessary to achieve the goal, patients view a videotaped demonstration that is periodically stopped to assess their attentiveness to and comprehension of the information conveyed in the demonstration. Incorrect answers result in replaying the videotape and highlighting the information needed to correctly answer the question when it is repeated. The number of correct answers is recorded.

After all of the information has been comprehended, patients are asked to role play the skill. The enactment is observed for the presence/absence of the behaviors demonstrated on the videotape. If a behavior has not been performed or has been performed incorrectly, corrective feedback is given and the patient is asked to reenact the roleplay. The presence or absence of each of the behaviors during each roleplay is recorded.

Resource management problem. After each skill has been correctly role played, patients are taught to solve a set of "resource management" problems. These are potential difficulties patients might encounter when they attempt to gather the resources necessary to perform each skill. The training procedures are based on a model of the steps necessary to solve such problems. The model is shown in Figure 4.

The training procedures consist of the therapist's describing the skill and asking a series of questions designed to have patients actively consider each step outlined in the model. The questions are:

a) What is your goal in using this skill?
b) What is the goal of this module?
c) What must you have to (*skill*)?

(For each resource mentioned in c)
d) How would you get (*resources*)?
e) If you were to get (*resource*) by (*method in d*), what other positive consequences would happen?
f) If you were to get (*resource*) by (*method in d*), what negative consequences might happen?

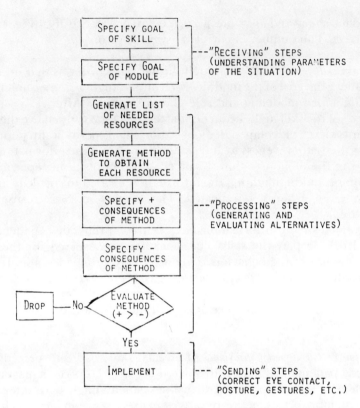

FIGURE 4. Procedural Steps in Resource Management

g) Do the positive consequences outweigh the negative consequences?
    (If yes, role play method generated by patient at option of the ther-
    apist.) (Assume that the (*methods in d*) were not satisfactory—what else
    would you do? Return to question d.)

Questions and the corresponding correct answers are available to the
therapist on a data sheet; therapists compare patients' answers to those
on the data sheet and institute a correction procedure if any answer is
incorrect. The number of correct answers is recorded.

Outcome problems. After patients have been trained to solve problems
involved in gathering the resources necessary to perform a skill, they
are trained to solve problems that might occur when they use the skill
and the environment does not respond in an optimal manner. These

are labeled "outcome" problems, and the training procedures follow the model depicted in Figure 5.

The training procedures begin with the therapist's reading a description of the attempt to use the skill, the response made by the environment, and the resources available to solve the problem posed by the environmental response. Patients are then asked questions designed to have them actively consider the steps outlined in the model. The questions are:

a) What is the problem?
b) Do you have time, money, skills, people to help?
c) What can you do to solve the problem?
d) Is (*method in c*) feasible?
e) If you (*method in c*), will you likely get your goal?

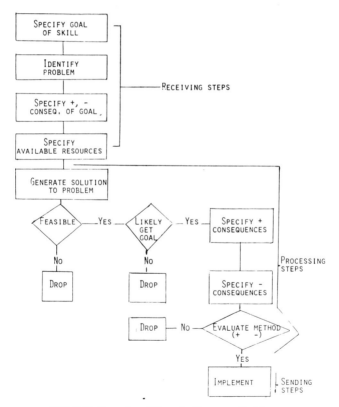

FIGURE 5. Procedural Steps in Outcome Problems

f) If you were to (*method in c*), what other positive consequences would happen?

g) If you were to (*method in c*), what negative consequences would happen?

h) Do the positive consequences outweigh the negative consequences? (If yes, role play alternative generated by patient at option of the therapist.) (Assume (*method in c*) doesn't work—what else would you do? Return to question f.)

The scoring of patients' answers, the training of correct answers, and the collection of data are all performed in the same manner as in the procedures to train the solving of resource management problems.

In vivo exercises. The in vivo exercises are designed to have patients perform in the "real world" the skills they have been taught in the training sessions. Patients are expected to independently collect the resources necessary to perform the skill, and therapists accompany patients on these performances to provide corrective feedback and to collect data about the quality of the performances.

Homework exercises. The homework exercises are much the same as the in vivo exercises except the staff do not accompany patients on their performances. Rather, data are collected whenever possible about the permanent products of an exercise that verify its completion. If there are no permanent products that result from the completion of an exercise, patients' self-report of completion is noted.

Booster exercises. The "booster" exercises are designed to refresh patients' skills after a period of inactivity. The exercises consist of many of the same role-playing, problem-solving, in vivo, and homework exercises used in the original training.

This intensive treatment "package" is designed for use with patients on an inpatient or outpatient basis. Since control of patients' psychotic symptoms is critical to the training process, program medical staff assume responsibility for monitoring and adjusting the neuroleptic drug regimen for each participant. The length of training and the modules selected for training are also individualized for each patient, since assessed social rehabilitation needs may vary substantially across individuals. The intensive treatment phase typically lasts for several months, followed by less intensive aftercare, including any needed booster treatment. Patients are treated in small groups with the highly structured initial components trained each morning. In vivo exercises are scheduled in the afternoons with program staff accompanying patients in the natural community environment.

COMPREHENSIVE SOCIAL SKILLS TRAINING: SUMMARY

Social skills refer to interpersonal behaviors necessary to accomplish interpersonal goals or to establish and maintain social relationships. In the short time span of 10 years social skills training for chronic mental patients has progressed from training a few topography or content responses in a few problem situations to comprehensive social and independent living skills training in many broad functional areas. Cognitive goal-setting and problem-solving skills have become essential components in current models of social skills. Focused instructions, modeling, feedback, and social reinforcement remain the behavioral techniques used in training, and most clinical researchers rely heavily upon videotaping for modeling and performance feedback. Training content is derived from systematic history-taking, behavioral probes on hypothesized difficult situations, consultation with the individual's significant others, and self-report assessment instruments.

Management of patients' psychotic symptoms, usually by a neuroleptic regimen, and extensive use of modeling are emphasized as essential elements in social skills training for chronic mental patients. Generalization of training effects outside the treatment setting remains an unsolved problem. However, the use of intensified training over many functional areas, including training trials in the community and "homework," appears to offer some promise for positive impact on patients' quality of life. Training procedures in such an intensive approach are equally focused on cognitive problem-solving and interpersonal communication skills. State of the art social skills training methods now appear better designed to meet the extensive social rehabilitation needs of chronic psychiatric patients.

REFERENCES

EISLER, R.M., BLANCHARD, E.B., FITTS, H., & WILLIAMS, J.G. Social skills training with and without modeling in schizophrenic and non-psychotic hospitalized psychiatric patients. *Behavior Modification*, 1978, 2, 147-172.
FALLOON, I., FLANAGAN, S., FOY, D.W., LIBERMAN, R.P., LUKOFF, D., MARDER, S., & WITTLIN,

B. Treatment of schizophrenia. In C.E. Walker (Ed.), *Handbook of clinical psychology: Theory, research and practice.* Kingsport, Tennessee: Kingsport Press (in press).

FINCH, B.E., & WALLACE, C.J. Successful interpersonal skills training with schizophrenic inpatients. *Journal of Consulting and Clinical Psychology,* 1977, *45,* 885-890.

FOY, D.W., EISLER, R.M., & PINKSTON, S. Modeled assertion in a case of explosive rages. *Journal of Behavior Therapy and Experimental Psychiatry,* 1975, *6,* 135-137.

HERSEN, M. Modification of skill deficits in psychiatric patients. In A.S. Bellack & M. Hersen (Eds.), *Research and practice in social skills training,* New York: Plenum Publishing Co., 1979.

HERSEN, M., & BELLACK, A.S. Social skills training for chronic psychiatric patients: Rationale, research findings, and future directions. *Comprehensive Psychiatry,* 1976, *17,* 559-580.

HERSEN, M., & BELLACK, A.S. Assessment of social skills. In A.R. Ciminero, K.S. Calhoun, & H.E. Adams (Eds.), *Handbook of behavioral assessment.* New York: John Wiley & Sons, 1977.

LIBERMAN, R.P., KING, L.W., DERISI, W.J., et al. *Personal effectiveness: Guiding people to assert themselves and improve their social skills.* Champaign, Illinois: Research Press, 1975.

LIBERMAN, R.P., WALLACE, C.J., VAUGHN, C.E., SNYDER, K.S. & RUST, C. Social and family factors in the course of schizophrenia. In J.S. Strauss, M. Bowers, T.W. Downey, S. Fleck, S. Jackson, & I. Levine (Eds.), The *Psychotherapy of Schizophrenia.* New York: Plenum Publishing Co., 1980.

MCFALL, R.M. A review and reformulation of the concept of social skills. *Behavioral Assessment,* 1982, *4,* 1-33.

PHILLIPS, L., & ZIGLER, E. Social competence: The action-thought parameter and vicariousness in normal and pathological behaviors. *Journal of Abnormal and Social Psychology,* 1961, *63,* 137-146.

PLATT, J.J., & SIEGEL, J. MMPI characteristics of good and poor social problem-solvers among psychiatric patients. *Journal of Psychology,* 1976, *94,* 245-251.

SERBER, M., & NELSON, P. The ineffectiveness of systematic desensitization and assertive training in hospitalized schizophrenics. *Journal of Behavior Therapy and Experimental Psychiatry,* 1971, *2,* 107-109.

STRAUSS, J.S., & CARPENTER, W.T. The prediction of outcome in schizophrenia II. Relationships between predictor and outcome variables. *Archives of General Psychiatry,* 1974, *31,* 37-42.

SYLPH, J.A., ROSS, H.E., & KEDWARD, H.B. Social disability in chronic psychiatric patients. *American Journal of Psychiatry,* 1978, *134,* 1391-1394.

TROWER, P., BRYANT, B., & ARGYLE, M. *Social skills and mental health.* Pittsburgh: University of Pittsburgh Press, 1978.

WALLACE, C.J., NELSON, C.J., LIBERMAN, R.P., AITCHISON, R.A., LUKOFF, D., ELDER, J.P., & FERRIS, C. A review and critique of social skills training with schizophrenic patients. *Schizophrenia Bulletin,* 1980, *6,* 42-63.

ZUBIN, J., & SPRING, B. Vulnerability: A new view of schizophrenia. *Journal of Abnormal Psychology,* 1977, *86,* 103-126.

Name Index

Subject Index